In Praise of *Luna's Life*

"Here is a beautiful portrait of a quietly heroic life. Luna Kaufman survived so much during the Holocaust years – being hunted and tortured, suffering the loss of her father, sister and other dearly beloved family members and friends. That tumultuous period was followed by years of oppression under a Communist dictatorship. Moving forward, Luna overcame illness, separation from loved ones, the rigors of immigration and the pettiness of bureaucrats; she went on to meet the challenges of work, family and community service. Through it all, she never lost a spirit of constructive engagement, positive embrace of life and the commitment to bring good into the world. In an inspiring way, this account reveals that with the will – and spunk – never to despair, the human spirit finds ways to get through the worst and go on to the best that life can offer. This book, then, is testimony not only to one extraordinary, very brave woman, but to the potential of the human spirit in all of us."

Rabbi Irving Greenberg, Chairman Emeritus
U.S. Holocaust Memorial Council 2000-2002

Blu Greenberg, Author

"I am thrilled that *Luna's Life* will reach a wide public to inspire and guide people young and old with her philosophy of life. The Luna that I have known and loved for many years radiates in these pages. She is a gentle force and guiding light for many. In this book, her inspiring words extend the gift of her life to all who read her legacy of optimism and inclusive engagement. I see forged in these pages her strength, wisdom and concern for building a better world, one more beautiful and humane because she lived in it."

Reverend David M. Bossman, Ph.D.
Executive Director, Sister Rose Thering Endowment
Seton Hall University

"Luna's story of her life after the evils of the Holocaust is unique in her willingness and ability to bring people together, especially Catholics and Jews, to defeat the evils of bias, prejudice and bigotry. I highly recommend this book."

Dr. Paul B. Winkler, Executive Director
New Jersey Commission on Holocaust Education

D1468559

Luna's Life

A Journey of Forgiveness and Triumph

by Luna Kaufman

Proceeds benefit the Sister Rose Thering Endowment at Seton Hall University

COMTEQ™
PUBLISHING
MARGATE, NEW JERSEY

Published by:
   ComteQ Publishing
   A division of ComteQ Communications, LLC
   P.O. Box 3046
   Margate, New Jersey 08402
   609-487-9000 • Fax 609-487-9099
   Email: publisher@ComteQcom.com
   Website: www.ComteQpublishing.com

ISBN13 978-1-935232-03-2
Library of Congress Control Number: 2009922159

Book design by Jackie Caplan
Cover design by Irene Kaufman
Cover photo by Dan Creighton

Printed in Canada
10 9 8 7 6 5 4 3 2 1

Let's make it a better world

To my grandchildren...the joy of my life.

Manya   Andy   Evan

Elena   Sasha   Dora

Byc zwyciężonym i nie ulec, to zwycięstwo
Zwycieżyć i spocząć na laurach, to klęska

To be defeated and not to succumb, is a victory.
To be victorious and rest on your laurels, is a defeat.

Marshal Josef Pilsudski (1867-1935),
First chief of state of an independent Poland

Table of Contents

Author's Note to the Reader

As I complete the writing of this memoir, I would ask the reader not to consider this book a historical or academic account of the Holocaust. Rather, it is written from my own memory of the events of my life. It is strange to me that after many years of living since those days—years that have included much turmoil and much joy—I have developed a selective memory. Exact *dates*, as such, are not important to me. As a matter of fact, it appears that I have a kind of mental block regarding this issue, yet the *facts* of what happened are inscribed in my memory as if they occurred only yesterday. Therefore, I have recovered every detail in my own mind over long periods of reflection and remembering, and I have done little outside research, trusting in myself and in the truth. This account of events is therefore suspended in time.

I was very fortunate to recover a number of old pictures from family and friends in Israel, Hungary and the United States, which I am happy to share with you at the opening of each chapter. In one miraculous coincidence, I received a picture from Zinek Finder, a fellow inmate of my father's from the concentration camp in Plaszow. I hope readers will gain a clearer visual understanding through these photos from my life.

Luna Kaufman

Sister Rose and Luna, Israel 2000

*"The love of your hands stretched to us inspired us.
It is by joining hands that we will lead a better
world for generations to come."*

Luna Kaufman, 1983

Preface

Luna Kaufman has lived an uncommon life, which she has chronicled in these memoirs. She has shared the lessons of her life with many people over the past 60 years, including the Seton Hall University community. Luna is one of many Jews and Christians who have found a place at Seton Hall to study and advocate for true understanding and tolerance between these two faith traditions that worship the same God and live on the same earth.

Since 1953, less than a decade after the end of World War II, Seton Hall has been home to a cadre of Catholic priests, rabbis and scholars who have made better relations between Jews and Christians their lifelong mission. It started with Monsignor John Oesterreicher, the Austrian-born priest who was inspired to institutionalize this cause at this university and founded what came to be a vibrant community that spoke out when no one else did about anti-Semitism in the post-war world, that chronicled the history of intolerance of Jews and laid the foundation for dialogue and for forgiveness of past errors.

Monsignor Oesterreicher was not, strictly speaking, alone (he attracted an audience for his written works and supporters for his Judaeo-Christian Institute)—but it was a lonely path on which he trod in those early years.

Sister Rose Thering, a Dominican nun from Wisconsin, became a professor of education at Seton Hall, and her "passion" (as recently chronicled in an Academy Award-nominated documentary film) was to tell the truth about the Jewish people and to erase the lies that had found their way into people's hearts and minds. Nothing was going to stop her in her mission. I know, because I worked closely with her at Seton Hall, and in her last years, after I had become president of the university, I felt the wonderful and sometimes withering way she had of prodding and promoting and scolding and living for her cause of tolerance and love among all people, especially for and with the Jews.

And along with Monsignor Oesterreicher, a succession of dedicated priests and lay people, Catholic and non-Catholic alike, lent their time, their great talents and, importantly, their treasure to achieve his vision of Jewish-Christian unity and friendship.

Into this "mix," Luna Kaufman came, attracted by Sister Rose's outreach to her. Luna had survived the Holocaust and emigrated to the United States from Poland, with her husband. She had raised a family here and had begun to carry her own message of reconciliation, to tell her own story truthfully to the younger generations coming up in the world.

As a loving parent, a member and later president of her temple and a dedicated member of her local community, Luna brought great energy and experience to the rest of us—and she wound up serving as the chairwoman of the Sister Rose Thering Endowment for Jewish-Christian Studies here at Seton Hall. She continues, even as an *emerita* to serve and to lead that institution and to inspire us all.

The strength of character that enabled her to survive imprisonment during the darkest time of the 20th century shines through even today. It is evident on the pages of this book, which is published by the Endowment, with the support of Seton Hall University, and my encouragement as someone who is grateful to call Luna Kaufman my friend. She has taught me so much, just as she has taught countless schoolchildren to whom she has spoken, just as she has taught fellow priests and nuns, just as she has taught her colleagues on the board of the Endowment and on the committees and commissions on which she has served so ably for decades.

In fact, I am pleased to note, as this book is about to be published, that Seton Hall will award Luna an honorary degree at our 2009 commencement ceremonies in recognition of her achievements and her example.

A remarkable life, a remarkable woman: Luna has proved to be a walking university in herself, and all who know her are thankful to God for her life. I am very glad she has chosen to share that incredibly rich life with us in these pages.

Monsignor Robert Sheeran
President of Seton Hall University

Foreword

I am proud that my dearest friend was a Catholic Dominican nun: Sister Rose Thering.

I am a Jewish woman from Krakow, Poland, who survived the Holocaust with my mother after being enslaved for four years in the depths of hell called concentration camps. I lost my father and 15-year-old sister. We, and millions of others, paid dearly for the actions of hateful, intolerant, and fanatical leaders.

Throughout the Holocaust and since, we survivors took upon ourselves an obligation to ensure that the Jewish people neither disappeared nor lost their humanity. For many of us, our wartime experiences sparked a need to teach tolerance and mutual respect. We feel we must use our lives constructively as a debt to the non-Jews whose help on our behalf threatened their own existence and to our liberators who sacrificed their lives to free us. We are grateful that our emergence out of Hades was often greeted by the embrace of people seeking to conquer the evil that had tried to annihilate us. No one was more successful in this quest than Sister Rose.

It was this nun's tireless efforts that helped pave the way toward the Roman Catholic Church's formal repudiation of anti-Semitism in a landmark document issued in 1965 by the Second Vatican Council. It was this nun who traveled over 54 times to Israel, leading groups of clergy and others to familiarize them with the political, social, and cultural realities of—not propaganda about—the Jewish homeland. It was this nun who led the educational vanguard in teaching about the Holocaust, not just as Jewish history, but also as a roadmap to encourage vigilance and stymie the roots of prejudice that harbor the potential of giving rise to another genocide.

At a Holocaust remembrance ceremony in 2006 organized by the New Jersey Commission on Holocaust Education, one of the commissioners, Abdalbagy Abushanaber a refugee from the Darfur genocide, publicly expressed his gratitude to the Commission. He thanked the panel for opening his eyes to the atrocities of the Holocaust and the imperative to teach all its aspects to future generations in order to prevent its recurrence. He said the work of the Commission taught him how to begin to confront the issue in his country.

The gentleman from Darfur unassumingly summarized Sister Rose's mission. She worked every day of her life to teach the world the need to ensure that future atrocities will be prevented. Sister Rose planted a seed. It is up to us to nurture it. I for one vow to continue her work and nudge her mission ever forward.

My parents, Mania & Marek Fuss, Krakow, June 15, 1923

Mania, Luna, Niusia and Marek Fuss 1929

Chapter One

My Krakow

My life's journey, which has taken me through three continents, began on November 28, 1926 in the majestic medieval city of Krakow, Poland. Born 15 months after my sister, I led a carefree childhood, surrounded by scores of caring and loving family members. I attended a 150-year-old school with only two other Jewish girls in my class.

After hours of being confined to my elementary school desk, I welcomed the daily romp home through the streets of Krakow and the Planty, the thin park that ringed the old city. At the age of seven I proudly strolled the long walk home—six blocks—unescorted except by my sister Niusia. Only a year older than me, with golden braids and a slender figure always adorned in immaculate, tailored clothes, Niusia was beautiful, fun-loving, and responsible. Like mother, she had a serious attitude toward all of her endeavors, particularly her school work for which she consistently earned high grades. Niusia's fine reputation among the teachers paved the way for me. Though I was mischievous by nature like my father, many of my pranks were overlooked since no one expected anything other than perfection from the sister of Niusia. Eventually, of course, my teachers caught on to my antics, dubbing me "Bolshevik" after the rebellious communists in the early days of the former Soviet Union.

Buoyed by the freedom of each school day's end and the independence our parents had granted us, Niusia and I would skip merrily past historic features that graced every city block. We would run around the trees and pathways of the Planty, erected by Krakow's history-conscious fathers where the original city walls and moat had formerly blocked passage to outsiders. Stopping en route for childhood adventures, we would breathe in the springtime aromas of the rainbow-colored flowers that spelled "Welcome to Krakow" and play hide-and-seek in the autumn trails carved from golden leaves and shiny fallen chestnuts.

At the end of our daily walk through the Planty, Niusia and I would arrive at a large intersection. Immediately across the street was the majestic building that housed the main post office, and on the opposite site stood the printing house of *Kurierek*, the city's main newspaper. Every day young delivery boys stood outside, awaiting the last edition that sent them racing through the city streets shouting, "The Latest News!" At that intersection Niusia's conscientious side would overtake her. Without exception she would firmly grab the hand of her adventurous little sister to prevent me from landing under a passing streetcar. At the next corner we would turn onto a fork in the road. On one side was the fortress-like Bank PKO building, where our family banked, and on the other side was our beloved four-story cream-colored apartment house at 13 Wielopole Street, built at the beginning of the twentieth century by a grandfather I never knew.

The length of the trek home resulted from our attending a school located outside the local district. The year we were old enough to be enrolled, the nearby school, which our mother had attended as a little girl, was filled. Niusia and I were assigned to Konarskiego, located just below the towering, medieval castle of Wawel. This course of events had its advantages for a romantic like me who, when classes grew tiresome, could delight in imaginary horsemen scooping me up and carrying me to a world of royal Polish fantasy.

The centuries-old Wawel sits dramatically atop a hill in Krakow's center. Behind its fortress walls are the august buildings where noblemen had lived for centuries, but which in the 1930s I knew as a dignified and massive museum filled with mementos of past grandeur. A wide, sweeping path leads to its apex, which is crowned with a gilded, shining dome on the magnificent cathedral. The kings who ruled Poland are buried in marble graves in the crypt of the cathedral, whose bell tolls melodically every hour.

On one corner was the modest tower of Queen Jadwiga's residence. The queen—whose beatification by Pope John Paul II I had attended in Krakow in 1994—had arrived from Hungary in the fifteenth century at age 12 to take over the throne. She was elegant but not pretentious, with a slender, dainty figure. Though she died childless a dozen years after ascending the throne, this young woman left behind a remarkable legacy: her royal jewels, which were used to establish hospitals and the Jagellonian University. Legend has it that All Saints Church on Grodzka Street was built around a stone where Queen Jadwiga rested her foot to remove a jewel from her shoe, giving it to a worker to pay for food and a doctor for his sick child. The indentation in the stone is allegedly her foot's imprint.

Growing up in a city where majestic history and beauty are so inextricably woven and everywhere present, my childhood fantasies were consumed with images of royalty. I visited the Wawel as frequently as possible, gliding across the highly polished floors with felt covers on my shoes to avoid scuffing the floors and standing transfixed before ornate tapestries that related stories of ancient days. My favorite chamber was a ballroom with a grid on the ceiling from which sculpted heads of court ladies and gentlemen adorned in decorative hats peered down, their imaginary figures dressed in glamorous styles of silk and satin, dancing across the large floor. On balmy summer nights my family and I often attended concerts in the castle courtyard under star-studded skies. Surrounded by the medieval balconies, I kept waiting for the appearance of royal family members.

Though 13 Wielopole Street was not a royal castle, it was our beloved home that grandfather Josef Schneider, my mother's father, built on a lot that had been owned by the family for generations. The house was in a non-Jewish neighborhood, and the Schneider children grew up with many Christian friends. It was a lovely house that contained 16 apartments on four floors. After the building was completed, grandfather, who had a great sense of humor, moved to the top floor, joking that he wanted to protect himself from garbage that might be thrown at him.

My grandparents had seven children: five girls and two boys. My mother, Maria, was their youngest, born on July 17, 1892. A serious and gentle person, my mother was an independent thinker. She and her closest sister, Helen, whom she closely resembled, spent many hours fashioning elaborate matching clothes. Helen chose the more common path of marriage at a very young age, moving with her husband Julek to Dziedzice, a town in Silesia near the German border. My mother rejected a string of possible suitors and decided instead to journey eastward to Lvov, where much to the chagrin of grandfather she enrolled in an accounting school. It was a great shame for a girl from an affluent home to take a job. After graduation, mother returned to the family home, taking a position as an accountant at the railroad station.

During her single days, mother's closest companion was her older brother Solomon, nicknamed Salek. Also unattached at the time, Uncle Salek was an architect educated in Berlin. With his handlebar moustache and black velvet cape, he cut a very impressive figure. Mother and Salek moved in bohemian circles, attending literary clubs, concerts, and theater.

Mother's single days came to an end when, at the age of 31 (an advanced age for marriage at that time), the matchmakers succeeded. The groom was my father, Marek Fuss, who had settled in Krakow from eastern Poland upon returning from a Russian war prison. A wedding was planned at the family homestead. Sadly, grandfather passed away a year before this happy event. Grandfather had been a highly regarded citizen of the city, and I was told the entire city council of Krakow attended his funeral.

Grandmother died two years after my parents were married, between my sister's birth and mine, leaving mother in the role of hostess for the extended family.

Our apartment was filled with antiques, crystal, and china acquired over the generations. My most revered family possession was an antique clock, which grandfather, a member of the National Museum, had been privileged to purchase. The clock woke me each morning to an aria from Flotov's opera *Martha*. Its silver dial reflecting the morning sun always seemed to me to welcome the new day.

Father opened a soap distribution center, and mother's accounting skills came in very handy. They worked together, maintaining the office at home so that they were constantly present in our daily lives.

Despite a wide age span and differing degrees of religious observance, Schneider family ties were very strong. There were about 50 of us. Most of the aunts, uncles, and cousins who did not live in our building had apartments within walking distance, and those who moved were for the most part only a short train ride away. But our home at 13 Wielopole remained the center where all the relatives gathered.

On brisk winter mornings our maid started the needed fires in the beautiful tile coal stoves that lined a corner in every room in the apartment. The midday main meal of the day was often fragrant chicken soup with homemade noodles and dill, set on a freshly starched white linen tablecloth. Our entire family shared this early afternoon dinner, which was timed to our return from school. The conversation around the table was always lively, with Niusia and me relating our school adventures and mother and father discussing current events. At the end of the meal our parents returned to work, and my sister and I were free to play. Going out of the school district prevented us from getting together with our classmates who lived too far away. So we joined our friends and cousins in the Planty on sunny days, or we ran between apartments on afternoons when the Polish weather was foreboding.

Although my fantasies focused on royalty in luxurious gowns waltzing through the lavish salons of the Wawel, my preferred play activities involved roughhousing with my cousin Julek, whose family lived on the second floor of our apartment house. I especially enjoyed chasing boys who liked a more sedentary activity level!

Another apartment I loved to frequent was on the third floor, where mother's older brother Henry Schneider lived with his family. Uncle Henry was married to Cyla, from a prominent German Jewish family. Cyla embodied in elegance what she lacked in beauty. She and Henry had two children, both of whom were educated in Berlin: Lutka, a pharmacist and a very good pianist, and Leon, an engineer, who brought sophisticated erector sets from Germany that occupied many hours of my time. Their stately apartment was strewn with Oriental carpets and antiques enriching the ambience.

Uncle Henry was a beloved figure in the neighborhood. With his bushy moustache and salt-and-pepper crew cut, he resembled our beloved Polish General Marshal Pilsudski, under whose command Poland was liberated in 1918 from approximately 200 years of partition. Pilsudski, called *Dziadzio* (Grandpa) by Polish children, was one of the country's most admired heroes. Polish Jews were also enamored of this leader who embraced civil rights.

A wounded veteran of World War I, my General-Pilsudski look-alike-uncle spent much of his semi-retirement in the Planty entertaining passing children by carving little figures from chestnuts and telling stories. On summer evenings the music from his violin poured through the open windows, attracting many appreciative listeners.

Coincidentally, Uncle Henry and Pilsudski became deathly ill at the same time in 1935. Not wanting to upset Uncle Henry with news of Pilsudski's sickness, we cut out of the newspapers the stories on that subject before giving it, holes and all, to Uncle Henry. Outside our house, neighborhood children kept vigil, awaiting reports on Uncle Henry's condition. Their cries filled the air when he died—on the same day as Pilsudski.

Just as the children in our community sobbed when Uncle Henry passed away, all of Poland cried when Pilsudski died. I remember his body being taken to several big cities in a glass coffin, where thousands of people gathered to view it. When they brought his body to Krakow, it was placed in the cathedral of the royal castle. Outside the window of my classroom the long line of mourners transfixed my eight-year-old mind. Deeply affected by the death of a beloved leader, I joined the crowd. It took many hours to reach the casket. My parents, who had arranged a formal dinner for the owner of the firm where my father worked, had no idea of my whereabouts. Although their dinner plans were thwarted by a frantic search for me, I escaped punishment. I attributed their leniency, in great measure, to their patriotism and love for Marshal Pilsudski.

When it was too cold to play outside I visited the fashionable millenary salon of my cousin, Ecka Timberg, located inside her apartment, next door to ours on the fourth floor. Ecka was my mother's niece. She had moved into the apartment with her sisters, Manya and Lola, and her younger brother, Salek, following the untimely death of their parents.

Ecka was statuesque, elegant, and blond. Her salon attracted many prominent and glamorous women who brought swatches from new outfits, which they matched with hats. I spent many hours working with Ecka, learning to fashion elaborate hats by steaming felt on wooden forms and decorating them with ribbons and feathers.

My Krakow childhood was filled with loving relatives, wonderful playmates, beautiful parks, friendly streets, and awesome fantasies. There were few days that I would have traded for a life in any other place at any other time.

Fuss Grandparents – Mania, Niusia, Marek-Pesia, Noah-Rudenko, 1926

Chapter Two

The Fuss Family

Marek Fuss, my father, was a newcomer to Krakow. The second to youngest of nine children in an Orthodox Jewish family, father was born in 1891 in Starzawa in eastern Poland, on a large estate with a manor. The children were educated at home. Grandfather Noah Fuss was a stately and stern master of the house as well as a Polish patriot who served in a nineteenth-century Polish uprising. Wearing a fur-collared coat with his long, white beard blowing in the wind, grandfather liked to inspect his property in his carriage pulled by a pair of white horses and guided by liveried coachmen.

Grandfather was the official town delegate to Emperor Franz Josef of Vienna, visiting the Austro-Hungarian emperor whenever a petition needed to be brought. On one occasion the emperor visited Starzawa and was welcomed by a rabbi and priest, together with hundreds of town residents. The emperor greeted the rabbi first, explaining that Judaism was older than Christianity.

In contrast to grandfather's austerity, father and his younger brother, Julek, were the family pranksters. One day, bored with their studies, they climbed two poplar trees flanking the road that led to the estate. They each tied themselves to the top branches, swinging until the treetops joined to form an arch. The trees were tall and thin, and no potential rescuer dared climb them. Apparently, it took a good amount of negotiation to get them to surrender. I believe the deal was that grandmother would administer the punishment rather than grandfather.

An adventurous, curious young man whose soul sought broader horizons, father was discontented living at the isolated estate. As a teenager he therefore made a decision that forever altered the nature of his relationship with his father. Defying grandfather's orders, he escaped from Starzawa to attend a prestigious secondary school in Krakow, the Jacek Gymnasium. Grandfather disowned him for his act of disobedience, refusing any contact with his son.

Father's school years were characterized by limited income and flamboyant adventures. Unable to return home for vacation, one summer he and a friend built their own wooden bicycles, taking off on a tour of Czechoslovakia. They rode from one factory to the next, charming and befriending the wealthy industrialists who housed them and loaded them with products made by their companies.

By trip's end the boys rode new bicycles, owned beautifully tailored school uniforms, and had received as gifts sets of china and crystal for which Czechoslovakia was famous. Not having a home, father sent it all to Grandmother despite his ban from the house. Grandmother, cognizant of the hardships father endured as a student, secretly smuggled money and food to him.

When he was a senior at the gymnasium, father required surgery to remove polyps from his nose. Since there was no health insurance at the time, grandfather came to Krakow to pay the bill at the hospital's office. He did not visit father in his room. His pride would not permit him to see a disobedient son.

Father's graduation coincided with the start of World War I, and he was drafted into the Austrian army as an officer. Tales of his experiences as a Russian war prisoner, filled with a sense of romance and adventure, were the favorite bedtime stories of Niusia and me. Sitting in a chair sandwiched between our rooms, father told us how he had worked at an agricultural school where the nobility came for fox hunting. I pictured beautiful ladies dressed in luxurious furs, arriving on snowy nights in big sleds with bells attached to their harnesses. A good horseman who was raised on a farm, father seemed to have enjoyed the assignment.

As the war continued, father was transferred to Moscow. The time was the beginning of the Russian Revolution, and father found he needed to earn money. Unlike the situation in World War II, prisoners of war during the previous conflict were permitted to live on their own with some supervision and were responsible for finding the cash to buy food for themselves. At first father discovered a market for umbrella repair, which yielded decent earnings, but then realized that embroidering vestments for priests was more lucrative. With this job father learned, and emphasized to us, the importance of hand skills that could cross language barriers and provide income regardless of location.

Being a prankster, father exchanged his army identification tag with a friend shortly after their enlistment. At the beginning of the war this friend was killed, and father was captured as a Russian prisoner. When the army collected the dog tag from the body of his friend, they notified my grandparents that their son had been killed. Devastated, the family observed the ritual seven days of mourning and spent three years trying to reconcile the loss of a son.

The elation the family must have experienced when father returned at the end of the war was the vision of many of my daydreams. For father, however, joy at the reunion was tempered by finding his parents living in a house rented from local peasants after their manor had been burned down.

Prior to World War I my grandparents had lived on a leased estate since Jews were not permitted to own property. After the war, Poland was liberated from approximately 200 years of partition, and an independent Poland emerged in 1918, permitting Jews to be landowners. Father contributed his substantial back pay as an Austrian officer, collected over three years, toward the purchase of a new estate for his family. They moved to Rudenko Lackie in far-eastern Poland, near the Russian border, where the local population of mostly illiterate peasants spoke Ukrainian.

Rural life did not appeal to father, and after tasting Krakow he decided to seek his fortune in the royal city. He started his career working for the American Jewish Joint Distribution Committee. But after observing some fellow workers steal goods arriving from the United States to help tradesmen establish their lives, his disillusionment caused him to seek employment elsewhere. His next job was with the Hupert Tea Company, but he finally wound up working for Czwiklitzer Soap Company, managing the district office.

Once, over a month-long school vacation when I was nine years old, mother took Niusia, me, and cousin Jozek Hilfstein, to Rudenko Lackie to visit our grandparents on their new estate. The railroad trip took us from Krakow to Lwow, where we had to change to a small local train, then climb aboard a coach in which we rode for hours over bumpy country roads. In total, the trip took 15 hours.

For us sophisticated Krakowians used to living in high style, arriving at a house, however imposing by local standards, that was lit by kerosene lamps and had well water and outhouses was quite an experience. Grandmother, who was in her nineties, greeted us warmly with a great spread of freshly baked bread and homemade preserves from fruit grown on their farm. The farm workers lived in an adjoining village in small houses. When we visited the village they climbed over their fences to glance at the people from the city; our fashionable dresses and manners were foreign to them.

The long years did not soften grandfather, who barely acknowledged us for the entire month. Though we ate three meals a day at the same table with him, he never uttered a word. Niusia and I assumed he did not speak Polish! It was only on the day we departed that he spoke to us—in eloquent Polish. We later learned that his original anger at father had been exacerbated by father's choice of a bride who did not speak Yiddish and was not sufficiently religious. The anger he had nurtured for much of a lifetime had been transferred to my sister and me on our trip to Rudenko Lackie.

During our month at the farm, Niusia and I spent much time with Uncle Julek, a dapper and handsome squire who had married a wealthy girl from an adjacent estate. They lived in an elegant house despite the lack of electricity or plumbing. He maintained a stable of beautiful riding horses and was a voracious reader. Uncle Julek devoted much of his time to experimenting with growing hybrid vegetables and fruits, for which the rich soil in that part of the country was very suitable.

Although the distance from dense population centers and lack of mass transportation prevented local sales of Uncle Julek's products, our family benefited when a railroad car arrived in Krakow every winter loaded with produce. Packed inside were a wonderful variety of apples never seen in our part of the country and radishes as white as snow and as large as melons. Grandma included her delicious preserves and dried fruits. Father made delicious blueberry and cherry wine and set up barrels of sauerkraut with apples, supplying delicacies to the whole family, as well as friends, throughout the cold winter.

In the winter when farming did not occupy his time, Uncle Julek was busy solving crossword puzzles and entering contests. He won many prizes, including beautiful paintings, which were shipped to our house in Krakow since mailing them directly to the rural post office in Rudenko Lackie was no easy matter.

Father delighted in the small successes achieved by his brother, and I delighted in my father. As a young girl I always considered myself to be my father's daughter. He taught me how to ride a horse, shoot a rifle, and engage in many other skills ordinarily avoided by girls. I felt as though I was the boy he had wanted. When I answered the office phone, I would introduce myself as "Mr. Fuss's daughter," and when the puzzled caller asked where Mrs. Fuss's daughter was, I would say, referring to my sister: "She is in the other room." I was my father's companion, and I cherished our time together.

The wit and storytelling abilities of father brightened my days. Yet, his jolly nature did not prevent him from imposing strict discipline, albeit with a smile. When Niusia and I were in second grade he gave us rectangular chrome watches with bracelets, an unheard-of gift for girls our age. But with the present came a condition: "Now there will never be an excuse to be late." The giving was a metaphor for the life lessons father set forth. The great degree of freedom Niusia and I were accorded was also laden with responsibilities.

Father never held grudges and never spoke ill of grandfather, despite the harsh treatment grandfather had inflicted on him over the years. I admired father for his kindness and the love of family he exemplified by appreciating virtues and tolerating shortcomings. He was my hero, the star who lit up my happy, youthful life every day on 13 Wielopole Street.

Aron Fuss Graduation, Krakow, 1939 –
Standing, Naftali Fuss, Ecka Timberg and Oskar & Niusia Fuss; Seated, Jacob,
Marek, Lea, Aron, Sender, Mania and Luna Fuss

Chapter Three

War Comes to Us

When I was 12 years old and beginning to prepare for high school, my parents were preparing for refuge and my country was preparing for war. My parents' mental preparations had begun three years earlier when they had considered emigrating to Palestine.

My father's closest friend from gymnasium—which was what we called secondary school—was Mr. Landau. He and his wife had two daughters, and the younger of them, Wisia, was a classmate of mine. Wisia was petite with large brown eyes and black hair. Despite father's close relationship with Mr. Landau, the quarrelsome relationship between him and his wife made me dislike visiting their family. Since I had been raised in a house filled with love and harmony, I found it difficult to be exposed to a family that could not get along. Nonetheless, the Landaus were a constant presence in our lives.

Mr. Landau was a chemist who was seeking a career change, and Palestine—still largely nonindustrial at that time—offered it. He jumped at the opportunity to become a representative BATA, a popular shoe company, and opened a store in Tiberias, on the shores of the Sea of Galilee.

Mr. Landau frequently wrote us letters from Tiberias, and the sections father read to us were filled with optimism. We gathered to listen to the descriptions of this sunny land with tall palm trees, beaches, and an abundance of bananas and oranges—a luxury in light of Poland's short and limited fruit season.

Niusia and I fantasized about Palestine. We imagined ourselves strolling in gossamer dresses on the sunny beaches of the Sea of Galilee, bathing in the sunshine, sporting beautiful tans year-round, and saying goodbye to winter coats and gloomy, rainy days. We dreamed about this country where the sky was bright blue most of the year and where we could set a date for a picnic from April until October with the assurance it would not be rained out. We were excited about the prospect of emigrating.

Mother and father were protective and undoubtedly conveyed to us only the positive images written by Mr. Landau. After all, the majority population in Palestine in 1935 was Arab, and the Arabs were hostile to the increasing settlements of Jews who brought a European lifestyle. The climate was hot, and the conveniences that had been a way of life for the Europeans were nonexistent. Tiberias, where the Landau family settled, was a small town connected by dirt roads. Since the Landaus struck out on their own, in contrast to the Zionist *chalutzim* (pioneers) who established collective communities, they were forced to fit into the local lifestyle. Coming from a city like Krakow, which was rich with centuries of culture and a vibrant and affluent Jewish community, the newcomers faced a way of life that must have required significant and often unwelcome adjustments not mentioned in the excerpts of the Landaus' letters father read to us.

The images of paradise Niusia and I harbored burst abruptly one day. Only a year after the Landaus' emigration, a wire communication arrived at our house informing us of Wisia's death. A letter followed, explaining Wisia had contracted diphtheria one night. The sprawling city of Tiberias lacked phones and transportation. When Wisia's fever climbed high during that night, Mr. Landau rode a bicycle on the dirt roads to another part of the city where a doctor resided. The infection closed her throat, and although her family tried to help her breathe, they were helpless without the aid of the doctor. Despite being advanced in years the doctor struggled with a bicycle up the hill to the Landaus' house, but did not arrive in time to save her life.

Wisia's death was the first time I had experienced the loss of a contemporary, and its impact shattered our desire to emigrate. The message we heard behind the tragic event was that—threat of war or not—Palestine was not an acceptable alternative.

Adding to the problem was that Zionists were perceived as leftists, since they mostly recruited young people to settle in Palestine on collective farms. Looking back, we can see that the collective farms were the only practical way to settle the country. At the time, though, having experienced communism as an Austrian war prisoner in Russia during World War I, my father was naturally very suspicious of any collective outlook.

Our large family had, moreover, lived for generations in the same region, and uprooting ourselves would have felt like both an abandonment of those we loved and a severing of our support system.

We contented ourselves thinking that Germany was the most civilized and liberal country in the world. We were convinced of this stereotype despite the sudden immigration into Krakow of thousands of German Jews. Our city was close to the German border and culturally attractive as a result of the Austrian occupation, which had lasted about well over 100 years. In the middle of the eighteenth century, the northwestern part of Poland had been partitioned; the west was annexed by Germany, and the east was under Russian occupation. The southwestern part of the country, Galicia, which included Krakow, became part of the Austro-Hungarian Empire. Led by the tolerant Emperor Franz Jozef, the occupation was nostalgically remembered by the Jews who, generations later, still looked with pride toward Vienna as a capital. Unlike armies in other parts of Poland, the Austro-Hungarian army allowed many Jews, including my uncle Henry, to serve as high-ranking officers.

The German Jewish refugees we met in Krakow had a strong air of snobbishness. Though they had been expelled from Germany in desperate conditions, they had continued to feel proud of their German nationality and considered themselves superior to Polish Jews. Their great influx created housing problems, and facilities previously occupied by organizations were converted into residential units. My father was a member of the Chamber of Commerce, the offices of which were hastily furnished to accommodate the new arrivals. My good-natured mother pitched into the effort to help make a home for the German Jews, but they expected to be served. I resented mother's acting like a maid to accommodate their demands. Besides, mother had her own responsibilities: working, raising children, and managing a household.

Our trust in Austria and Germany was not weakened by early reports about concentration camps—in the late 1930's they were not yet death camps—which we believed were constructed for political activists punished for their rebellious activities. After all, father had experienced a similar plight in Russia during the revolution. We thought Hitler was a crazy maniac unrepresentative of the majority of Germans, and he would never be allowed by the citizenry to implement the anti-Semitic programs he was candid in espousing.

Our rationalizations were affirmed by local Polish beliefs. With the invasion of Austria and Czechoslovakia, the Polish army began to feverishly prepare for defense with a fighting spirit that made us believe they had a chance.

Meanwhile—despite the evil—there were happy moments to celebrate. My cousin Aron, the son of father's brother Sender, graduated from the Jagiellonian University Law School in Krakow. Aron Fuss was a very bright and politically savvy student who was president of the Jewish students' association and had become a well-known speaker on the political circuit. He had campaigned actively for a Jewish senatorial candidate named Oziasz Ton, who even as a Jew, won the election. Since his family lived in the city of Rzeszow about two hours away, our home had become his second home.

The graduation was a memorable event in our family's life. Aron's father, Sender, a handsome Orthodox Jew, sported a long, white beard and wore traditional black clothing. Since anti-Semitism had spread through the university and physical violence against Jews was rampant in the streets, attendance at the graduation was laced with fear. I had been recovering from scarlet fever at the time, but nothing could have stopped me from attending. I remember family members surrounding Uncle Sender in an effort to hide him and keep him from being attacked by malicious students. Fortunately, he was not attacked.

Following the graduation proceedings, the family, as was typical, gathered in our house for a celebration. Three months later World War II broke out. Aron went to Lwow, dedicating himself to delivering food during a typhoid epidemic. During this selfless mission he caught the disease and died of its complications.

In the summer of 1939 a Krakow city law required all lights to be extinguished after dark as a protection against bombing attacks. We put shades on the windows, and voluntary patrols roamed the streets at night searching for even the slightest beam of light, suspected of being a signal being sent by spies. Older adults received training as patrols and emergency personnel in anticipation of younger men being drafted into the Polish army.

Feeling like an invincible and patriotic 12-year-old and easily lulled by feelings of patriotism and trust, I considered the Polish army to be too valiant to be defeated. I was swayed by the handsome soldiers in khaki green uniforms with shiny gold buttons, and even further assured by visits from my handsome cousin, Zylek Timberg, wearing his tailored cavalry uniform and tall hat with its bright red band.

Father rationalized Germany's annexation of Austria in 1938 by maintaining that Austria was a Germanic country willing to ally with its larger and more powerful neighbor. Regarding Germany's occupation of Czechoslovakia, father believed this small, affluent country could not repel the German military force, which needed the sophisticated Czech industries for its war effort. The Polish army, on the other hand, said father and many others, had liberated our country from occupation in 1918 and would surely be a match for the invaders. In retrospect, I do not think my parents believed this rhetoric, but having no alternative they convinced themselves and us not to worry.

Matters other than war occupied my mind that year. The summer of 1939 preceded my first year of high school, where I would again accompany Niusia on long walks and the promise of older girls' conversations. New friends and a new wardrobe awaited. My navy coat-dress with its white collar and colored bow tie revealing my grammar school grade made way for fashionable clothes. Mother took us to the fabric store and then the dressmaker where clothes went from the imagination to our closet.

The dress I most remember was a beautiful scotch plaid of red, green, and yellow. It had pleats that stretched from the shoulders to the hem, buttons on the back, a white collar, and sleeves with white cuffs. Since I feared that mother would not have agreed to have the dress cut if she had known the extent to which my skin itched from the wool, I kept the discomfort to myself.

Niusia and I were outfitted in the same dresses, but we did not look the same in them. My sister was very fair and slim and much taller than me. She dressed with great care and wore matching shoes, gloves, and even undergarments. My clothes received much more abuse, and I almost took pride in making them appear well-worn.

That summer I spent a lot of time with Niusia and her friends, all of whom tolerated me. Although 12 years old, I was not quite ready to date and defensively ridiculed the teenagers. I enjoyed spending time with them and parading around the promenade, observing their flirting behavior. The entire world seemed to me to blossom with romance. Even news reports warning of spies and teaching us how to wear gas masks did not spoil the romance of the moment.

Most of the news was kept at a distance from the children, who did not read the newspapers. There was no television, and the few radios that existed generally required earphones. The news that ultimately filtered down to our ears was sanitized. I do not even remember hearing about *Kristallnacht* (the Night of Broken Glass), when Jewish synagogues, institutions, and books throughout Germany went up in flames. November 9-10, 1938, marked a dramatic and nightmarish turning point in Germany's treatment of the Jews: thousands were beaten, deported, and killed. A reign of terror had begun.

September 1, 1939, was a beautiful, sunny day. That morning, as mother prepared breakfast, as father got ready for work standing by the bedroom window and shaving with his straight razor, and as Niusia and I fantasized about high school, which would begin imminently, we heard a sudden call from father to approach the window. We witnessed what appeared to be a small plane going down in flames over the Krakow airport. Our apartment on the fourth floor in the old part of the city, where few tall buildings stood, gave us clear vision of the air space above the airport. Father enthusiastically applauded what he believed to be a military training mission. We did not know then that this had been a real German bomber plane and that its downing had been one of the events signaling the beginning of World War II.

We scrambled for a radio, which confirmed this fact. Subsequently we heard the howl of air raid sirens and orders shouted from the streets commanding us to leave the top floors of buildings in case of falling bombs. Our family took a small supply of food and gas masks and headed for father's office on the ground floor of 13 Wielopole Street. Our fear of a gas war scared us more than anything else. When the immediate threat dissipated, we returned to our apartment.

In a short time the streets were swarming with people carrying little bundles of their most essential belongings, preparing to embark on a long march eastward to escape the Germans, without any specific destination. With no trains, few private cars, and horses being used for military purposes, we had no transportation save our own feet. Many people thought they would be best off vacating the city while the soldiers repelled the enemy closer to the borders. We continued to have confidence in the Polish army. We believed Poland's prosperity over 20 years since World War I had equipped its army to fight Germany even better than it had in the first war, when Marshal Pilsudski managed to liberate Poland from its approximately 200 years of partition by Russia, Germany, and Austria.

After the first day of the invasion, the Polish currency was frozen. Since valuable items like gold and precious stones could be carried, many of the refugees hoped that the few pieces of jewelry they had brought would bring them the means to pay for shelter and food. Mother sewed jewelry into the lining of garments, which she distributed to father, Niusia, and me in case we were separated.

The emigrants came from the areas that bordered Germany. After war had broken out, Poles from Silesia in western Poland had taken to the streets and migrated east, hoping the Polish army would stop the invaders at the border. The family of Aunt Helen—mother's elegant sister—and her customs-officer husband, Uncle Julek, were among this group.

Aunt Helen and Uncle Julek Hilfstein were frequent visitors to Krakow with their two sons, Oscar and Jozek. Five years older than my mother, Aunt Helen moved, after marrying Uncle Julek, to Dziedzice, where Uncle Julek became a customs officer on the German border. The move had saddened mother. She missed Aunt Helen very much.

Despite their age difference, the two sisters looked like twins. Aunt Helen was tall and statuesque. She and Uncle Julek liked to attend balls in Krakow, for which she always looked elegant in her beautiful gowns. Once, when she and Uncle Julek were the leading couple for the opening cotillion at a ball, Aunt Helen wore a black lace gown with a Maria Stuart collar and diamond jewelry, and Uncle Julek wore a white tie and tails. The compelling image of this refined couple whose lives were so entangled with ours played into all the fantasies of royalty from which native Krakowians could not escape.

Our house on Wielopole Street had been home to Aunt Helen when she was growing up. It represented security, a comfortable place to huddle in times of disaster. On their eastward journey Aunt Helen's family arrived on our doorstep. Their bags, all that they could escape with, were filled with what they considered to be their most valuable items. They had abandoned their beautiful home in Dziedzice, filled with antique furniture, oriental rugs, exquisite artwork, and most of their possessions.

Like many of the people passing through Krakow from the west, they had been frightened by the proximity of the entering army that they had experienced firsthand. Only a day after their arrival at our house they joined thousands of others marching toward Russia in the beautiful early-autumn weather. I felt brokenhearted to part with my beloved cousins. For days after they left I glued my eyes to the window, envisioning their tired bodies trudging down the street.

The Hilfsteins were not the only ones who left the family in the first few weeks of the war. My cousin Salek Timberg had a new car. Salek—a Victor Mature-look-alike whom I idolized, an athlete six years my senior who took me skiing for the first time, was a member of the Maccabi club who had had the courage to defend Jewish honor against the roving groups of anti-Semitic Poles who had beaten Jews. Two days after the outbreak of war, he was hired to take several people to Lwow, the most easterly Polish city at the time, close to the Russian border. The roads were fraught with danger, and we begged Salek not to accept the job. My invincible cousin, however, felt the pay was too excellent to pass up, particularly given the need to make car payments and the uncertainty of the future. My goodbye to Salek was drenched with tears of young love and familial love. I felt an agonizing fear grounded in the chaos of the moment, influenced by powerful childhood memories and a terrible, foreboding vision of what was to come.

Events were happening so rapidly that choices—which were more abundant than any tangible item—were often based on instinct rather than rationality. The day after Salek's departure, our family faced a major choice. One of the Christian tenants in our apartment building worked for a utility company and had a truck, which they were planning to use to drive eastward. They offered our family four spots on the truck, one for each of us, but gave us only minutes to decide whether to join them. The opportunity seemed priceless.

We dressed hastily and packed our most valuable possessions in small bundles. It was so difficult to gaze around the apartment and choose which items would come with us and which would stay. The family home was filled with three generations of memories, all of which seemed equal in value. But there was no time for sentimentality.

Though I am sure my bag was filled with items that felt important to a 12-year-old girl, what they were eludes me today, except that I do recall my decision to lug my new winter coat purchased for me by cousin Moishe Fuss from Belgium who had just visited Poland over the summer vacation. The weather was still warm, the coat was heavy. But we believed the war would be over and the Germans chased out before the first winter winds blew across Poland. Including my coat with my baggage was almost an omen.

Belongings in hand, my family approached the stairway. The familiar four flights of stairs I had bounced up and down for a decade suddenly seemed to slowly descend into an abyss. When I reached the second floor I sat down and refused to continue. I suddenly could not imagine riding in an open truck through throngs of people with low-flying bomber planes hovering overhead. I could not bear to let loose the grip of my feet and my emotions from the one place that had always enveloped me in security.

My father hunched over me, simultaneously attempting to persuade me to move forward and hesitantly listening to my logic, unsure himself of the correct choice. Finally, in the last moments of decision making, feeling that he would never forgive himself if something happened on the trek eastward, he agreed to stay. It was a decision built not on rationality, but on emotion—and perhaps premonition.

The next morning we learned the truck had been bombed when it had reached the edge of Krakow, and all its passengers had been killed. The neighbors who had offered us the space had also decided not to go, so they were not among the victims. It was our first very hard lesson about the unpredictability of our wartime destiny.

Our fantasies about Polish defense were smothered faster than the fire that brought down the German plane at the Krakow airport on September 1. The occupying German forces met no resistance when they entered Krakow within three days of the invasion.

The next morning, as the pale autumn sunshine filtered through our apartment curtains, we awakened to the sound of German songs accompanied by the thunderous, rhythmical pounding of marching boots on the streets below the windows. The inevitable had happened. Terrified, I had for my sole psychological defense my fantasy that the Polish army would come to our rescue.

There was nothing gradual about the crisis we faced. Everyone ran to the food stores to accumulate groceries. Perishable goods, which had generally been purchased daily since there were no refrigerators, were the first to go. The shelves were quickly emptied of flour, potatoes, and coal—the only means of cooking and heating.

Most of the businesses closed, and father found himself without work. The banks were shut down, and our assets inside them were frozen. Father had always stressed to Niusia and me the importance of earning money and keeping savings in a bank account to purchase items for which we would have special appreciation. We had been saving our money to buy bicycles, putting the Polish equivalent of pennies into the bank each week and watching them grow into more substantial sums. We had almost reached our goal. Just two months before, over the summer, we had gone shopping to pick out the most beautiful models. But when the banks closed, the value of our Polish pennies—and the bicycles that had promised us newfound independence—evaporated.

While the food and money shortages brought unwelcome complications, the school closings punctured holes in the dreams of a 12-year-old whose entire previous year had been geared toward attending high school. Gone were the daily occasions to parade in beautiful clothes; gone was the internal controversy about wearing the itchy plaid dress with the pleats from shoulder to hem. Gone were the occasions to observe the dating scene of the older kids; gone was the assurance that one day I would be an older kid whom someone younger would want to observe. Gone were the lessons tailored to a more thoughtful crowd; gone was the challenge of learning about subjects that promised to make my mind race. Gone were the private walks with Niusia; gone was the promise of metamorphosis from childhood to adulthood in the context of a city alive with history, tradition, culture, intelligence, and romance. When the school doors were locked, I despairingly felt a figurative *zamkniente* (closed) sign write itself across the immediate future I had mapped out for myself.

A few days after the occupation had begun, father came home accompanied by a German officer—a robust, jovial character. Although we were initially frightened as father introduced us, we immediately learned this soldier had been an officer who served—and had been friends—with father in the Austrian army during World War I. The meeting brought us a momentary sense of security.

We questioned the "scare tactics" of the Poles that preceded the invasion, and began to think about the Germans as soldiers who wore different uniforms but who came from a highly regarded culture that had been allied with the Austrian Empire under the good Kaiser Franz Josef. After all, Jews in Krakow had lived and prospered under Austrian occupation for well over 100 years with relative harmlessness. Indeed, to some extent, the thought of living under Austrian rule seemed like a more pleasant prospect than living under the largely anti-Semitic Polish government of that time.

Daily life, however, did not confirm the hopes that the German officer's introduction had brought. Every morning we awoke to newly glued posters on the round kiosks announcing additional restrictions on the Jews. Each regulation was written in a manner suggesting that it would be the last and that compliance would result in a hands-off policy. One of the first regulations provided that Jews were permitted to shop only in specially designated grocery stores containing a much smaller supply of food than the grocery stores available to non-Jews.

Next, the Germans began arbitrarily picking Jewish men on the streets to perform dirty manual labor under terrible conditions. This regulation did not keep father at home, and each time he left the apartment he said, "Don't worry. I am only going around the corner." But we never knew on which corner a truck with German soldiers would be waiting to grab passing Jews and escort them to clean latrines or sweep stables, beating and mistreating them as they worked. For us, father's exits from the apartment provoked terrible anxiety. We planted ourselves next to the window from the moment he departed until he returned.

Within two months of occupation the Germans issued an order for all Jews over the age of 13 to wear white armbands imprinted with the blue *Magen David* (Star of David). My thirteenth birthday had not yet arrived, and without the band I could have used the streetcar, keeping in contact with members of the extended family and obtaining food and other resources from stores closed to Jews. But mother, father, and Niusia were required to wear it, and I did not want to have any special privilege to which they were not entitled. I was determined to wear my band with its white and blue colors standing out on the background of my navy blue coat. In fact, I worried that the blue might fade with washing, and I embroidered the star into the white band to be more distinctive. It made me feel defiant and proud of my heritage. I considered the band my badge of honor.

The daily barrage of restrictions became a way of life. Incredibly, we somehow adjusted. After all, we rationalized, Jews had always been singled out for discrimination, even if these regulations were more severe than past ones. We could not imagine the conditions of our lives at that moment as a permanent reality—or a reality that could grow grimmer.

The weeks of anxiety wore heavily on all of us, alleviated only by the joyous return of Aunt Helen's family to Wielopole Street. They had been exposed to bombing on the open road, and their food supply had dwindled. Endangered and desperate, they reversed their course and moved in with us. Seeing them created such joy that we forgot that the war had begun to rage.

But I never again saw Cousin Salek or heard anything about his fate.

The joy in having our favorite cousins live with us was so great we barely noticed the way we had crammed eight people into the four rooms of our house. Jozek and Oskar were only a few years older than Niusia and me, and their presence fostered an active social life. Oskar was a talented pianist and singer who performed frequently on our grand piano. Young, handsome boys congregated at our home, often enjoying card games in our salon. I fantasized about relationships with them, becoming infatuated with each one anew every few days.

Popular, older girls who had previously refused to acknowledge me suddenly sought invitations to our house, hoping to meet some of the boys. I found their behavior amusing and teased them mercilessly.

In the first few weeks after the invasion we illegally held school classes in private homes. Arrest was threatened if our actions were discovered, and with time the endeavor became too dangerous—we had to give it up.

The streets were hazardous, crawling with German soldiers who found many reasons to arrest, beat, or haphazardly shoot people. Within the walls of our familiar apartment, however, we felt as secure and comfortable as butterflies in cocoons.

We had no income, and all the money in the banks had been frozen. Father's factory was closed. Always enterprising, he found a formula to make soap from lard, and he sold the new product. Mother and Aunt Helen also contributed meager sums to the family income. Through their ingenuity they conjured up tasty "cheese cakes" made from potatoes, which they sold. I embarked on an enterprise to knit sweaters and socks from old garments, combining wool from two sweaters of different colors into intricate designs. One time I managed to unravel a beautiful blue sweater with multicolored knobs, knitting the yarn into a two-piece bathing suit for myself. Looking back, I wonder where I was planning to use it. But simply creating it gave me pleasure, and the fantasy of wearing it on a beach somewhere made me smile internally.

Conservation of our resources required as much inventiveness as ways to earn money, and father was well endowed with ideas. Worrying that our shoes would wear out, he bought scraps of leather for us to attach to the soles, ensuring that the scraps would fade before the soles gave way.

Refusing to go to the barbers assigned to service Jews, father bought a pair of clippers, and made the mistake of agreeing to let me cut his hair. It was quite a risk, since he knew I found laughter in all kinds of pranks. I gave him a "punk" haircut, leaving his head in stripes. Fortunately for me he had a sense of humor. While we all had a good laugh, father had to walk around for a month with a totally shaved head, which was not exactly fashionable.

Our "enterprises," together with the sale of our valuable possessions, provided us with income for a while; it also occupied our time. We redefined the meaning of "necessities," and we somehow continuously found items to sell to satisfy our needs.

Coal for cooking and heating was one of the most important essentials for us to live as comfortably as possible under the circumstances. Father managed to make occasional deals for coal that arrived by horse-drawn wagon and was deposited on the street in front of the cellar window. The building janitor who had once had the job of shoveling it down the chute now considered the job beneath his dignity. Father and I took the task in stride. We grabbed shovels and dumped the coal into the cellar. Niusia, a perfect lady, abhorred the idea of work that left her covered with black dust; the concept embarrassed and humiliated her. For me, in comparison, it was a great game. Somehow many of the tasks intended to humiliate the Jews had the effect of amusing me.

Within a few weeks of the invasion the Germans began systematically plundering homes, taking with them whatever they desired. One day we heard their boots banging on the wooden stairs of our apartment building, climbing up to our fourth-floor apartment. The sound brought panic. Their visits were known to be for the purpose of taking people or belongings.

Three officers dressed in uniforms with medals, shining boots, and guns on their hips appeared at our front door. We froze, feeling raped, as they silently marched through the apartment, assessing what they felt to be desirable loot. A truck waited downstairs, prepared to load their pickings.

Our atrium-like salon was a large, bright room with a gold-framed mirror flanked by ceiling-high ficus trees. The floors were covered by detailed, maroon Oriental rugs, and in the corner atop the safe an antique clock chimed an aria from Flotow's opera *Martha*. The officers noticed immediately the grand piano standing under a beautiful French tapestry mother had embroidered. It was obvious to us the piano would be a targeted object to take—a form of entertainment for girlfriends at the boisterous parties the officers hosted nightly.

When they asked who played the piano we hesitantly pointed to Oskar, whom they commanded to perform. Despite Oskar's trembling hands, music flowed from his fingers seemingly with ease and charm. The soldiers stayed for a half hour, listening to and admiring Oskar's performance of Chopin and popular music. I imagined they were surprised by our degree of civility, quite different from the images of Jews presented in German press caricatures at the time. The officers chose to leave our apartment empty-handed.

The incident confirmed our shoestring hopes that the Germans were a culturally sensitive people. Their appreciation of art left us with a false sense of security. We could not comprehend that characteristic existing side by side with the utter brutality we later witnessed.

A very popular German song rang true for us: *Es gait allies foriber, es gait alles forbai, nach jedem December comes vieder ein May.* Translated into English, the lyrics state: "Everything passes by, everything ends, after each December again comes May." Those words became the motto of our lives for the next six years.

Chapter Four
Bronowice

Niusia and Luna, Bronowice, 1941

As long as we were enveloped in the security of the home that had been ours for generations, the war felt surreal. The new reality, of course, swept through the streets: Jewish stores displayed the Star of David, Jews wore white and blue armbands, and the city crawled with soldiers in German uniforms. But inside our apartment little had changed. The grandfather clock still chimed its aria; we gathered around the table covered with a white linen tablecloth three times a day with our enlarged family; and our sense of humor had not yet dimmed, though conversations lingered much longer than they once had. No one was in a rush to go to work or attend school.

Every morning we reluctantly ventured out to read the latest posters that had been mounted on the kiosks overnight. Their messages never spelled good news.

March 5, 1941, was a bleak morning. The posters declared that all Jews were to leave the center of the city within a few days. For my family and me the announcement marked the first jarring impact of the war. Abandoning the house built by grandfather—the house where mother, Niusia, and I were born; the house in which every corner, every inch, was familiar and held memories of childhood joy; the house that had protected us as the war raged for a year and a half—was a frightful and cruel prospect.

Equally distressing was the notion of leaving the house to the Germans, who intended to occupy and loot all apartments within the city. Grandfather had been a great lover of antiques and art, so our apartment was full of items he had collected during his long life. How merciful that he had died before the war and did not live to witness this destruction.

We had only a few days to dispose of our family legacy. Not wanting to leave behind any objects of value for the Germans, my parents arranged with Nela, the daughter of our tenants, the Zaczeks, to store valuable furniture at her home just a few blocks away. In this way our dining room furniture, which had been designed by my mother in 1923 for her trousseau, the large needlework mother had embroidered in 1935, our grand piano, and other objects important to us became the furnishings that filled the home of Nela, who had fled with her family from western Poland after the German invasion and who had been living in a large but empty apartment.

The panic-stricken Jewish population began to search feverishly for new living quarters outside the city center. My parents found a room in Bronowice, a small town at the end of a streetcar line. In exchange for rent a peasant family agreed to share their small, gray apartment with us.

We loaded onto a horse-drawn cart a few remnants of our lives. Since it had been decreed that Jews could not ride streetcars, we embarked on a long foot march to Bronowice. Where the streetcar tracks ended, so did city life. There were no suburbs around Krakow. Paved streets gave way to dirt roads. From the moment we walked over the city limit, we were forbidden to re-enter, an act that carried the risk of arrest or deportation.

Neat but primitive houses—two-story whitewashed abodes—dotted the roads of the countryside. Local people rarely ventured into the city. Their horizons were limited by the town's boundaries. A hand-pumped well supplied water, and hot water for washing required heating in large pots.

The fears that accompanied leaving our home gave way to an initial hope that this small, out-of-the-way town might prove a good hiding place as opposed to a large street in the city center. Niusia and I thought the town was so gloomy the soldiers would not be interested in bothering us there. If our parents had a different assessment, they did not share it with us. Instead they focused on keeping our spirits high.

But sharing the small apartment and tiny kitchen with unsophisticated people whose lives differed greatly from ours was difficult. A poor Jewish barber lived in the basement. Almost as soon as we arrived mother set out to spruce up the apartment by setting out doilies and a few small but familiar objects we had taken with us. We filled shelves with books considered a luxury by our barely literate landlords. We set the table in a more elegant fashion than they did, even under the dire circumstances. They were kind to us, but our way of life must have been as strange to them as theirs was to us.

The barber had very crude manners. He constantly appeared unwashed, and his facial features gave off an aura of sadness. He was alone. I don't know if he was a bachelor or had lost his family. Much to my dismay, mother took pity on him and included him in our mealtimes. He talked with mouthfuls of food, and his comments were routinely negative. I fought with him constantly, particularly resenting his expectation that mother would serve him. He loomed like a big shadow at the table. He did not share our sense of humor, which was our only escape from the troubles that filled our daily lives.

Our relatives had moved to other villages, everyone scrambling to find available housing. This was the first time our extended family had been dispersed without the ability to communicate. We could not cross the city line or use transportation. There were no phones, and mail was unreliable. Our support system was severely damaged. We felt isolated.

The only family members who lived within walking distance of Bronowice were Aunt Helen Hilfstein and her family. One day Niusia and I embarked on a hike to visit them, discarding our armbands so we would not be spotted as Jews. Since we had to circle the city, the walk took several hours. The weather was nice, and the stroll through fields and villages was pleasant. We dressed in freshly starched cotton dresses to present ourselves nicely to our favorite cousins.

En route we encountered two German soldiers. I had been lagging behind Niusia, enjoying the fragrance of the field flowers. My sister, with her tall and lovely figure, big blue eyes, and stylishly wrapped golden braids, walked in front. One of the soldiers stopped to admire her, remarking, "How good-looking the German girls are." When I—a shorter and rounder figure—came into view, he snapped: "The Polish girls are so clumsy." Niusia and I shared the luxury of a good laugh at the expense of their prejudice and ignorance.

The Hilfsteins welcomed us with hugs and kisses. While their living conditions were not any better than ours, the visit gave us all a wonderful boost.

Such excursions were risky. The probability of the soldiers realizing we were Jewish and forcing us to clean latrines was very likely. The hours of absence provoked anxiety in our parents, but they understood the need to give us some freedom and the semblance of a normal life. I am sure mother sat by the window throughout the day, awaiting our safe return.

In comparison to the more remote villages where Jews were forced to settle, Bronowice's location was good. Its proximity to the city made it possible for our Christian former neighbors to reach us by streetcar. We had arranged with some of them to sell our possessions and bring us money or food.

I remember Mr. Zaczek visiting us one day. He was elderly and breathed with difficulty as he climbed the flight of stairs to our second-floor apartment. Mr. Zaczek, who was a big, burly butcher, brought us a package of ground meat, and he was visibly distraught when he saw our poor living conditions. He had hidden the meat in his coat pocket since it was illegal to supply Jews with food. If caught, he could have been arrested and imprisoned in a concentration camp.

Despite our grim living conditions, we found creative ways to maintain our collective family spirit. Mother baked "cheese" danish consisting of cheese-flavored potatoes, selling them to supplement our meager income. Since my favorites had always been pasta and potatoes and these staples were still available, I did not suffer from hunger. Mother was also very inventive in her soup recipes. With vegetables readily accessible in the country, a new dish appeared on our daily menu. We called it *Ein Topf Gericht*, a whole meal in one pot containing vegetables, grains, potatoes, and, if available, a small piece of meat for flavoring. We cherished each spoonful.

Buying new clothes was impossible, so we made alterations and imaginative repairs. I embarked upon an enterprise to design pins and necklaces from tiny, multicolored beads I had collected as a child. Now I turned my play into an occupation, giving new life to old clothes with additional decorations. Amazingly, there was a market for my creations, which I designed in the shapes of bow ties and daffodils and red cherries on green stems. A daughter of a childhood friend of mother who had traveled with her to Lwow when she studied to become an accountant and later became Aunt Helen's sister-in-law—a young woman named Wanda Fail—sold my work at a country market. I also found another customer, a dressmaker who ordered beadwork for the trim on the clothes she designed.

My successful enterprise introduced me to the business world. I was inspired by father's World War I stories about how he had repaired umbrellas or embroidered priestly vestments to obtain income. Indeed, my parents' experiences only 20 years before, when they had learned to accept the inconveniences brought by war—and then enjoyed the ensuing prosperity—helped to make the situation tolerable for us. While my beadwork efforts did not earn a fortune, they brought in enough money to supplement our resources, especially since the rationed food was inexpensive. Perhaps equally significant, the satisfaction of creating original pieces of work diverted my thoughts from the grim realities.

Living in isolation in the country, where newspapers were published only by official authorities and therefore sanitized and where possession of telephones or radios was illegal, we were lulled into a false sense of security, hoping our tormentors had forgotten us. I could not divest myself of the thought that one day we would return home. Our constant state of denial helped us to survive. We did not think about the future. We could not have anticipated what would come.

With time, the isolation turned into loneliness, and we craved contact with family and friends. After only several months in Bronowice, the Germans issued an order for us to move to the ghetto they had created across the river from Krakow in the neighborhood of Podgorze. Not knowing what would await us, we welcomed the idea of reunification with the Jewish community.

Niusia with bead bowtie fashioned by Luna, 1941

Chapter Five

The Ghetto in Krakow

The Krakow ghetto was built in the spring of 1941 in the section of the city called Podgorze. While the Germans had intended the 320 apartments in Podgorze to house 16,000 people, eventually the number swelled to 19,000. The ghetto was intended to confine all the Jews to one area, making it easy for the Germans to control them. The Germans had made the cleaning of streets or military latrines, as well as other other demeaning tasks, a way of life for the Jews. Now, the Germans no longer had to figure out which city residents were Jewish. They only had to come to one point and load a truck full of people within minutes.

We were moving back to the city of Krakow, but it was not *our* Krakow. Podgorze, on the other side of the Vistula River, had been a blue-collar neighborhood with only a few pleasant residences. It was much newer than the medieval center of town that had been our familiar stomping ground. Despite the proximity of Podgorze to the city center, I had never crossed the river before the war.

Erecting the ghetto in Podgorze necessitated the installation of barbed wire around its perimeter. All non-Jewish residents were evacuated and forcibly moved elsewhere, leaving their small apartments empty for Jewish habitation. Again we had to liquidate most of our meager possessions since with each move our belongings had to fit into smaller spaces. The impact of the first move had been the most devastating, since it entailed leaving not only objects, but also our home, our neighborhood, and our memories. By the time we were forced to part with more possessions on the trek from Bronowice to Podgorze, we accepted that aspect of our fate without much reaction. After all, we had no closets for extra clothes or cupboards to store dishes. It was enough to have dishes for one meal, and then wash them for the next.

The entrance to our assigned second-floor, two-room apartment was in a courtyard. Little sunlight found its way through the small windows that opened into the dingy courtyard. We shared our two rooms with the Spielmans, an ultra-Orthodox family: parents, a 15-year-old son named Moniek, and a 17-year-old son named Romek. Mother, father, Niusia, and I shared half a bedroom with the Spielman parents, dividing our family quarters by a bedspread hanging across a string. The boys had a second room to themselves.

The Spielmans' observant ways were more foreign to us than those of the peasants we had lived with in Bronowice. Our assimilated way of life in Krakow had not included following many religious customs.

The Spielmans had little tolerance for our way of life. Though mother was familiar with Jewish customs of *kashrut* (Jewish laws concerning food and cooking), nothing mother did was kosher enough for Mrs. Spielman, who demanded that we adhere strictly to laws regulating what we ate and requiring the use of separate dishes for dairy and meat. Her demand was almost impossible to meet in light of the scarcity of dishes and available (and affordable) food. Moreover, the tiny, windowless kitchen had a coal stove with a surface that was not more than 3 feet by3 feet. Consequently, dividing the space between two women cooking for a total of eight people required great navigational skills—and much patience.

The ultra-Orthodoxy of the Spielmans did not apply only to food laws. Their observance of the Sabbath each Friday evening through Saturday restricted our lives in a way we were not accustomed to. Actions like writing, turning on lights, or cooking using a flame were considered transgressions. Before sundown on Friday we made *cholent*—a pot of barley with beans, potatoes, and meat, if available, which we left in the bread oven over the fire extinguished for the Sabbath. The coals stayed warm enough for the mixture to bake through Saturday. Admittedly, it was a delicious meal. Had it not been forced by circumstances, we would have enjoyed it very much.

The biggest advantage to sharing the apartment with the Spielman family was that Mr. Spielman was a baker. When food was scarce, we were never short of bread—indeed, not just any bread, but fresh, crusty, aromatic rye bread with caraway seeds. Sinking my teeth into the delicious bread was a great comfort to me through the stressful periods.

I can still smell the bread today.

We convinced ourselves that as long as we had enough food we would not only not starve, but we would have enough strength to conquer all obstacles. Mother supplemented the bread with daily hot meals she invented from potatoes, beans. and barley. Mr. Spielman supplied us with flour, which enabled us to add dumplings to our menu. We were never hungry.

The barbed wire that locked us into the ghetto also shielded us from the hostile world outside.

On sunny days we looked out on the hills beyond our confines, imagining that our world had not gone insane. After all, the grass was equally green on both sides, and on spring and summer mornings the songs of the birds transcended any barriers. For a while this false sense of security left room for us to live with some degree of uncomfortable normalcy.

It was not only the birds that crossed the ghetto's borders. Non-Jews who needed to travel through the ghetto en route to somewhere else were able to ride on the streetcar—doors locked—as it traversed Limanowska Street, the wide avenue where our apartment was located. Despite anti-Semitic slogans that too frequently burst from the mouths of tram riders, the sight of free people offered us a window into life on the other side, and sometimes, tools to help us survive.

Before leaving our apartment on Wielopole Street for Bronowice, we had given our household possessions to Mrs. Podworska, a kind Christian widow who was a tenant in our apartment building. Slowly she had sold them, accumulating cash. After we moved to the ghetto, she brought it to father, throwing bundles through the window of the passing tram. Once, as she attempted to throw the parcel, Nazi soldiers spotted her. Fortunately, they could not discern which face in the crowd Mrs. Podworska's package was intended to reach. Had my Jewish father been singled out, his punishment could have been the loss of his life.

But Mrs. Podworska's transgression had been noticed. A guard on board the streetcar approached her, slapping her face. Mrs. Podworska weathered the beating with dignity, and the episode did not deter her from returning. She knew her packages were our only source of income, and she was committed to helping us despite the danger. Her valiant acts were a key source of our survival as long as we remained in Krakow.

Despite endangering their own lives, some non-Jewish friends rode the streetcar through the ghetto to toss us money obtained from the sale of goods we entrusted to them. Newspapers were special treasures, since there were none available in the ghetto.

Additional income came from the sale of our belongings, but the less we owned, the less was available to sell to get cash for food. We no longer needed more than one pair of shoes, and the minimal clothes that would protect us from the cold of winter and keep us cool on a hot summer day were enough. Everything else was marketable, and the preferred black marketplace happened in whispers through Jews assigned to work outside the ghetto walls, where the barter was food that was less accessible on our side.

The best source of income, however meager, came from the sale of jewelry, which was easy to transport and hide. Diamonds were the most desirable commodities since they were worth more than other gems, yet their size allowed them to be hidden in the seams of garments. Despite announcements posted by the Germans throughout the ghetto ordering the turning in of all jewelry and furs at the risk of death for noncompliance, mother sewed valuable pieces into the hems of our clothes. She reasoned that if any of us found ourselves alone, we would at least have some share of our jewelry resources.

Our cramped and miserable living conditions notwithstanding, we refused to bow to any semblance of disgrace. No matter how scant the amount of food on the table, we set it atop a tablecloth. We spruced up the apartment by creating doilies from old clothing and decorating in any way possible. Every minor aesthetic feat gave us a feeling of home.

Since the curfew was 9 p.m., we had a lot of family time together each evening when we dined and basked in the memories of pre-war life. During this period I gathered detailed information about father's family that I had never known before. He spoke about his parents' beautiful estate, his large extended family, the many nieces and nephews who lived in the compound, and the singing and rejoicing that accompanied holiday celebrations around grand tables. He laughed as he recalled pranks he and his younger brother Julek had orchestrated. His stories transported us to a world of fantasy that, in the circumstances of the ghetto, seemed much more compelling than even my childhood musings about Queen Jadwiga dancing in the Wawel.

One evening we decided to gather around the table for a seance in which we asked many questions and expected the responses to be in the form of knocks against the table. Father was very skeptical of extrasensory perception; he disapproved of our going to fortune tellers. But understanding the activity that night included no one outside of the family, he witnessed our venture with skepticism from the side of the room, a smile upon his face. Finally wanting to prove the falsity of the table's responses, he threw a question into the middle of the circle, asking how many siblings he had. Although no one around the table knew the correct answer, somehow the table knocked the appropriate number of times.

Father's view of fortune tellers was not altered by the miracle of the table. Eventually, we learned what lay behind his closed-mindedness on the subject. Upon graduating from gymnasium in Krakow during World War I, all the boys were drafted as officers for the Austrian army and assigned to the front lines. During a farewell party, someone introduced a game in which he wrote a fortune with wax on plain paper, and then inserted it into a bottle with ashes that clung to the wax, creating an image of a message.

Apparently, one of the boys did not understand the trick and gave great weight to the fortune that emerged for him, which portended his death fighting in the war. According to father, this episode so agitated the boy that he went into an adjoining room and shot himself. After that episode, said father, he had disdain for fortune telling, whether authentic or contrived.

I think, however, that the real truth was that father did not want to hear what the future held for us. He would allow almost nothing to break the strength of his spirit; he was our cheerleader and felt the responsibility of helping us sail through the roughest of moments. A jolly, optimistic man who knew that we leaned on him for moral support, he could not afford to think about the negative directions to which any fortune teller would have been forced to point.

Our familial sense of security was rooted in each other. Our greatest fear was separation. Upon our arrival in the ghetto, father and Niusia were assigned jobs almost immediately and were forced to work outside the ghetto walls each day. Mother and I hailed their return over and over as the biggest event of each day. We were relieved with the knowledge of their safety, and they showered us with news from the "real world" outside the barbed wires behind which we were imprisoned.

Before the appearance of a posted order demanding that all ghetto inhabitants work, I too was assigned to jobs that changed daily. One day I was taken to the airport, where I was forced to scrub the floors on my knees. At the end of the day the soldiers beat the other girls and made them repeat their jobs, spilling buckets of water the girls were required to mop up with little rugs.

I did not immediately understand why I was spared the humiliating and painful punishment. When I returned home, I learned that my sister had been working in the same place several days before and, as always, had done exemplary work. Despite the differences in our appearance that had led the German soldiers in Bronowice to identify Niusia as German and me as Polish, the family resemblance seemed obvious to these soldiers. I believe they thought Niusia had returned and had confidence the job would be done well. No one inspected the mess I had made. Still, it was a cold winter day and my clothes got wet, which made the long trip home on an open truck very uncomfortable.

Some days when it snowed I was taken outside to shovel the streets. While most of the other girls felt debased by the work, I looked forward to a day in the brisk fresh air. Meticulous in performing my job, I was determined to keep my head and spirits high. I felt there was nothing dishonest in the work, despite the occasional jeering of passersby relishing the site of Jews at hard physical labor.

One day an order was posted demanding that every ghetto inhabitant work. We were required to report to the *arbeitsamt* (employment office)—a large building a block away from our apartment. German women dispensed each assignment regardless of qualifications. Most sought after were the few available jobs inside the ghetto, which was perceived as being in a more secure zone than areas outside. Beyond the walls, beatings of workers were frequent and terrible winter weather provided no excuse for performing outdoor jobs slowly.

I was very fortunate to receive a plum work assignment—plum, not only because my job was indoors in a brush factory just around the corner from our apartment, but also because I was even paid piecemeal for the brushes I produced. The factory was run by Hasidic Jews shrouded in long black frocks and sporting unkempt beards. They came from the Orthodox sections of Krakow and spoke mostly Yiddish, a language not understood by many of us. The Hasidim had little tolerance for our differences in religious belief. They demanded that boys cover their heads and that sleeves hide the elbows of girls. They resented the lifestyle to which we continued to cling, which celebrated the free mixing of boys and girls and in which the rules they established for the celebration of the Sabbath and the prohibition of mixing dairy and meat products fell by the wayside. We felt little in common with our Hasidic bosses.

Ironically, the challenge of making the best and most brushes gave me a sense of accomplishment. It took me little time to develop the skills to make a decent number of brushes each day, and the few pennies I earned went a long way toward purchasing food. Moreover, in the face of the world that was continually trying to make me feel inferior, doing a job well gave me satisfaction. This twist of logic was one of the internal secret weapons that helped me maintain my dignity.

Another internal source of sanity came through my relationships with peers, especially teenage males. In the brush factory I developed a friendship with several boys—especially, two, one named Max Frayman and the other Dziunek Steinlauf. They worked on the drilling machines making wooden boards for stringing the brushes. With our friendship came a better supply of the boards, enabling me to sharpen my skills, produce more brushes, and generate additional income.

For all of us teenagers school had been interrupted. Doing manual labor was a novelty, and we felt kinship facing our adversaries, the Hasidic bosses. After work hours we maintained an active social life. We usually met on the corner of Limanowska Street, laughing and acting like teenagers anywhere in the world. We attended "concerts" and "parties" in the apartments of friends who were fortunate enough to have instruments. Singers were particularly popular, since the space requirements for their concerts were not very demanding. On nice evenings we strolled in the ghetto, seeking to be revived by fresh air after long hours in the dusty factory. Sometimes we climbed

Krzemionki Hill on the edge of the ghetto where Oskar Schindler, the German businessman well known for employing and saving a few hundred Jews who worked in his factory, was reputed to have sat on his horse, overlooking ghetto activities.

One day my sister's boyfriend, Mundek Bigeleisen, was rushed to the ghetto hospital with appendicitis. The hospital was an old, dilapidated building containing white metal beds, and it was serviced by Jewish doctors and nurses assigned to this job. They had virtually no medical supplies and very little food. Patients relied on whatever was brought from home.

Mundek's parents were no longer alive, his sister had the flu, and my sister contracted jaundice. It therefore became my responsibility to deliver food to Mundek. I delivered far more, however. My packages were wrapped in laughter—an antidote for the spirit, but not for the newly sewn stitches across Mundek's flesh.

The visits to the hospital were filled with a sense of romance. In the bed adjacent to Mundek, surrounded by guards, was the handsome young leader of the underground, who I think was Szymek Drenger, who had been injured during his anti-Nazi activities.

Szymek and his young wife, Gusta, had formed a resistance movement comprising untrained Zionist youth groups whose 160 members sprang from different ideological perspectives. Despite their philosophical disagreements, the resisters worked in unison, taking advantage of the minimal number of weapons accumulated from successful raids against Germans. Other appeals for weaponry generated no help. Among his other talents Szymek had developed great skill for falsifying papers needed to move in and out of the ghetto.

I had little knowledge of the activities of his organization, but we had heard about him and had made him our hero. I did not know he was the leader of the group to which my cousins, the Wolfs, belonged and which had made attempts to sabotage German war efforts. Though my young friends and I were attracted by the courage and dynamism of the resisters, most of the adults considered the movement to be an exercise in futility. After all, we were no match for the well-equipped and organized German army, and although each outbreak by the resistance fighters cost many casualties on our side, it did little damage to the oppressors.

Dreaming of the day when they would land on the shores of a free Jewish state, the resistance fighters under Szymek waged a valiant fight. Of 160 members, only 20 survived to witness the birth of the state of Israel. They proceeded straight from the war zones of Poland to fight in the war of independence.

As for Szymek and Gusta, it was their wish to die together if fate required. Their wish was fulfilled on November 9, 1943, when they were murdered in prison.

For a short period after the Germans had issued the order requiring all ghetto inhabitants to work, mother did not get a work assignment. Convinced that the possession of working papers would provide additional protection against deportation from the ghetto, which had begun in its earliest phases, I went to the *arbeitsamt* to obtain a job for mother. Work assignments were very difficult to obtain, and I do not know why I applied in her stead.

The young German clerk asked me if I knew how to knit, since she needed to finish making a sweater for her fiancé by the next day, and it was missing the entire back. In fact, knitting was a skill I had mastered at a very early age. Although it was nearly impossible to imagine completing the project by the next morning, I took the job.

When in the past I had encountered a shortage of wool while knitting, I had learned to wet the finished garment and then stretch it to a desirable size. Working through the night on the German clerk's project, the old trick served me well. Applying this technique, I was able to meet my deadline. Grateful, the clerk assigned a precious brush-factory job to mother, and from that time on we never separated. I wondered what had become of the sweater after it was washed.

Within days all the people without jobs became the object of an *aktion* (deportation). Although the Germans said the people slated for the deportation were being resettled to the east, we did not believe it. We were powerless, however, to do anything about it. The intimidating *Schutzstaffel* (Protective Echelon, or SS) with their polished uniforms and staccato, snarling, commanding voices were very well-armed and ready to shoot at the slightest movement that did not comply with their orders. We clung to the hope that if we obeyed, we would have a chance to survive. In any event, we had no weapons, and acts of defiance caused the Germans to shoot other Jews. Indeed, this group-punishment methodology worked well.

The deportations had dual purposes: thinning out our ranks and creating panic that would allow the Germans to better control those who remained.

Not having been assigned to any jobs, mother's sisters, Aunt Sala Isenberg and Aunt Helen Hilfstein, as well as Aunt Helen's husband, Uncle Julek, were all taken away. So were the parents of many of my friends. Those of us who remained were almost numbed by the combination of events and daily realities of life. The struggle to merely exist left us very little time or energy for mourning. Despite stories that had begun seeping into the ghetto describing the horrors of the execution of those who had been deported, we continued to believe—rather, to deceive ourselves— that our loved ones had been resettled. This psychological defense mechanism enabled us to keep whatever sanity we had left.

After the *aktion*, the part of the ghetto where the Hilfsteins had lived was liquidated, and the borders shrank by half. Oskar and Jozek, the Hilfstein boys, were left homeless and without parents, so they moved in with us. So did the sister of Mrs. Spielman (who was not religious, easing some of the tension in the apartment), together with her two daughters. One of them, Sydzia, was a 19-year-old dancer who, because of an unfortunate fall just before coming to the ghetto, was paralyzed from the waist down. The Nazi policy of intolerance for handicapped people made us fear for Sydia's life, taking our minds off our own familial losses.

The Germans forced Poles residing in nicer apartments in the city center to move into the former ghetto quarters, thereby leaving vacant the desirable housing for the conquerors. The apartments remaining within the shrunken ghetto walls became further swollen with more displaced Jews.

In the aftermath of the *aktion* and the subsequent reduction of the ghetto, there were 13 of us living in the two rooms on Limanowska Street. In light of the problems that loomed outside our doors, however, the crowding inside barely fazed us. Six of the 13 were teenagers; I was the youngest, and Oscar, the oldest, was eight years my senior. In the evenings we played games, told stories, and used our imaginations to entertain ourselves. I enjoyed being included in this group.

This sense of momentary calm existed despite the tremendous losses we suffered. We experienced the existence of only one toilet and the lack of privacy or running hot water as only minor inconveniences. We dressed under blankets, and we hung a large blanket in the corner of the kitchen to hide the small basin in which we washed, mostly in cold water. Heating water on the stove was difficult because the surface was needed to prepare meals. We pretended to go on as though life were normal, afraid to display any sign of despair for fear of upsetting the delicate balance on which our very existence depended. All of us gazed at each other through brave eyes, trying to convey a sense of courage we did not truly feel.

Eventually, the most dreaded turning point came to pass. In the beginning of 1943 father and Niusia were assigned permanently to live outside of the ghetto. The prospect of missing father's smiling face and daily hug was more than heartbreaking; it ripped asunder my system of internal defenses. Prior to that moment, no matter how awful the situation, the inner strength I always seemed to muster had felt directly linked to father's protection.

And parting with Niusia, who had been my lifelong mentor and friend as well as my sister, seemed like an impossible blow to bear. I could not imagine life without her. Only 15 months apart in age, Niusia and I had always shared our friends, our school, and our secrets. Our loving protection of each other had sustained my personal security. Having been forced to work at different assignments from hers throughout the ghetto period had been difficult enough for me. The thought of coming home each day from the brush factory in need of relaying the day's events and looking at our sparsely covered supper table bereft of Niusia and father stabbed at my heart in the most unrelenting way.

I cannot even begin to imagine the pain and anxiety the separation must have caused mother. To watch a child walk down a path that you know is almost certain to end in death—whatever your mechanism for denial—and to be rendered completely powerless to change fate is a torture worse than death. And mother simultaneously lost father, with whom she had been linked for 20 years in an unbreakable unit. They had always made decisions jointly, both in our personal lives in and running the business together before the war. While not overly demonstrative, the deep and tender love they shared radiated between them. I could not conceive of how mother would cope without seeing the smiling eyes of one of her two children and the support of her beloved life-mate.

But on the morning we said good-bye, we dared not show each other the pain. We pretended our parting was only temporary. The realization of any other possibility would have been impossible to bear. We parted as if it were any other workday, somehow hoping that without a big farewell, the ones leaving us might miraculously walk through the door when evening came. But evening came, and no one walked through the door. Despite the 11 people who continued to share our two-room ghetto apartment, the space felt empty.

From that day on, mother and I almost never separated. Although we would not speak about the absence of father and Niusia, hoping that our silence would reverse the terrible reality, we awaited their return.

But it never came.

Neither mother nor I could have imagined a day more frightening than the one when father and Niusia were forced to leave, but even that illusion was shattered on a beautiful morning on March 13, 1943, when the mandate was issued for us to evacuate the ghetto. After posting the order on walls throughout the ghetto, the SS soldiers roamed the ghetto with vicious dogs searching through apartments to ensure no one would be left in hiding.

We were ordered to pack one valise each, mark our names in white paint, and throw it over the balcony outside our second-floor apartment into the courtyard. We were then directed to report in front of the ghetto gate on Limanowska Street. The "privilege" of going on a march to a concentration camp called Plaszow, located three miles away, was to be limited only to able-bodied people who had permanent work assignments. This was the second time that knitting the sweater in exchange for mother's work assignment had paid off. Her working papers had become her passport to Life.

Two of my cousins, Dora and Giza Horowitz, ran through the chaotic crowd toward us—women in their early twenties desperately cradling their infants, who were considered useless in the concentration camp to which we were to march. The Germans tried to rip the children from the mothers' arms. Dora and Giza resisted—a crime for which the immediate punishment was to be coerced into watching the torture and subsequent execution of their infants.

The two valiant women, whose weddings mother helped arrange in the house of Uncle Yehiel Horowitz (her widowed brother-in-law and the father of Esther Wolf, who resided in our house) thought that mother could devise a solution.

At the moment memories flashed before my eyes. Uncle Horowitz was a stately and imposing man with a snowy white beard. Now he was hiding in the ghetto. Before the war he had owned a textile business in the center of town frequented by consumers for upscale suit fabrics. He was an Orthodox Jew who came from a long rabbinical line. Though mother and father kept a kosher home observing the Jewish dietary laws, Uncle Horowitz, cognizant of the less rigid standard which we applied to the Jewish laws, did not drink even a glass of water in our house.

Niusia and I had speculated that he had not always been so religious. The large red velvet photo album containing pictures of all the family members showed him as a younger man wearing no yarmulke. No matter: he penciled it in on one of his visits.

Since Uncle Horowitz had 10 children, weddings in his home were frequent events. In conformance with Orthodox Jewish rules concerning gender separation, I remember the rooms filled with men in black coats and hats, chanting and singing joyously. In others, elegantly dressed women entertained themselves. As a little girl I had free rein among all the rooms. Uncle Horowitz presided over the kids, greeting us with a smile in his sparkling blue eyes and handing us special candies. I loved entering this mysterious world filled with ancient customs that made me feel closer to my Jewish roots, though I was glad not to have to adhere to the traditions when we returned home.

Seeing the terror in Dora and Giza's eyes transported me immediately to the reality of the moment. Terrified by thoughts about what might have happened to father and Niusia, mother and I clutched each other and joined the sea of humanity representing what remained of the population of the Krakow ghetto progressing toward Plaszow, numb and bereft of any emotions. Pandemonium filled the streets as the Nazis shouted frightening commands in German and families were torn apart. Children and old people, both of whom were considered burdensome because they could not be productive enough to merit the bowl of soup we would receive each day in the camp, became instant targets of the firing squad.

Everyone marching held onto his most prized possession: working papers, the permit to live for the moment. We had already begun to realize the chances of survival were slim, but the will to live was strong even if life was a more difficult choice than death. We could not permit our tormentors to win, and the only fight we could wage was for survival.

The three-mile march to Plaszow seemed endless. Suddenly, as we neared the gates to Plaszow, mother noticed that she was missing her muff, which contained her work papers. We fell into total panic, since their absence would have been a certain death sentence. With mountains of belongings covering the streets, a search for the muff seemed useless. We slowed our pace, trying to let people pass us by, delaying our arrival, hoping for some miracle . . . which came.

Out of nowhere we heard a cry in the crowd: "Mrs. Fuss! Mrs. Fuss!" The voice belonged to Halina Poss-Ragozzoni, a friend from the brush factory who had found the muff and opened it, then embarked on a search to find us. I don't know how many times she called mother's name. Had she thought about the odds of locating us in the thousands of people, she might not have been so determined. Even in those circumstances, some people grabbed for the smallest straw in the effort to rescue a life.

By day's end, all that was left in the ghetto were streets littered with bodies and blood that flowed through the gutters.

We later learned that neither Dora nor Giza had stopped fighting the executioners, and both had therefore perished that day alongside other young mothers who refused to surrender their babies. I found solace in knowing that their deaths offered them shelter from the nightmare of living with the cruel memories from which they would never have been able to escape.

I was among the youngest allowed to survive that terrible day. I had just about reached the age in which entrance to Plaszow was considered permissible.

Marek, left, with boys in Barakenbau Camp, 1942

Chapter Six
Plaszow

There was an alternative to Plaszow: instant death. Outside the gates of the labor-concentration camp, the Nazis methodically selected those among us—only 8,000 made the grade—who appeared able to work. The "unprivileged" were marched up to a hill inside the confines of Plaszow. They were ordered to dig long ditches, and then undress completely, since the Germans did not want to waste clothes on dead bodies. Humiliated and afraid, the victims were commanded to line up on the edge of the ditch, where machine gun shots—one per person—methodically toppled them, dead or alive, into their final resting places. The blast of bullets signaled their demise.

Those of us who remained were taken on a three-mile march that lasted a seeming eternity, finally entering the gates of hell: Plaszow. Barracks the length of long barns—our sleeping quarters—were grim and crowded. Now we were to share a space not with nine people, but a few hundred women. Narrow bunk beds, the width of army cots, lined the wooden walls three layers high, each one accommodating two women. SS guards in tailored uniforms and shiny boots swarmed around the camp, guns hanging over their shoulders as a warning against any act of disobedience. There could be no hesitation in carrying out any order they might shout. The speed with which their fingers could find the trigger could outrace a bolt of lightning.

Awaiting the construction of our workplaces, where we would advance the German war effort, our captors invented a slew of meaningless and exhausting jobs in our initial days in Plaszow. At first we were assigned to carry boulders from one side of the road to the other. When we finished, we were commanded to carry them back to the original side. We were never permitted to be idle except when we slept at night.

My life-saving defense mechanism was an ingrained, unyielding attitude to make the best of any situation. While the physical labor broke the backs and spirits of many of those I worked with, I viewed it as an opportunity to be outside in the fresh air as opposed to the dingy, stuffy brush factory where I had worked in the ghetto. The weather was beautiful, and the warm sun felt good on my back.

Within a few weeks the useless tasks yielded to work aimed at bolstering the German military. Work barracks were erected, and mother and I resumed our jobs making brushes at a Plaszow work barracks. Others were assigned to a garment-factory barracks making military uniforms or to mechanical workshops.

The barracks were built with large windows, which allowed the guards to exercise control over us from the outside. The windows faced a road that led to the hill where the mass graves were dug. The liquidation of the ghetto, with its thousands of inhabitants, took weeks, and from the windows of our work barracks we witnessed long lines of people streaming up the hill from where we could hear the gunshots. We always knew when the ditches were too full because the gunfire would be delayed—until new graves were dug.

Recognizing faces in the parade of people marching to their tormented deaths was the most insufferable part of this terrible event. One day I saw the twin brother of Uncle Julek Hilfstein among the victims. I could hardly contain the blood racing through my veins. I felt helpless watching him marching so downtrodden. He must have sensed the pointlessness of protesting, which would have brought severe beatings before his death sentence, and he walked with resignation to his violent end.

Knowing the fate suffered by many of our family members, friends, and neighbors, we considered nothing more important than staying alive in the moment. Delaying death became our main goal.

To my eyes the guards appeared enormous. Most striking and frightening was the commandant, a man named Amon Ghett, who carried a big whip he was always ready to use. Ghett marched with a harlequin Great Dane and a menacing entourage whose loud laughter sent shivers down our spines. The sadistic satisfaction they derived from haphazard, spontaneous beatings or shootings of inmates was intended to strip us of any semblance of humanity.

In Plaszow, the reality of this war, of this Holocaust, finally hit us. We were captives of monsters.

One sunny morning we received a surprise order: to clean and whitewash the exterior of our barracks, buildings about which our captors had never cared. We were even ordered to dress neatly and comb our hair carefully. The commands puzzled us: amid such horror, why should attention be paid to appearances?

The mystery was soon solved. A large delegation of the Red Cross International had arrived to inspect the conditions of the facility. The observers saw what they perceived as a healthy, vigorous workforce carrying stones. Despite viewing young girls and other frail people bending under the weight of carts loaded with heavy stones, they somehow concluded we were being treated decently. They did not even criticize the three tiers of bunk beds made of hard board without bedding, each the size of an army cot and accommodating two people.

The Red Cross officials did not go to the kitchen to see the gray slop with mysterious floating objects that was called "soup," nor did they taste the gooey brick which was our bread. And they did not walk up the hill to see the ditches full of freshly killed corpses, some of them still barely alive.

Before that day we had worshipped the Red Cross as a protector of human rights, but after their inspection, we lost hope. We realized that not even the Red Cross considered us human, and that there was no one left to speak on our behalf. We felt totally abandoned.

News of Niusia and father sifted to us from people who came to Plaszow from Emalia, the factory connected with the Barakenbau lumber yard, where they had been assigned. Emalia was not far from the ghetto, yet the distance was impenetrable for us. We knew they were alive. Despite the irrationality of our dreams, every day we hoped to see them.

Several weeks after arriving at Plaszow, on our day off, what felt like a miracle happened: Father appeared at Plaszow together with a group of laborers from Emalia. They had been given permission to pay us a visit.

I was simultaneously overjoyed and heartbroken by father's appearance. He was obviously exhausted from hard labor. His clothes hung on his emaciated body, and his eyes had lost the spark I had loved so much. He attempted to smile, but despair filled the lines in his face. He wore a knapsack in which he brought a pot of milk soup with dumplings; he had wrapped the pot beneath his clothes to keep its contents warm. Access to a stove had not been denied him, though I could hardly imagine how he had been able to gather the ingredients, cook a soup, and risk the danger of sneaking it to us.

Mother, father, and I sat in virtual silence, relishing the moment even more than the delicious soup. Throughout my life, father's love had sustained me morally and emotionally in the worst circumstances. I had always envisioned him as a cuddly, loving man with a great sense of humor. But on that day in Plaszow father was not laughing.

Father filled in the blanks of our curiosity about him and Niusia. He explained they had been assigned to work at Emalia with Christians imprisoned by the Nazis. Mrs. Podworska still managed to smuggle some money to them, and that was how they were able to purchase a limited amount of food on the black market.

At the end of the day mother and I felt justified in the dreams we had nurtured, of setting eyes once again on father and Niusia. We looked forward to a visit from Niusia in the same way father had come to Plaszow, and we eagerly awaited father's return. But there was no next visit. Nor was there ever a visit to Plaszow from Niusia.

Father, however, had received a personal reward that day in Plaszow. He had watched mother and me imbibe with relish the soup he would provide for us, for the last time. This milk-dumpling soup was the most delicious treat I ever ate. So much love had been poured into it.

The Germans kept meticulous count of the people living in the barracks. Each morning we were all required to stand in formation in front of our barracks until every person was accounted for. Sometimes the numbers did not check exactly, and the count took many hours. Every night someone was required to be on duty, prepared to give a count of all the inmates in the barracks. The report had to be recited in German, using precise wording and rhythm.

Once, when it was my turn on duty from 3 to 5 a.m., the welcome nighttime quiet suddenly yielded to the loud, acrimonious sounds of shooting and the heavy footsteps of soldiers' boots. The doors of our barracks were thrown open, and Commandant Amon Ghett and his entourage stormed into the room. I don't know how tall he was, but in that moment he appeared to be more than 10 feet tall, hovering over me with his black-and-white harlequin Great Dane at his side.

Enveloped in fear and panic, with my memory momentarily frozen, I realized my life depended upon a correct report, which consisted of a specific greeting and a count of women in the barrack that night. I jumped to my feet, stood at attention, and blurted my report in German in a daze. I felt as if an unknown voice was speaking for me.

Ghett and company left as they had come, without uttering a word. Once again the sound of a few hundred women sleeping peacefully, unaware of the drama that had just unfolded, filled the barracks. It was springtime. A hint of the dawn's pink sunrise streamed through the window, the smell of early morning dew seeped through the cracks in the walls, and a bird sang its high-pitched song. The season's promises of renewal flourished on the other side of the barbed wires, cut off from the climate that relentlessly persisted on this side.

How I envied the birds their freedom! A month after my liberation in 1945 I took an American reporter on a tour of the Auschwitz death camp. In the museum the Poles had erected on the site, I saw a painting depicting a silhouette of a man resting his tired body on a shovel in front of barbed-wire fences, longingly looking at a single bird on a tree outside the fence. How well I understood the scene. It could have been me the night of Ghett's visit to the barracks. . .

Despite living in constant fear I could not keep myself from small acts of rebellion. Perhaps it came with the nature of my age, or maybe it was my way of proving that I still had some control. One day we were ordered to turn in all the jewelry still left in our possession. The one thing I refused to part with was a beautiful sterling silver dachshund on a chain, a prized gift from my beloved cousin, Salek.

Of all my cousins, I adored Salek the most. Only six years older than me, my six-foot-tall, blue-eyed, blond cousin with the physique of Hollywood actor Victor Mature, was the heartthrob of all my girlfriends. Despite our age difference he often included me in his outings. Salek was a member of Maccabi, a Jewish sports club. With him, at the age of nine, I went skiing for the first time. We embarked on the adventure early in the morning, going to the little Krakow hills of Podgorze, where later the ghetto was built. Salek broke his ski at the beginning of the day, but not willing to give up, we went to his workshop where he spent the whole day repairing it. We were oblivious to time and did not return home until 10 p.m., much to the worry of my panic-stricken parents and relatives.

Though Salek was admittedly not the most reliable escort, the rebuke we received left me brokenhearted. I especially admired Salek's courage. Just before the war broke out, groups of Polish students roamed Krakow's streets, beating Jews. One day when Salek returned home he greeted my father with his lips tightly closed. It did not take long for my father to make a funny comment and Salek's broad smile revealed two missing front teeth. My shocked father asked what had happened, and Salek replied: "Uncle, you should have seen my opponent!" We later learned that the Maccabi club had organized a bunch of strong young men, including Salek, to confront the attacking students. Jews were generally not inclined toward physical retaliation, and only a few participated. Salek's chivalry sealed my perception of him as my greatest hero.

For my ninth birthday Salek presented me with one of my most cherished possessions. While it was not customary for children to have much jewelry, my cousin gave me a beautiful sterling silver dachshund on a chain. Until I was forced at the age of 14 in the Plaszow concentration camp to remove all my jewelry, the necklace never left my neck.

Declining to leave my treasure in the hands of the Nazis, I buried it next to my barracks and never saw it again. On my 65th birthday, my daughter Irene had a jeweler replicate the dachshund with great precision. I must have described it in vivid detail.

While this may seem an insignificant incident in the face of being constantly exposed to the sound of gunfire and the sight of people being tortured or killed, it gave me a feeling of satisfaction. Anyone in uniform was an adversary, even a Jew assigned to some kind of policing post. Initially some Jews had volunteered for this service as a way of protecting their families. While some of them maintained their humanity, others became as brutal as their German captors.

Our ranks were steadily decimated with ever-changing categories of people being marched to the hill. One day our captors took inmates they considered too young; the next day's victims were those they decided were too old. It was impossible to determine which criterion they would employ each day. We focused on outguessing them, speculating on what to do to our appearances to fit the image we could only hope they would not want to destroy.

Since I was more assertive than mother I assumed control of family decisions. Mother was a strong woman, but her gentle disposition led her to avoid controversy. She had great confidence in me, which enhanced my own self-esteem even in those circumstances.

One day, seemingly out of the blue, I insisted that it would be safer for mother to conceal her white-gray hair. Always meticulously swept back, her hair had been that color throughout my life. Mother was elegant but modest, never using cosmetics, and she was repulsed by the thought of dyeing her hair. Moreover, the payment for such a service was our meager day's bread ration. Nonetheless, I insisted. She submitted to the process, which was performed by another inmate.

Several days later gray-haired people were marched to the death-hill, considered by the Germans to be too old to work. Once again, mother was granted an extension of life.

Few inmates attempted to escape Plaszow. The biggest impediment to escape was the camp's location in open fields, surrounded by two rows of electric barbed wires, with watchtowers equipped with searchlights situated every few hundred feet of the camp's perimeter. The entire surrounding area was brightly lit and guarded by vicious, roaming dogs. The camp was also located a long distance from any area where one could seek shelter. People living outside the camp were afraid to hide us. The Germans had imposed the death penalty for them and their families in retribution for any such act. Moreover, some people who lived in the areas outside the camp were ready to report runaways in exchange for the reward of five pounds of sugar, or perhaps just the satisfaction of turning in a Jew.

The greatest deterrent to escape, however, was the collective punishments the Germans would inflict on all the camp inmates. Cognizant of the sense of community among Jews, the Nazis held everyone collectively accountable for any infractions of the rules. Each escape cost the lives of many people who knew nothing about it. Daily head counts in the mornings and evenings revealed missing inmates within hours.

I knew very little about the underground or its activities, other than that it existed. Few people wanted to confide such dangerous information in me, a 14-year-old. And I preferred not to be privy to secrets that could put anybody in jeopardy.

One beautiful, sunny day, three young men who, we believed, were connected to the underground, escaped. It took only hours for the Germans to capture them. Ghett decided to make an example of the consequences of their behavior. We were required to gather in front of three gallows atop tall platforms, surrounded by so many uniformed, gun-toting soldiers, it appeared as if the entire German army were present.

A public hanging was announced. Just before joining the ranks of Jews ordered to witness it, I convinced mother to hide on a top bunk bed. She assumed I would join her, but I was too scared to hide. Being in the open and seeing what was happening gave me a false sense of security. In the last minute I slipped out. There was no time to argue, and we could not bring attention to our plot. Despite the realities surrounding me I believed myself to be as invincible as most teenagers. I experienced a sense of great responsibility for my mother, whom I saw as being more vulnerable than me, and my somewhat spontaneous actions were too unpredictable for her to control. Trusting my instincts was my *modus operandi,* which proved to be as effective as any other.

Jewish policeman Iciu Salz, the youngest son of the brush factory Hasidic bosses, was selected to do the hanging. Though in the factory he was known for his brutality toward the Jews, this job exceeded any behavior to which he might have acquiesced. Yet he had no choice. We stood for what seemed like hours around the gallows, required to witness the procedure.

One of the boys emerged on the tall platform with his head held high proudly reciting the *Sh'ma,* a sacred Jewish prayer declaring unity with God. The other was hung instantly but his noose broke on the first attempt. Despite the international convention requiring a hanging victim to be released in this circumstance, the boy was brought to the noose a second time. All the while he never stopped reciting the *Sh'ma*. I admired the dignity with which he died this most awful death.

The torture did not end with the deaths of the three who had unsuccessfully attempted to escape. After the hangings we were required to march single-file in front of the gallows, our heads turned toward the bodies. As we passed by, each tenth person was pulled from our ranks and laid on a table to receive a lashing of horse-leather whips against their bare buttocks, tearing their skin mercilessly. My cousin, Esther Wolf, Joel's mother, was among those beaten that day.

It took weeks for the whipped bodies to heal, and infections exacerbated by malnutrition set in. Yet no one was permitted to stop working for a day. The punishment served to ingrain the lesson of the futility of rebellion or escape.

This experience hastened my maturity. I resolved not to develop relationships with boys or to form any attachments that could expose me to additional losses or hurt. Having to worry about the loss of my immediate family was more than I could handle. I started to build a wall around myself, a self-created cocoon.

The work in the brush factory was consuming, and I responded by setting personal goals of bettering my skills. This focus, together with preserving my only dress—a black cotton *dirndl* with white polka dots, red piping, a fitted bodice, and a gathered skirt—enabled me to maintain a sense of self-worth.

My brush-making abilities became known to my bosses, and when an order came from Ghett to produce brushes for grooming his horse, I was selected to make them. I felt proud of the quality of my work, caring little about the destination of the product. I did not realize, however, that with the assignment came an order to deliver the brushes in person to Ghett's house. This was a frightening prospect.

The commandant's imposing white house stood down the hill, isolated from the camp. It was known for famous parties where factory owner Oskar Shindler was entertained along with notable Nazi henchmen. In the midst of the slaughterhouse where we were imprisoned was this oasis, equipped with a sophisticated library and record collection. Apparently Ghett and his cohorts were unfazed by the contradiction between their island culture amid a sea of atrocities.

Not given a choice, I frightfully embarked on the walk to Ghett's forbidden world. I held my breath until I reached the spectacular, large kitchen where I was told to deliver the brushes. The employees in white jackets hovered over steaming pots of fragrant food, which at that moment was not at all tempting. I wanted only to get out alive. One never knew when an officer would get an urge to use me as target practice for entertainment.

Fortunately I did not encounter any officers. I promptly handed over the brushes and started on my return trek. The starving diet of the inmates was no secret to the cooks, however, and one gave me a package of ground meat, wrapped in paper. How exciting was the prospect of bringing real food to mother, even if we had to eat it raw. I flattened the package and slipped it securely under the bodice of my dress, on my stomach. I feared that if it fell out or was detected, penalties would be suffered not only by me, but by the well-intentioned cook as well.

I felt almost giddy. Suddenly as I exited the kitchen, Ghett's Great Dane, the black and white giant, appeared, heading straight for me. For a second I believed that my fantasies of feasting on the raw meat would give way to the dog feasting on me. He approached me slowly, smelling around my body, but miraculously he went on his way, leaving me to go back to the barracks with my treasure. Mother and I shared the meat, relishing every morsel. This was the greatest culinary treat we enjoyed at Plaszow.

After the first few months at Plaszow, the initial frenzy of activities subsided and we settled into daily routines. Amid the constant shooting and hunger to which we almost became adjusted, we worked 12-hour shifts, alternating days and nights. Summer was quickly coming to an end, and the prospect of winter was intimidating. Light shone through cracks in the wallboards where we knew the cold of winter would settle. Undoubtedly heating would be very sparse. Still, we believed that now the Germans would leave us alone. We feared any new move.

Chapter Seven
High Holidays in Plaszow

The inmates at Plaszow acknowledged Jewish holidays in their own ways. I did not eat bread on Passover, and I fasted on Yom Kippur. These choices gave me a sense of belonging to the community and brought me warm memories of joyous family celebrations. I did not feel that a public display of the observance contributed to its importance. Moreover, punishment on the part of the Germans was brutal and extended to anyone in the vicinity of the lawbreaker.

The weather was beautiful on Rosh Hashanah—the Jewish New Year—in 1943, and the Germans took advantage of the warm, sunny day by strolling around the camp looking for signs of religious adherence. The managers of the brush factory, the Salzes, were Hasidic, and consequently they refused to work on Rosh Hashanah. Instead, they arrived at work wrapped in their large white prayer shawls and prayed in front of the windows.

Within minutes the soldiers spotted the defiant act of the Salzes and stormed the workshop, gun triggers ready to fire and big whips in their hands. There were about 50 of us in the room; panic-stricken, we were ordered to continue working.

The soldiers arbitrarily chose seven older people. They laid each of them across the edge of a table, ordering them to lower their pants. After the most brutal of whippings the victims were shot. Though my back was turned to the action the piercing sounds of the wailing, the swishing of the whips, and the fire of the bullets filled the room and the hearts of all who were there.

The brutality did not end with the death of the seven older people. Still hungry to whip, the soldiers picked out a few young men, among them a newly wed Hasidic teenager with rosy cheeks. His beautiful bride, a resolute young woman, was working with us. She rushed to the soldiers, seeking mercy for her beloved. Seeing that the young man's life had meaning to someone, the laughing soldiers shot him after they finished the cruel beating. They let the other whipped youngsters, with their mutilated bodies, live.

Throughout this ordeal I sat at a corner table by the door, my hands working automatically as they strung the horsehair with wire. I functioned like a robot, frozen into repetitive action. Several people who worked near me slipped out the door during the confusion of the event, recognizing that all of us were targets until the soldiers' bestial instincts were satisfied.

If ever I imagined a hell, this was it.

Every now and then I lifted my eyes to look at mother, sitting at the far end of the room, her eyes reaching for me in panic. She was too deep in the room to have a chance to escape. While I contemplated following my comrades out the door, I knew that leaving mother in this hell would have been too torturous for me. However, equal danger lurked outside since we were required to be in the workplace during the day. I decided to stay at my station.

As a teenager, I felt invincible and thought that death could not touch me, despite the room full of corpses and splattered blood.

It is hard to remember how long this nightmare endured. It felt like an eternity. Finally the ruckus quieted down, and the Germans began to leave.

One of the soldiers, whose hand was paralyzed, was called Willie the Hand. The most vicious of the lot, Willie the Hand was responsible for most of the shooting that day. As he was exiting he stopped behind me, standing for a while as I mustered the strength to continue to work. Suddenly I heard a click sound next to my head. I thought it was his silver cigarette case, and though my hands shook I was not deterred from performing my job. For a second my eyes sought out mother, whose face had turned white and immobilized. She was 50 years old, but her silver hair and ashen skin now made her look ancient. I assumed the events that had preceded the moment had mortified her. Mother was a very gentle and compassionate woman, and a strong reaction was to be expected.

After some time had elapsed—I do not know how long—I heard Willie the Hand leave, slamming the factory door behind him. Outside, the soldiers proudly assessed their accomplishments. Those of us who remained sat dazed.

It was then that I learned that the click sound had come from the gun of Willie the Hand. After pulling the trigger he had looked around the room, awaiting reactions. In the absence of a voice of protest, he had apparently decided that it was not worth his while to reload a gun for someone unimportant to anyone. I cannot imagine the courage it took for mother to remain silent and restrain her emotions, seeing this killer behind her teenage daughter and understanding that a reaction would have meant my death.

After the soldiers' departure, we harbored bitter feelings toward our Hasidic bosses. Casting blame in the wrong direction, we thought that the observant men had given the soldiers an excuse for this atrocity. We still believed that if we lived within the framework of the Germans' orders, we had a chance to survive. It was our only hope.

While normally it would have taken a long time to recover from the events that took place on Rosh Hashanah of 1943, acts of genocide occurred daily with such speed that we had no time to digest any single circumstance.

Chapter Eight
Skarzysko

It was one more dreary day in a long stretch of dreary fall days, typical of weather patterns in Poland at that time of year. We were working in the brush factory, rushing to fulfill our daily quotas. The gray, rainy weather contributed to our collective depression, and the hours dragged by slowly, prolonging the nightmare our lives had become.

Suddenly the door to our work barracks swung open, and a group of *Ordnungdienst* (*Jewish Police,* or *OD,* made up of camp inmates), darted in to announce a special "selection" of people, allegedly for immediate transfer to another camp.

We knew about "selections." Every day people were selected to march up to the hill of death. We were certain they were inventing a story about transfer to another camp to ensure our cooperation.

The blood frozen in our veins. We waited to hear who would be chosen next. Each of us desperately hoped for an adjournment of this death sentence, but the workbenches emptied quickly as the selection proceeded.

In horror I watched the finger of an OD point to my mother. Always dignified, even in this situation, she rose quietly, slowly walking to join the group selected for "transport." She looked sadly in my direction as if to say good-bye and ask forgiveness for not being able to provide me with a better life.

After the deportation of father and Niusia, mother and I had completely leaned on each other for moral support, terrified of separation and the loneliness certain to follow. The thought of remaining in Plaszow without her was more than I could bear, and the only solution seemed to be to join her and share her fate. When our eyes met she understood my intention. She was desperate to stop me, believing it was the only chance of saving my life. But I was determined to join her. Since the police implementing the action were Jewish, I was able to walk over to the crowd of people selected for deportation.

I had heard that after execution, the Germans collected the better clothing of the inmates, which they then distributed in Germany. Recognizing that the chilly weather was a prelude to winter and warm clothing would be in demand, I was determined to ensure that my coat and shoes—the only treasures I rescued during the liquidation of the ghetto—would remain in the possession of people I cared about. No German kid would get to wear my clothing while my Jewish friends froze. The coat had been a gift from father's nephew, Mojsie Fuss, who had visited us from Belgium in the summer of 1939. He had bought Niusia and me coats to ensure that we would enter high school in style. My coat was still in good condition, as were my fairly new lace-up leather boots.

Certain that my hours were numbered, I decided to leave my bare-bones wardrobe behind. Almost in a trance, I unlaced my shoes and handed them to Halina Poss, the friend who had found my mother's ID on the way to Plaszow. Halina had always taken great pride in wearing beautifully polished shoes, and those on her feet in Plaszow were showing extensive wear. I then removed my coat, and set it on the workbench for use by anyone who might need it.

As we were ready to depart, Greshler, a kind OD, offered to retrieve my coat, but I rebelliously refused, giving me a sense of control over the situation. We embarked on a long march through drizzling rain and a chilly wind to the detention barracks down the hill in a remote spot of Plaszow. The half-mile march felt like the longest I had ever taken.

Convinced we were walking to our deaths, mother maintained a slow gait, and soon we found ourselves at the end of the line, escorted by a young OD. The tension between him—a Jew serving the Germans—and us was unbearable, and it finally broke within me. With great fervor I accused the OD of victimizing us to obtain better conditions for himself: using our lives for his advantage. I asked: "How can you, a Jew, collaborate with the Nazis in killing other Jews? You also have a mother; how can you lead mine to her death? You will bear this guilt for the rest of your life!"

The OD grew weary of my bitter accusations, and he offered to clear the way for our escape. At that moment, however, we were very close to the German headquarters. Dogs and searchlights heavily guarded the area, and an escape attempt was a magnet for the firing squad. This was not the concern of our guard, who walked ahead, allowing us to attempt to flee. He perhaps felt magnanimous about the help he was providing, and he knew that if it backfired, our deaths would not be blamed on him.

I was not going to let him get away with clearing his conscience by placing us in the heart of danger. Besides, I was no great hero, and escape frightened me too much. Hoping to punish the OD for his collaboration, I called him back to let him know we had not tried to escape and that he was committing a crime by delivering us to the Germans to be killed in our passivity. My outspokenness was both naive and risky, but it helped to assuage my fears. It was my weak attempt at some form of retaliation.

By the time we reached the detention barracks the hour was late, and we had to wait for morning to learn our fate. It is hard to describe the sounds of wailing and grief that long night. There was hardly a soul who thought we would live beyond the next day. In an effort to shorten the time and the sadness locked into it, I went to sleep. As a teenager I continued to cling to a feeling of indestructibility, hoping that if I only endured the night, I would find a solution in the daylight hours. I could not believe this was the end of my life.

Much to our surprise, with the arrival of daylight the guards came to escort us to the cattle cars used to transport Jews to concentration camps on railway lines. They had told us the truth after all: We were being shipped to another camp.

The transport awaiting us contained some blankets and clothes thrown on the floor—indications that they expected us to live. By morning I had become quite cold in my silk dress, but the kind OD Greshler had ignored my objection to bringing my coat and had thrown it onto the pile that turned up in the train. That coat was my source of warmth during the cold winter that followed in the next camp. I do not remember what mother wore to keep her warm.

The cattle car was like a wooden barracks on wheels. We were loaded so tightly that there was hardly room to sit. The lack of air and the stench emanating from the pails into which people relieved themselves, made the trip unbearable.

It is difficult to tell how long we traveled. The trip began in early morning, and when we arrived at our destination, it was dark. The train traveled a whole day over a distance that normally would have taken one and a half hours. Ultimately it came to a screeching halt. Outside we heard the barking of German soldiers, and the door of the cattle car was flung open with a big bang. What our eyes beheld through the misty darkness was a frightening forest without a trace of life.

Again alarmed, we pondered our fate. We thought that if the Germans had wanted to shoot us, they would not have spent the time and money to transport us to this place. We had seen that the economy of extermination had been very carefully calculated. To our captors, each of us was only a pound of flesh efficiently disposable after squeezing the last drop of usable energy. Since our incarceration in Plaszow had lasted only a few months at this time, we still had enough energy to put to some use. The question became, what kind of use lay ahead?

We came to the conclusion that we had been given an extended lease on life, if only for another short while. But any delay gave us new hope that the Allies would win and we would survive.

After what seemed like a long march through the Black Forest, stumbling over stones and branches, we reached a camp called Skarzysko, where we were greeted by shouting members of the OD with whips in their hands. At Skarzysko the Germans had largely ceded the reins to cruel Jewish commandants, ready to perpetrate the same forms of brutality as their German rulers in exchange for privileges. Only rarely did the Germans need to patrol the grounds. Our enemies at Skarzysko were Jews.

The OD were well fed and were dressed in tweed jackets, riding breeches with inseparable whips in their hands, and highly polished boots, as if ready to go on horseback. Their appearance was in great contrast to the inmates, whom we saw emerge through the darkness like ghosts. The skeletal bodies of the latter were wrapped in large paper bags; their skin was yellow and their hair orange. The apparitions seemed to be crawling toward us from all directions, shuffling their feet slowly and eventually surrounding us. Their big eyes, protruding from hollow faces, looked at us with envy. At least we still resembled human beings.

Now we had an inkling as to what faced us.

We learned that the inmates were from Lodz, and they had worked with TNT and picric acid in the production of ammunition for the German war effort. Those chemicals had not only destroyed their clothes, but they had colored their skin and their hair and had also damaged their lungs and heart. We had reached another grim turning point: We had escaped the shooting in Plaszow only to endure a torturous death from malnutrition, contamination, and disease.

Mother and I were devastated, but we were determined not to give up. Our only way to conquer the Nazis, we told ourselves, was to survive. Our goal was to outlast the tyrants, and we felt that the fight, in its new form, had just begun.

We were assigned to sleep in wooden shacks lined with three-layer-high bunk beds stretching down the length of the building in two rows, one on each side. In the middle of the barracks atop a little iron stove hung a single bulb suspended on a cord. The walls contained many cracks through which the howling wind seeped into the room, and the faint fire in the stove was incapable of providing heat for the large space.

When we first entered our barracks we found the floor covered with the clothes and blankets that had traveled with us on the cattle car. I managed to get a blanket, and mother and I found ourselves the first night on a bunk bed with another mother and her daughter and niece. The girls were older than me and very pushy. They grabbed our blanket, pushing us to the edge of the bed. I was very angry, but mother always advocated for peace, refusing to allow me to fight. Retreating instead into a childish belief that whoever wronged me would pay for it, I let my anger and bitterness go. I believed justice would take its own course.

My first escapade upon reaching the barracks was to go on an outing to the latrine, where we were not allowed to go after the curfew. The latrine was a long building without doors, containing only a wooden board stretched across the length of the room, holes punched out every foot or so, with a ditch underneath to catch the refuse. There were no stalls and no privacy, and the stench was suffocating. The only concession to our dignity was the separation of latrines for men and women. There was almost always a long line for the latrine and little time to use it.

I delayed my visit until the last minute, and consequently I found myself heading back to the barracks dangerously close to the curfew. Suddenly the lights went out, and the camp, bustling with people just moments ago, became deserted, dark, and silent. I knew I was required to report to my barracks at once, but my physically and emotionally drained body could not increase its slow pace. I mistakenly turned in the wrong direction, running into a large crate, which appeared to be a garbage container.

As I came nearer, the true contents of the crate became clear: skeletal corpses with limbs and heads spilling over the sides. The bones were covered with the paper-thin tallow skin of people who die of malnutrition. This was a receptacle filled with the daily casualties, intended to be discarded when it overflowed. Horrified, I shuffled my feet in the direction I believed led to my barracks.

Through the darkness the harsh voice of a Jewish policeman startled me. He was yelling at me for not observing the curfew. The image of the container of corpses froze in my mind. I had suddenly lost hope for survival and no longer cared about my fate. To my mind, being shot seemed preferable to the fate of those skeletons that had undoubtedly suffered an unbearable decline before death rescued their souls. I ignored the angry voice, continuing on my way. The policeman had not been accustomed to being dismissed, however, and he responded by catching up to me then escorting me to my barracks, saving me from the trouble that would have been mine had I been discovered by another policeman or a German. The name of the policeman was Melech Goldberg, a character whom I later learned was notorious for his viciousness.

The Skarzysko camp was administered by a Jewish woman from Lodz named Fela Markowiczowa, who had been named commandant. She lived a very privileged life together with her entourage, who included family members and friends. Amazingly they lacked nothing, and in return for their good fortune they were allowed to control the inmates, stealing provisions and robbing the few valuables some inmates had managed to smuggle into the camp. Though the Germans did not give the Jewish guards guns or knives, the guards often used their whips to beat inmates mercilessly, killing them with blows to the head. Men were their preferred targets.

Melech Goldberg was Markowiczowa's assistant. He was a crude and brutal man. Always dressed impeccably, he paraded around Skarzysko carrying a big whip that he used frequently to inflict deadly blows. It was Goldberg's job to conduct the weekly selection for extermination, the victims of which he first treated to vicious beatings.

In the few years before coming to Skarzysko I had witnessed the brutality that humans are capable of, but I had been able to find some level of rationalization by convincing myself of black and white divisions between the perpetrators, who were German, and the victims, who were Jews. That distinction, that last line of understanding, crumbled when we arrived at

Skarzysko. Here Jews continued to be victims, but here Jews were also perpetrators.

Within the first few days of my stay in Skarzysko my internal fury at the situation exploded. The target at whom I could not help directing the tirade was Goldberg. Much to my surprise, this henchman's response was not violent. Rather, he attempted to justify his actions. Twisting the realities of his atrocious behavior, he stated that when the Germans ordered him to deliver a hundred people, he selected only individuals who were very sick and did not stand a chance of survival. Had the selections been left to the Germans, they would have chosen healthy inmates, fully aware that the sick ones would die anyway and they could thereby double the casualties. He complained that people condemned him unjustly. He did not address either the unnecessary cruelty with which he carried out his orders or the benefits, like food and nice clothes, he received.

Throughout my captivity in Skarzysko, whenever my path crossed Goldberg's, he would insist on continuing the conversation, bent on changing my perception of his role.

The pushy bed-mates and I separated after a few days, and then I shared a bunk bed on the third level, too narrow for even one person, with Lola Adler, a friend from the brush factory in the ghetto. Mother, who was considered old, was assigned to a lower-level bed in order to spare her the climbing. Our bedding consisted of a burlap "mattress" filled with straw and a coarse gray blanket. The burlap was loosely woven, and I managed to pull out threads, which I used for sewing.

In Skarzysko I was able to obtain from one of the Polish workers at the camp a truly luxurious item: a needle. This tiny object was very precious in that it gave me the ability to earn some additional bread and soup by sewing and repairing clothes for other inmates. It also enabled me to keep my "wardrobe" in a more "stylish" condition.

As inmates we had only one change of clothing, yet we attempted to dress neatly. I still owned my prized navy dress school uniform with the mother-of-pearl buttons. The button-down dress covered anything I layered under it to keep me warm. Now that I was beginning to outgrow my winter coat, I decided to remodel it in time for the upcoming winter. I enlisted the help of a coworker who was a tailor, and we produced a very stylish suit. It took many hours of hand-sewing to accomplish my masterpiece, and I felt very proud of it. Making it gave me great satisfaction, proving to myself that I was able to create something new in the midst of this hell.

I also made a few colorful scarves from rags used to clean the machines in the bomb factory where we worked. The rags were made of discarded clothing, and frequently we could find scraps of colorful fabrics from which I could fashion scarves or even make alterations and trim for tattered dresses. My inventive creations earned me a good reputation, and my "free time" was put to good use. Using my ingenuity reminded me of the extent to which I could sharpen my skills and maintain a positive attitude. It was key to affirming a sense of my humanity and dignity—and as a practical matter, it provided us with extra rations of sorely needed bread.

Personal hygiene was another important aspect of maintaining dignity. The washroom—a long unheated barracks with rows of cold water faucets over a continuous metal sink—was next to the latrine. In the winter icicles hung from the faucets, but the pipes never froze because they were in constant use by long lines of people. Soap was available only rarely and for the purpose of ridding hair of lice. But washing was a function of civilized people, and we could not abandon it.

To maintain our sense of humanity, we needed to create some sort of spiritual nourishment even in the midst of the horror that greeted each day. While it had not been possible at Plaszow, the environment in Skarzysko left some room, however scant, for bare levels of entertainment. In our barracks, the little stove, which was the warmest spot in the building, became the cultural center for evening gatherings. Following exhausting days of work, the hungry women huddled around it, engaging in intellectual discussions, reciting poetry, composing music that reflected our collective misery, or singing melodies reminiscent of wonderful moments that had once filled our days.

In the dim light of the solitary bulb of the night, we often allowed ourselves to be transported to a world of fantasy, the images of which lifted our spirits and helped us to endure the cruelties. We spent many evenings listening to tales of the life that would await us after the nightmare. Dreaming aloud about tables piled with delicacies and elegant clothes and beautiful houses and concerts and theaters, our gloomy surroundings momentarily faded together with our hunger and cold. I felt like the character in Hans Christian Andersen's fairy tale *The Little Match Girl*—the little girl dying from the poor conditions around her who, using her last match, saw in its flame romantic promises of a good life.

Theater at the camp was not limited to our barracks. The "campus queen" Markowiczowa enjoyed theater, encouraging inmates to produce a revue that so delighted her she invited the German supervisors to watch it. The "success" of the performances gave us a brief respite to smile, lifting our otherwise dejected spirits.

We also tried to pepper our lives with some form of socializing. While many girls had "cousins"—male partners who frequently provided them with additional food—my social life revolved only around girls. Seeing the rate at which young men perished, I did not want to expose myself to another loss. I found room for only one main attachment—mother—and for a few girl friends, like Mala Hofnung-Sperling. I had originally met Mala, who was my age and also from Krakow, in 1939, following enrollment in the high school we had never been able to attend. We had both gotten jobs together in the brush factory in the ghetto, and then our paths ran parallel throughout the duration of the war.

The nights were always too short. We worked in 12-hour shifts, not including the long marches to and from the factory. After a few stolen moments around the stove or at a performance or socializing, there was little time to sleep.

The daily routine at Skarzysko was very demanding. The 200 grams of bread—one meager slice—that resembled a block of clay and the gray water presented to us once a day as soup, provided little nourishment after an interminable day of hard work. The soup was brought to the barracks in large kettles carried by starving men who bowed under the heavy load but nevertheless fought for the privilege because there were always a few spoonfuls left for them. Since the rations of the men were equal to those of the women, I believe the former, with their bigger bodies and harder work assignments, suffered even more. I was fortunate since I never needed much food and the hunger did not have as negative an impact on me as it did on many others.

As fortune would have it, mother, Mala and I were initially placed in the same work assignment: the last stage of production of large bombs, which we jokingly referred to as "calves" due to their size. The assembly line, where the TNT-filled shells were capped, was on tracks in the middle of a large hall without doors. The shells had holes in the top, where we were required to install an anchor made of a warm ring of paraffin and paper and insert a stick, which I suspect was dynamite. Mother's role was to cap the loaded shells with a pointed tool. Though the area of the room where she worked was drafty, she was at least able to sit, and she did not have to exert hard physical labor. Men lifted the 115-pound bombs onto the track prior to their reaching mother.

Mala and I were assigned to a small, well-heated room with a hot plate for the paraffin. When a bell rang, we were summoned to the main hall to install the paraffin, heated to the appropriate temperature. For a slave labor camp, our work assignment was as good as a happy dream. The room was warm and the work was easy. Even better: the space served as a lunch room for local Polish slave laborers who, still living in their homes, brought lunches each day. Frequently they gave us their leftovers. For them, these were only scraps of food, but for us, they were feasts. I savored small portions, always putting aside some for mother. Once a hunchback man brought Mala a treasure unheard of in the camp: a whole sausage, which she shared with many of us. The limited exertion and extra food shielded mother, Mala and me from the physical and mental deterioration that hounded other inmates.

Starvation was so rampant that we used all our resources to obtain additional food. Like other inmates, mother even resorted to pulling out her gold crowns to trade for bread. I was so sorry that I had been blessed with good teeth. Some prisoners sold pieces of their clothing to other prisoners to make patches for their clothes. Any item that could be translated into the food trade was fair game.

In these ways—a roof over our heads, sharing a bed, a tiny heater in a barracks housing hundreds of people through cold Polish winters, two items of our own clothing per person, holes in long wooden boards for toilets, and scavenging for scraps of food—we were able to survive, albeit barely. But a few months after our arrival a typhoid epidemic broke out, seriously undermining our efforts to maintain ourselves.

There was an infirmary at Skarzysko, called a *Krakenstube,* built to prevent the spread of illness to other slave laborers who were needed to continue manufacturing the weapons of death at no cost to the Germans. The *Krakenstube*, however, had almost no medications or medical supplies and could not curb the devastation wreaked by typhoid. We were informed that the Red Cross refused to supply us even with aspirin since we were not considered prisoners of war but rather "an internal problem of our country."

Recovery came to those nurtured by family members and friends who had not been stricken by the disease. The doors to the *Krakenstube* were never locked, and healthy inmates were permitted entry to take care of those who were sick.

I suppose this was one time when having Jews at the head of the camp benefited us. They reported the problem to the Germans as an outbreak, not of typhoid, but rather of influenza, which did not sound as dangerous. The sick people were relegated to separate barracks and stacked on the crowded bunks. With the disease consuming worn, emaciated people who, in their ill condition had no ability to obtain the small rations of food allotted to us, the death rate skyrocketed. Indeed, there were so many corpses that the orderlies could not remove them all each day, and sick people were often forced to lie next to dead bodies for days. Out of the 2,500 inmates who had come to Skarzysko from Plaszow, 900 perished from typhoid.

Although mother and I both contracted typhoid, we were fortunate in that the disease did not catch up with us at the same time. Mother came down with it first, and I was able to take care of her. Every day after work I collected her daily food ration and brought it to the *Krakenstube*, feeding her through her delirium.

After she recovered, I contracted typhoid, and mother took care of me in the same way I had looked after her. Since there was no one to help the sick, the attention we gave to each other proved again to be life-saving.

Among the many people killed by the typhoid epidemic were the mother and aunt of the pushy girls who had shared our bed and took our blankets when we had first arrived at Skarzysko. I could not rid myself of the feeling that the injustices they had heaped on us had been avenged, however cruelly. The girls had been left with their precious blanket, but I still had my beloved mother.

Mother and I returned to health much sooner than one would expect under the circumstances. Though our energy was depleted, we were alive, and that was what counted.

After my recovery from typhoid, my appearance, though gaunt, was presentable in the context of this mad world. I returned to work, where the factory temperature kept my body warm and the Polish laborers continued to give us additional food scraps. My skin was tan in the early spring from the long daily walk to the factory, my clothing was enhanced by scraps of fabric I had found around the camp, my navy coat-dress still created a neat appearance, and my braids were long. I even made a comb from a piece of ivory I had found in the factory. A dense comb was a great treasure since it served as a tool to comb out the lice that infected us all.

One day Walter, the German assistant commander of the camp, walked across my path. When he saw me he grabbed my chin. Walter was handsome, tall, and young. My short height reached only to his chest, and I could not see his face. Frozen, I stared at the body of this hulk of a man, this giant in a perfectly tailored dark green uniform with shining buttons. My knees buckled under me. Mother, standing nearby, turned ghostly white, anticipating the resounding noise of a slap across my face.

Walter slowly reached inside his pocket and pulled out a pair of scissors, proceeding to trim my eyebrow, which had a tendency to turn upward like a Mephisto. After he completed his task he stepped back to admire his masterpiece, then departed without uttering a word. I was left trembling like a November leaf.

Not every encounter I had with the Germans had such a once-upon-a-time (if one can call the encounter with Walter that) ending.

It was a beautiful spring day in 1944: flowers had begun to bloom along the road to the factory, and the free birds were singing in their spring-feverish voices; they had infected me with their upbeat mood. I had just made a lovely red polka dotted scarf for my dress. That day my hair was nicely braided, encircling my head. I felt as good as it was possible to feel in the camp. A ray of hope even dashed through my mind.

In the factory when the bell rang summoning us to bring the paraffin, I entered the room skipping, a smile pasted on my face. That day the old German commandant of the camp, Hecht, whom we called *Dziadek* (Polish for grandfather)—a very tall man hunched over from old age—stopped me, insisting I looked too well and seemed too happy for an inmate of a concentration camp.

Furiously Hecht shouted an order assigning me to work on the presses in the toxic picric acid factory, where people turned into scarecrows eaten alive by the figurative chemical crows within three months' time.

My mood sank like the *Titanic*. I thought I had finally reached the end of the survival road.

My new assignment began the next day. The presses where I was appointed produced explosive underwater mines. The work hall had several presses, and each one was served by four people. The daily quota was very demanding. Before the war Polish laborers at Skarzysko had worked only two hours at a time and wore gas masks, receiving milk at each break to counteract the poisonous chemicals. They had been required to produce 350 pieces a day. By comparison we were required to work 10 hours a day with no breaks (admittedly two hours a day less than other branches of the factory) and produce 1,650 pieces each day. If the quota was not filled, the entire team faced severe punishment in the form of brutal beatings, having the daily food ration withheld, or being forced to stand in the shooting range.

My entrance into the hall my first day on these presses was greeted with neither welcome nor relief: Not only was I among very few women, but I was the youngest and smallest. The teams could not imagine meeting their quotas with me as a member.

Always up for the challenge, I decided to prove that my presence would not cause a problem. I launched into the job with fervor, bent on overcoming my physical shortcomings by compensating with ingenuity. Each piece was produced by pouring picric acid into a mold, then placing it under a press to produce a cube. I developed logistics—such as which hand to use in reaching for the molds—guaranteed to save fractions of seconds on every move, cognizant that since the moves were repeated hundreds of times a day, those fractions would save appreciable amounts of time. Understanding that it would take a little time to break me in, some of the other teams contributed a few pieces to us, enabling us to meet our quota in the initial phases.

My teammates were very receptive to my innovations, and within a few days we not only met our quota, but we repaid the teams who had provided assistance during my apprenticeship. The mutual support of the teams was remarkable.

I felt so proud to have overcome yet another obstacle.

But my feeling of victory did not last long. It took only a few days for me to resemble the typical picric acid ghostly figures. My lungs began to suffer from their exposure to the corrosive acid. My skin yellowed, my hair turned orange, and my fingernails appeared stained from a lifetime of nicotine use. My skin and clothing became saturated with the horrific odor of the bitter powder that flew into the mouths and noses of anyone who came near me.

No amount of washing could erase the extent to which the chemical had embedded itself. It was difficult for my bed-mates to sleep when I crawled into my spot between them, though they were kind and understanding. Mother was horrified by my fate. The neat appearance I had fought so hard to maintain disappeared.

But my sense of dignity remained. I would not allow my spirit to be broken. I was driven to prove that nobody could crush me.

After three weeks at the picric acid presses I became ill. About an hour after arriving at work one day, I felt my body burn with fever. Afraid to slow down my team, I asked the Jewish foreman to find a replacement for me. He was a short man from Lodz who, to compensate for his inferiority complex, strutted around shouting orders and doing his best to stay out of the press room and avoid the picric dust contamination. He closely guarded his position as supervisor, which he assumed gave him the right to act in a superior manner.

That day there were no replacement possibilities other than the foreman himself—a fate he did not wish to undergo. He angrily refused to replace me, accusing me of laziness. Understanding the futility of my appeal for help, I summoned whatever strength I could find to continue working.

Miraculously, at that moment Commandant Walter, the German soldier who had trimmed my brow, passed by the window to inspect the factory. Though Germans ordinarily did not enter the building for fear of exposure to the picric acid, Walter noticed that I was not working with my usual fervor.

Through the window he asked me: "What is wrong with you, Little One?"

Knowing the fate of the sick, I would not admit feeling ill to a German, so I insisted that I was all right. Walter did not believe me, and he came into the hall to touch my forehead, which was burning with fever. He ordered the foreman to replace me immediately, then he told me to lay down on the boards in the storeroom and rest until the end of the shift. By then I had begun to cough and spit blood, a sign of what we called *hasagowka*—the illness caused by the picric acid's presence in my lungs.

My coworkers later told me that they had verbally attacked the foreman for being so cruel to me, and ultimately he asked me for forgiveness. About a month later I saw him dragging through the camp, sick and skeletal in appearance. Again I thought that someone had paid the price for mistreating me. I have no idea if he survived. When I last saw him, he did not appear as if he had a chance.

After work mother and Mala led me to the *Krakenstube*. Upon seeing me—the symbol of stalwart strength—in this weakened condition, the chief Jewish doctor named Haendel lamented that if I were to succumb, no one had a chance of survival. Apparently my image of indestructibility had spread beyond myself.

The *Krakenstube* was a barracks with two rows of bunk beds. Burning with fever, I was grateful for being able to enter this more sanitized room with mattresses larger than the army-cot-sized ones in our barracks, and comparatively comfortable for two people to share. I was fortunate to find as my bed-mate a friend my age from Krakow named Felicja Schechter. As was the rule in the *Krakenstube*, we were given clean sheets and clean nightgowns.

All the doctors in the infirmary were Jewish. The Germans seemed to want to give the appearance of caring about our health. Yet lacking medications and supplies, the doctors could do very little for us. They visited us daily, however, stocked with kind words and stories that transported us to beautiful, imaginary places.

Doctor Rothbalsam, the youngest of them, was in charge of the *Krakenstube*. He was kind and handsome, and his mere presence worked like medicine. Fela and I planted our imagination in the tales of his student life in Paris, picturing ourselves looking ravishing as we strolled down boulevards in elegant clothes with young male admirers in tow. Since there were no mirrors in the infirmary room, our images could not be contradicted.

Another doctor, Adam Wasserstein, also came daily, bolstering our health with kindness. The care provided to us by the doctors made us feel protected. In time—probably about a month—the clean room, bed rest, and uncontaminated air restored my health. While I had to wait for my orange hair to grow out, my skin returned to a human color.

Knowing that my return to the picric acid factory was likely to spell death, the doctors prescribed the continuing need for me to remain in the infirmary long after my fever had subsided. This was very courageous of them. Punishment meted out for such a transgression ranged from a severe whipping to death.

One of the great gifts of the spring of 1944 was the distant sound of Russian artillery. From the windows of the infirmary we could even see flames far away. We anticipated the quick advance of Russian troops, smelling liberation as sweetly as the fresh blooms outside. For a short time the camp became electrified by inmates' hushed giddiness.

Unfortunately, however, the Russians did not seem to be in a hurry, and the delay gave the Germans time to organize the camp's evacuation. With the decimation of the German ranks on the eastern front, those of us who were able-bodied were seen as an even more useful and economically efficient workforce than in the years before. Rumors began that we were to be taken to another ammunition factory.

One day in July 1944, as we looked out the window of the *Krakenstube,* we saw German soldiers, accompanied by dogs and *OD,* heading in our direction. We immediately understood the implications: Sick people would not be worth transporting.

Melech Goldberg, the brutal *OD* whom I had met my first day at Skarzysko, was among the group. Suddenly he rushed forward, out of his position, entering our barracks. He grabbed Fela and me, throwing us out the back door in our nightgowns before the Germans entered.

Since the first day I had met Goldberg he had tried to prove to me that he treated people with kindness. I suppose his rescue of Fela and me gave him sense of redemption. Had he been caught, he would have paid for the momentary kindness with his life.

The rest of the women in the infirmary who were considered sick and unable to work, including a Mrs. Fortgang, her daughter, and her sister Mrs.

Rubin, the mother and the aunt of a friend from the brush factory in Plaszow, were rounded up and executed prior to our evacuation.

Escaping the *Krakenstube*, I darted in my nightgown into the barracks where I had been housed with mother and Mala, overjoyed at our reunion and at another deliverance from death. The entire camp was gripped by a palpable tension as the Germans had begun dismantling Skarzysko. The inmates deemed not fit to be a part of the Germans' plans were executed the first day that work stopped. The rest of us no longer went to work; we strolled the grounds aimlessly, awaiting some resolution.

For the first time since incarceration, a faint ray of hope for survival and even physical recovery appeared on the horizon. After several days we were again loaded onto cattle cars, embarking on another trip that seemed to last for days. The train was windowless, so we had no idea which direction we were headed or what the duration of the trip was.

Luna's Hasag prison dress
(Photo by Mike Allison, courtesy of U.S. Army)

Chapter Nine
Leipzig

When the doors of the cattle cars opened we found ourselves at another work camp site of the ammunition manufacturing company Hasag, which also owned the factory in Skarzysko. This new camp, however, was located outside the borders of Poland, in Leipzig, Germany.

Upon arrival we were assigned numbers, which from that moment replaced our names in yet another act of humiliation. My number was 648; Mother's was 255. We were then required to pass "medical" examinations and undergo lice control. Our bodies had to be totally sanitized. We were stripped naked, each woman waiting for hours for her check-up. Upon finding lice German soldiers would shave the woman's hair, leaving her with a bald head. Despite the fact that we all had lice most of the time during our incarceration, women whose heads were shaved felt terribly humiliated. Hair was the only inseparable adornment that could not wear out and that reminded us of our humanity. While the one set of clothes all of us had been allowed to keep showed its use over the years despite our constant maintenance efforts, hair framed our faces. When we looked at our reflections in windowpanes from the neck up, our hair told us that we still looked decent.

Mother and I were very fortunate; we were not ordered to have our heads shaven.

After the lice-check the Germans took from us the last of our possessions, which consisted only of what we carried on our backs. I had to part with my most prized possession, my masterpiece, the remodeled suit that I had created in Skarzysko from my school coat. The coat, initially designed for me to wear proudly en route to an anticipated illustrious secondary school career, maintained its air of dignity despite its relegation to the shoulders of a concentration camp inmate. Like me, the coat had survived indignities unbefitting to its physical stature. Throughout my imprisonment I had felt a sense of inanimate friendship with the coat. Letting it go was akin to saying good-bye to a loved one.

Next we were marched, about 100 women at a time, into a great white, tiled room with shower heads spread across the ceiling. In Skarzysko we had grown accustomed to cold water washing in wooden barracks with holes in the boards that allowed the wind to blow on our freezing, wet bodies. The sudden luxury of a tiled room felt unexpected and suspicious. Moreover, by then we had heard about the gas chambers the Germans had constructed at concentration camps where the substance that eked through the shower heads was lethal gas rather than water. The descriptions of the gas chambers had mirrored the appearance of the room we were entering,

Our blood froze. We did not know what to expect. What a relief it was when the water—which was not ice cold—started to flow generously. We were even given soap! When we finished washing we were forced to exit through a different door so the incoming group would not see us and therefore would be forced to undergo the same horrific anxiety of not knowing whether the shower heads would rain water or gas.

Mother and I walked to our building assignment and were delighted to see that our quarters were in a brick structure. Another "luxury"!

No more wind howling through the cracks. No more darkened chambers. A bright light streamed through big, unbroken windows in the large and clean rooms, each housing up to 600 women. Mala was assigned to an adjoining hall since she worked on another shift.

Physically we felt good. We had been able to wash thoroughly with an abundant amount of water and with soap for the first time in two years. We were issued new white cotton shirts and clean covers for our mattresses, which were filled with new aromatic straw. No perfume would have brought more joy than the aroma of that fresh straw.

Our four-level-high bunk beds were the only place where we could rest after work, since there were no chairs, benches, or tables in the rooming quarters. I had the top bunk, close to a window that let in a good amount of light. Mother's was just below mine.

Our striped prison dresses did not arrive for a few days. This was fortunate for me because I had come to Leipzig straight from the infirmary at Skarzysko. The fact that we could not work without the camp uniform gave me additional time to recover. For three days our daily activity was wandering around the camp in our white underwear.

The extravagance of free time was surpassed only by the decency of the food—in its quantity and quality—at Leipzig. We received one bowl of soup a day with a bread ration that was much larger than any we had gotten over the previous two years. The soup was delicious with two varieties provided: milk-based with dumplings or thick pumpkin. The kitchen was run by Russian women soldiers who were prisoners of war—and excellent cooks. While other women assigned to the kitchen stole food provisions, selling them to outside workers, the Russian women did not. Indeed, they cooked using all the ingredients given to them.

Today I always order pumpkin soup when I find it on a restaurant menu, but none tastes as good as that offered in Leipzig.

Our brand-new uniforms were clean, lice-free, gray-and-blue-striped prison dresses. Because of my small stature the dress I was given appeared to swim on me. Since it was important to me to look decent, I managed to make a needle from a wire and pull thread from the burlap mattress to make a hem. There were also black threads in the mattress, which I used to embroider my number—648—and mother's number—255— into our uniforms so they would not fade in the washing. In this manner I converted a potential feeling of dehumanization through numerical identity into a source of pride. A few days later I found a yellow plastic machine belt, which I converted into a belt to accentuate my figure under the uniform.

One of my great finds at Leipzig was a piece of hard plastic that I was able to carve into a fine comb with the help of a metal file. The one I had made at Skarzysko had been confiscated when I arrived at Leipzig. I shared this luxury item with my friends. Keeping clean was a constant battle since few women had combs or soap.

One day soon after we had arrived in Leipzig a female SS guard named Anna Lisa stopped me. She called other women to circle around me, praising my neatness and the creativity with which I had adorned my uniform. The rest of the time I was at Leipzig Anna Lisa made efforts to help me, frequently giving me extra soup, which I shared with mother.

Anna Lisa, whom we called "Little Doll," was very decent to all of us inmates. She treated us like human beings. When we arrived at Leipzig in 1944 we believed the end of the war was likely—there were occasional sightings of American planes bombing nearby towns and rumors that the Russians were progressing west—and we surmised that humane treatment on the part of SS guards might be motivated by a desire for postwar positive testimony on their behalf. Whereas gossip that circulated about the commandant at Leipzig, for instance, pegged him as a mass killer in previous camps, to us his behavior was mild. Grateful for bearable conditions, we did not dwell on the possibility of previous atrocities.

Wearing my uniform with its embellishments, I did not feel humiliated when I faced civilians working next to me. I was assigned to be a helper operating a metal lathe. The job posed little physical challenge, and working with metal ensured that I would be surrounded by clean air. My chances of survival increased.

We worked as a team of three on the lathe. There was a technician with us, a young Polish boy about 18 years old, whom I quickly befriended. Like many Poles, he had been shipped to work in Germany as forced labor; other Poles chose to engage in this work voluntarily. Unlike the Jewish factory workers, who received no compensation and were enslaved at the concentration camps, the Poles received minimal stipends and were free to live outside of the workplace.

Also on our team was our superior, an old German technician we called "Grandpa." All of us were supervised by a German professional engineer. The environment came the closest to resembling normal working conditions that I had experienced since the beginning of the war.

When I first began working on the team Grandpa stared at me continuously. Ultimately his reason became apparent: he had believed that only prostitutes and thieves were incarcerated in concentration camps, and to his mind I seemed too young to be a prostitute and too honest to be a thief. He expressed great surprise when I explained that my only crime was being Jewish. I found his innocence—or his appearance of it—shocking, since by 1944 anti-Semitic propaganda had been commonplace for a number of years in Germany.

Once on a snowy day I felt the urge to engage in a snowball fight. Not permitted to go outside during working hours, I persuaded my Polish cohort to bring a pile of snowballs indoors. The delightful battle between us ensued until Anna Lisa spotted us. Thinking he was hurting me, she came running to my rescue. We could not tell her that I had instigated the game, since despite her generally kind disposition I would have suffered dire consequences. My Polish friend, however, was not under her jurisdiction. Since Anna Lisa was powerless to punish him, we blamed the prank on him. We both had a good laugh later on.

Female inmates in Leipzig were not just Jews. They were from France, Hungary, Poland, and Russia. The Russian women were war prisoners. The others were incarcerated following sentences for petty "crimes" like smuggling bread or walking after curfew hours. There were also some partisans among them. But for us it was enough simply to be Jewish.

Nonetheless, although we were housed separately, we maintained the illusion of being equal to the others. Their presence brought color to our lives. On Bastille Day, the French women made paper hats and marched through the hallways of our living quarters singing French songs. When the Russian women refused to work in the ammunition factories, they were forced to stand outdoors for 24 hours, which they spent singing beautiful a capella songs. As military women, they were protected by the Geneva Convention, so despite the severity of their infraction the threat of death did not loom over their heads. Ultimately they won their battle and were assigned to the kitchen rather than the factory. We admired them for their resistance and their dignity—as well as their melodious voices. We were also the beneficiaries of their rebellion, since they proved to be excellent cooks.

One of the more difficult reminders of our incarceration was the daily requirement, regardless of the weather and the meagerness of our clothing, of standing outdoors on an *Appel* to be counted. This was the German method of ensuring that no one had escaped overnight or was hiding from work. Basically a roll call, the *Appel* took hours. The punishment for the smallest infraction, such as not marching in proper formation, was being kept standing in another *Appel* formation after work for hours at a time.

When the morning *Appel* was completed, we were forced to march a long distance to the factory. The shoes with which we had come to Leipzig had worn out, and we were issued wooden clogs. Once the calluses had formed and the sores had disappeared, the clogs kept our feet warm even in the winter. But the rough wood of the clogs was too hard for mother's sensitive feet, causing deep sores and requiring her to spend the last few weeks of our time in Leipzig at the infirmary.

The guards always looked for reasons to punish us. One day after work one of the SS women guards peered into the windows of our room and saw from the distance an inmate applying lipstick. Since there were no cosmetics in the camp, the woman's action signaled the fact that she had been in contact with the world outside the camp's borders. The SS guard stormed into our room, demanding to know who had applied the lipstick. Paralyzed by the potential severity of the consequences, the room went silent.

Our entire bunk of about 600 women were marched outside, where we were forced to spend several torturous hours standing in straight-line formation following a 12-hour night shift. I never wore lipstick and felt terribly angry that the guilty party would not own up to her act. Mother's quiet intervention convinced me to keep my mouth shut. I looked up to her for her wisdom, composure, and ability to bear her fate with dignity.

In retrospect I am self-critical at the anger I felt toward the woman who had applied lipstick. Though it seemed like a frivolity to me I now understand that, to her, the lipstick was a touch of humanity the way the hem on my dress was to me. Each of us clung to whatever shred of civilized life we could find.

By the winter of 1944 production was very important to the Germans. All able-bodied German soldiers were serving in the army, and we provided the cheapest possible labor. We met with little maltreatment (relative to what we had experienced before coming to Leipzig), since its impact would have slowed down production.

We did not dwell on the destination of our products. In Leipzig we were making small parts, the ultimate role of which was unidentifiable. We focused on gratitude for the relatively decent living conditions and the apparent imminence of the war's end. Our work hours seemed to be merely the way we were required to bide our time.

The 12-hour shifts were exceedingly boring. My repetitive job required installing metal rods in three machines. Four knives cut each rod into small pieces as it rotated. I did not know the purpose of the rods. Since I was small and female, the engineer assumed I did not understand the workings of the machinery. My teammates called me *die Kleine*—German for "little one"—and despite my handiness and good mechanical skills, I played into their stereotype. The situation left room for me to entertain myself with pranks that only I understood. For example, I reset the knives so the machine produced rejects. Now the broken knives could not cut, and the twisted rod would swing in front of the machine. After the malfunction was under way, I would run to the foreman, pretending to be distressed because the machine had broken. Sometimes it took many hours to repair it while I continued my pretense of concern.

Holding up production and wasting metal were serious crimes, particularly in light of the severe shortages. The offenses were possibly punishable by death. For me, though, the incidents were merely ways to amuse myself. I had not intended premeditated sabotage. Fortunately the overseers never suspected I knew what I was doing.

Nor did mother ever catch wind of my pranks, which would have mortified her. She had been assigned to work on a hand machine—some kind of small press—where she moved a lever hundreds of times a day. Though her work was also very tedious mother's sense of duty was her priority. She produced her quota diligently, sometimes even exceeding it. She also feared the consequences if she did not fulfill her obligations since the Germans were much harder on the older than on the younger women.

With the arrival of 1945 we believed the end of the war was near, and our hopes of survival increased. Rumors of Russia's victory spread. At Leipzig the SS guards believed our labor was necessary, so they continued to loosen the pressure under which we functioned and to improve working conditions. They even closed the factory for one day on Christmas. After the war we learned that in other camps German soldiers had spent this time executing as many inmates as possible.

In appreciation for our decent treatment the women decided to give a Christmas gift to Anna Lisa, and I was selected to create it. This was a pleasure for me because, although she was an SS guard, Anna Lisa had been for me a ray of sunshine in the cruel world of concentration camps. She had helped me to keep my faith in people and to maintain hope in the face of deplorable conditions.

I had no supplies other than a good imagination. I took a *Laufkarte*—a production sheet—and filled it in, spelling "Happy New Year." From scraps of fabric we used to clean the machines I made a doll dressed in a prison dress just like ours. On her sleeve I embroidered "1945" and in her hand I placed a piece of our metal production. The other inmates greatly admired my handiwork, but since the giving of presents was highly punishable I never had the pleasure of seeing Anna Lisa's reaction to the doll. That was all right with me; the satisfaction of expressing my feeling through the gift was sufficient. Eventually toward the end of our incarceration we were issued coupons as rewards for good work. The coupons enabled us to purchase a few luxuries like toothpaste, toothbrushes, pieces of soap, or combs and even shoes with wooden soles. However, the number of coupons, awarded in accordance with productivity, were minimal, and after several weeks few of us had enough to qualify for even a toothbrush. Mother received a few coupons each week. Once we rejoiced at being able to exchange them for a bar of soap.

For a long time, my performance did not qualify for the receipt of coupons. Only in the last weeks was I called by the chief German engineer to collect a few coupons, the total of which did not amount to enough to trade for any goods at all. When I reported to pick them up I boldly told the chief engineer that they would be good currency to buy a house after the Americans entered Leipzig. At that point the daily sight of Allied planes overhead had convinced us that liberation would greet us any moment. The chief engineer carefully peered around the room to see whether anyone else had heard my sarcastic comment. Finding an otherwise empty room, he let me go.

With the coming of spring, our hopes blossomed faster than the buds on the trees. Unlike the winter drill we marched back and forth to work in daylight, frequently witnessing American planes bombing surrounding factories. We waved to the planes as if they were able to see us. We felt giddy with hope. Surely those planes were our ticket to freedom. When the planes approached the area of Leipzig we refused to run for air-raid cover, eager to watch our Allied rescuers. Additionally the pilots would not have known there were occupants in the buildings they were bombing, and staying inside put us in jeopardy of friendly fire.

One day the alarm sounded when we were still in our bunk beds, and the Germans ordered us to go to the shelter. Very jealous of the right to kill us, they protected us from the fire of their enemies. We had just returned from a 12-hour night shift, and my body was falling asleep. I considered staying in my bed, but I was forced to go into the shelter. No sooner did I reach the door than a bomb hit a corner of the building, shattering my bed. Again I felt that my number had not yet come up.

In April 1945 a new group arrived at Leipzig, including many women from Krakow. They reported seeing my sister in Auschwitz, and mother and I rejoiced. This was the first news of Niusia we had heard since 1943. We were told that a cousin of ours from Belgium who had worked in the kitchen at Auschwitz had managed to smuggle extra food to Niusia and cousin Ecka. When the time came for a transport to depart from Auschwitz, convinced that they were being selected for crematoria, our Belgian cousin helped Niusia and Ecka to escape.

Mother and I entertained high hopes for a reunion with my sister. It took 40 years after the war for us to learn that instead of joining us in Leipzig, Niusia and Ecka were sent to Stutthoff, one of the most cruel camps. In the last days of the war they were all loaded onto ships that were sunk. Only a small handful were rescued by Swedish fishermen.

Chapter Ten
Death March

On a beautiful April day in 1945, when the sweet smell of freedom was within our reach, we were once again rounded up for deportation. Unlike our experiences in Plaszow and Skarzysko, there was nothing for us to take other than our depressed bodies. Even to the last second our monstrous German captors continued to deprive us of the gift for which we had been yearning for four years: LIBERTY. Yet we would not give up hope. Indeed, we were more determined than ever to endure whatever obstacles we would confront to reach freedom's destiny.

For several weeks before that April day my poor mother had been in the Leipzig infirmary recovering from wounds to her feet. The pus that had oozed was so severe that her wooden shoes stuck to her skin, and she had to soak them off. Despite her pain the prospect of separation from me seemed unbearable, and mother came out of the infirmary to join our ranks—clad in a pair of wooden shoes.

The Germans lined us up four abreast and started us on what was to be a hunger march. The only possession we were permitted to carry was a metal can with a string handle into which we were occasionally permitted to put water we might find by the roadside. At the start of the march we each received a handful of rice, which we soaked in our cans and ate, a few grains at a time, realizing this diet would have to last indefinitely. We supplemented the menu with those sporadic weeds and leaves alongside the road that were capable of growing in early spring. The days turned to nights and then back again to days and nights and days, and throughout the period we were hardly ever permitted to stop marching.

I do not know how many we were in total, but when I glanced around I saw a sea of human ghosts, slowly shuffling our feet. Along the road our camp of women was joined by inmates of other camps. Our striped prison uniforms easily distinguished us, even seen from the air. Ironically we served as a shield for the Germans who were guarding us. After all, the Allies would not shoot prisoners.

Indeed, I believe it was to save the lives of our German captors that the hunger marches had been orchestrated. Our guards were an arm of the military, and without us they would have had to report to the front line. Unlike the prisoners they were guarding, the SS soldiers were well-fed, alternating their shifts every few hours.

Mother, Mala, and I marched holding onto each other. Occasionally overcome by complete exhaustion, I would fall asleep walking. Mala, much more frail than me, would wake me so I would not cause mother to fall. She was so unstable on her sore feet. The open wounds on her feet worsened with every step, weakening her overall condition. Mala watched over her like another daughter, clinging to the only semblance of family she had left.

At night we could see the sky light up orange with the flames of artillery. We were isolated from any source of news or contact with civilians, and we could not understand why, though we saw fire before and behind us, no one was rushing to our rescue. It seemed impossible for the Allies not to see thousands of us in our prison uniforms on the roads. We felt forsaken.

We were forced to march through the days and nights without stopping. Fortunately the weather that spring was beautiful, saving us from enduring the additional burden that rains and winds would have brought. From time to time we were permitted to stop momentarily—a gift that we greeted with great relief. Although we could not imagine how the hunger march would end, the belief that it would end never faded.

One day we came across a group of Polish officers who were also prisoners of war. One tall, handsome man carried a whole loaf of rye bread with a golden crust—a delicacy we had not seen for years. He rested his foot on a stone, then pulled out a knife and proceeded to slice the bread and distribute it among us. I was among the fortunate ones to receive a slice, and I rushed with my priceless possession to mother and Mala. The three of us shared it, feasting on one crumb at a time. The fact that someone had been willing to share a loaf of bread with us renewed our faith in people and rekindled our strength to continue fighting for life.

After an eternity of three weeks the German guards divided us into groups of about 300 women each. They led our group into a barn full of soft, fragrant hay where we were able to rest our feet for the first time since leaving Leipzig. Although there was barely an inch of vacant space between us, no more luxurious bed seemed to exist in the world. We immediately collapsed into sleep.

When we awoke we saw daylight stream through the cracks in the barn walls. The 300 of us continued to lie in silence and darkness. Ultimately one woman peering through a hole spotted a pile of German uniforms in front of the barn, and we realized that our guards had left us behind. We did not know what to think or do; we had been deceived too many times over the years. We could not even discern which of our extremely compelling feelings was the most pressing: exhaustion, hunger, or fright. We had been so relieved to rest our bodies that we had stopped expecting to get food, and we no longer believed anyone would help us. We tried to keep quiet so we would not attract unwelcome attention outside the immediate safety of the barn.

In whispered conversations we wondered aloud how long we ought to stay in the barn and who might be brave enough to venture out. The latter question became moot, however, when—much to our terror—someone from the outside slowly opened the heavy wooden doors, the rusted hinges roaring like a lion.

Shock registered on the face of the German who opened the door. Dressed in a dark suit, riding britches, and shining boots, he had expected to see a few piles of straw and instead was confronted with 300 pairs of eyes staring out of emaciated, frightened female prisoners. We learned that he was a civilian who had been the caretaker of the now-abandoned estate where the barn was located.

Though our collective initial instinct was to fear the worst when we met this German man, we noticed that he had no gun and that he spoke softly. He immediately recognized our need for food, simultaneously realizing that feeding 300 mouths at this late point in the war was a tall order.

The German caretaker offered us a large mound of potatoes left from winter storage. He suggested that a few women be assigned to peel the potatoes and cook them in a mixture of water and milk. The offering sounded absolutely divine. The thick mush the women prepared was delicious. Its preparation and consumption all took place within the tight and darkened confines of the closed-door barn. We still feared stepping outside. We knew the supply of potatoes would last for several days.

We later learned how fortunate we had been that other food was not available to us at that time. Some rescued inmates who had been provided with ample food at other locations died from the excessive intake into starved stomachs.

The fresh water we received at that time was also life-saving. In addition to hydrating us it enabled mother to soak the wooden shoes off her feet again.

Cognizant of our desperate situation, a day after he found us the German caretaker tied a white handkerchief signaling surrender to his bicycle and rode into Risa, the closest town, near the shores of the Elbe River, where he sought assistance from the Red Cross. He returned very disappointed, saying they were not ready to offer any help. As we had experienced in Plaszow and Skarzysko, the Red Cross turned its organizational eyes away from us in indifference. So much of what defined the horror of our plight was that no one cared.

By the time the caretaker returned our fear of leaving our safe shelter had begun to dwindle. The caretaker explained to us that we were in the neutral zone between the western and eastern front lines—the same neutral zone where we had been marching for three weeks. Now we understood why we had seen flames on both sides of the road. Caught as we were between the British and the Russians, he surmised that it was unlikely liberating armies would reach us very quickly. His advice was for us to lay low and get as much rest as possible.

Chapter Eleven
Liberation

So now we are free!

But where do we go? What is awaiting us? What does it mean to be free?

Our dreams have come true, but what do we do with our new freedom? Sooner or later, we have to face the great unknown world that awaits us. Where can we rest our tired bodies?

I had been 12 at the outbreak of the war. I had lost my teenage years in the ghetto and camps, and with those years had vanished my high school education. At the age of 18, I felt totally unprepared to take responsibility for my life.

It was now up to us to find shelter. Even the meager daily soup and slice of bread we had been given in the camp suddenly had to be earned, or we would go hungry. And where would we get clothing?

Strangely enough, even though we had survived the horrors of the camps, we were frightened at the prospect we were facing. What would we do with our lives? Who would we become? There was nobody to tell us what to do, where to work, or how to act. The responsibility of freedom dampened the joy of obtaining it.

I was among the fortunate few to have my mother with me, but she was sick, and now, having my own children, I can comprehend what a nightmare it must have been for her not to know the fate of my sister or father. I was so grateful to have her—she was my greatest support—but at the age of 53, she appeared to me to be very old and in need of care. The sickness and trauma of the past years had taken a severe toll on her.

We stayed in the crowded barn where the Germans had left us, eating our potato soup and hoping for a miracle. It was not long before a Russian military transport drove through the town. Trucks and tanks carried a motley crew of young, vigorous soldiers covered with dust and bandages, some playing harmonicas and singing. They did not resemble the spit and polished German army of tyrants that we had faced in the camps.

The local German population may have been terrified of what appeared to them as invading barbarians, but we welcomed them with joy. Their warm smiles and shabby appearance made us feel very close to them. We had both spent the last few years facing terrible hardships. We felt a common bond and considered them friends. Unfortunately, they disappeared as suddenly as they had come, and we were left in the same bleak circumstances.

The next day two wounded Russian soldiers returned to town on a beat-up motorcycle. They rounded up the Germans and took all their watches, stringing them on their arms from wrist to elbow. Russia had not produced many luxury items since the Revolution, and watches were considered great trophies.

After they completed their watch mission the soldiers focused on us. They ordered the Germans to accommodate us in private homes, where we would get beds and food. They threatened to come back in a few days, warning that the town would suffer dire consequences if their orders were disobeyed. The soldiers never returned, but the threat did the job.

Mother, Mala, four other women, and I were assigned by the Russians to be housed in Olganitz, a small village next to Risa, on the large farm of an older couple. Several Christian workers from Czechoslovakia who had been deported during the war to work in forced labor assignments also lived on the couple's farm. The place was clean, and they had a modest amount of food—certainly more than enough to feed us.

I can still smell the beautiful aromas that emanated from the kitchen of that farmhouse. For the first time in years the food really resembled the home cooking we had known.

We found ourselves sitting at a table for the first time in four years, being served on real plates and using real silverware, eating potatoes smothered with onions, vegetables, and small pieces of sausage. For breakfast we were given a fresh glass of milk, which soothed my diseased lungs.

We were impressed with the beautiful German farm where we stayed as well as with others in the vicinity. The barns had clean concrete floors, and the brick buildings were spotlessly whitewashed. Beautiful flower gardens grew in the front yards. The living quarters were much more sophisticated than the Polish farms with the dirt floors that we had known.

Our room was bright and airy, shared by only three women. What a treat it was to enter a room with white starched curtains, real pressed linens, pillows and covers, and sunlight streaming through large windows.

How ironic that here in a German house we experienced a feeling of peace and security for the first time in five years. We pushed away thoughts about the past affiliation of our hosts. We needed peace and were willing to receive comfort from whoever offered it. We were totally spent.

The only thing we missed was communication with the outside world. There was no radio or newspaper, and only rarely did someone pass through town.

From time to time, individuals from outside the neutral zone would pass through the town to gauge the level of activity. Occasionally groups of American reporters arrived in what appeared to be shiny black limousines. Their cars were probably used Chevrolets, but to us they seemed luxurious. The reporters brought supplies of candy bars, which they distributed. Many of the women went wild at their first postwar taste of chocolate. I was too proud to take the candy, which in the end served me well. The chocolate was too rich for the stomachs of most of the former inmates, causing rampant sickness in those who ate it.

The town had no bakery, so every few days two women went to the adjoining town to bring a supply of bread for the village. One day it was Mala's and my turn. Still clothed in our prison dresses and pulling a little wagon, we marched on a country road. On the way we met Russian soldiers who were surprised to see us still clad in the uniforms of our imprisonment. They informed us that we had better find other attire—the war had been over for five days!

We forgot about the bread and raced back home to share the joyous news. Yet our happiness was tempered by our fear of facing the future. We did not know what we would find once we returned home. For most of us there was no home to which we could go back.

We lingered another few days. Ultimately some Russian soldiers "helped" us make a decision. One evening the commandant of the area arrived with his entourage of young men, an accordion player, food, and vodka. He was a high-ranking officer who was young and very handsome with a smiling face and a lust for life.

The commandant had heard there were girls in the village with whom he figured he could have a good time. At first the scene he set up looked like a great party. A number of us young women felt as though we were returning to the life of normal teenagers. Spending the last years in a concentration camp for women, however, had left us naive. Shortly we discovered that our idea of fun did not correspond with their intentions.

The soldiers' attitude conveyed a simple exchange: They believed they had fulfilled their military obligation, sacrificing their lives to liberate us, and therefore we now had an obligation to express our gratitude by sleeping with them. They considered our compliance a reward. Refusal meant rejection, raising the specter of violent retribution. We had heard reports about rapes and even a few deaths.

The commandant, who had brought a large diamond looted from Germans as a reward for the evening, decided I was a fit companion for him. Mother tried to no avail to tell him that my pink cheeks were a result of tuberculosis. I had to be very careful not to object to his advances so he would not be aware of the intended rejection. I decided to play for time, hoping for a solution. I appeared to be receptive and encouraged him to drink a lot. We danced and sang Russian songs, and I toasted him every few minutes, managing not to drink myself.

When he got really drunk I suggested he show the diamond to some of the other women. Diamonds had never tempted me; they look only like pieces of glass. Although pawning it might have produced the badly needed seed money for our new start, I was not about to sell myself for any price, let alone in front of my mother.

One of the women who saw the precious gem started flirting with the commandant, sitting on his lap. Older than me and rather unattractive, I suppose she was enticed by this handsome, rugged man with a large diamond ready to be given away. I guess in other circumstances I also might have found him appealing.

In the morning the woman wore the diamond on her finger. I was very proud of my manipulation and thought it was the end of this adventure.

About noon the next day a young Jewish doctor who had been part of the commandant's entourage presented mother and me with two valises filled with clothes for every season. The doctor told us that after the Russian commandant had sobered up, he realized I had manipulated him the evening before, and was planning to seek revenge that night. It was suggested that we leave immediately.

One of the valises given to us by the doctor contained clothing suitable for a mature woman like my mother, and the other had more youthful items. Looted from German homes, the clothes had been carefully selected. I remember the lovely chiffon dress printed with colorful sweet peas. It was so bright and airy—a far cry from the coarse blue-and-white-striped uniform stiff enough to stand by itself.

My dresses before the war had been much more tailored, generally adorned with Peter Pan collars befitting the style of young Polish girls at that time. This silky, flowing dress was my first fashion bridge to womanhood.

Within a few hours after getting the advice and the clothes from the doctor, mother, Mala, and I left for Risa, where trains were departing in the direction of Poland. We pulled a cart to transport our few treasured possessions on this long march.

The sea of humanity that swarmed about Risa was overwhelming. Everyone was trying to find a precious spot on open flatcars returning east. Built to transport trucks, tanks, and other heavy vehicles and equipment, the flatcars were vacant—leaving space for human occupancy—after their cargo was unloaded. It took only a short while for us to board a very long train. We were grateful for our good fortune in being able to find a train with an open platform as opposed to the dark cattle cars on which we had been transported from camp to camp.

The train moved slowly from town to town, riding on tracks that were not used for military transports. As long as the train was empty we were permitted to ride, but if cargo needed to be loaded we were required to get off and wait for another one. Many times we stood waiting for days on the tracks. A trip that should have taken several hours lasted a week. But we were in no hurry, almost happy to delay facing reality.

We shared the train with a group of Polish war prisoners who served for us as a shield against the Russians. Unlike us, they were returning home to families and lives disrupted but not destroyed. They were educated and handsome young men, most of whom had been caught as partisan fighters. The boys, Mala, and I shared a great camaraderie as we sang and flirted through the trip. Other than the "party" given by the Russian commandant days before, this was the first time in my teenage years since the ghetto when I was in company of the opposite sex.

Anti-Semitic remarks were a part of the conversation. Still feeling that Jews were in danger, we did not dare disclose our Jewish identity.

The supply of food was sporadic. When the train stopped we sometimes ventured into the nearest town and tried to get food. Having no money, we depended on the goodness of local residents to share with us whatever meager supplies they had.

In one German town I found a small farm with a goat. We needed food and had no other source at the time, so I took the goat over the protests of its owner. I had seen so many mothers protesting the ripping of their children from their arms that I felt justified in taking a mere goat to supply us with sustenance.

We shared our bounty with our 20 or so traveling companions. One of the men, a young Polish veterinarian, slaughtered the goat. We built a fire and roasted it, providing a feast for all of us.

A few days later Mala and I went to town looking for bread, but upon our return we discovered that the train—with mother and our belongings—was gone. Mother and I had managed to survive the whole war together, and now we were separated! I was devastated, imagining mother's despair when the train pulled out without me. Yet we both knew the destination to which we were heading: 13 Wielopole Street in Krakow. Mother would arrive sooner.

Two brothers who traveled with us were from Poznan, a city near the German border. When the train stopped in their town they invited Mala and me to spend an evening at their parents' house. The prospect of a good night's rest was very enticing, and we accepted their invitation.

We witnessed with envy their wonderful family reunion as they fell into the arms of their parents and siblings. Their family welcomed us warmly, sharing a beautiful feast at a table covered with a white linen tablecloth and delicacies we had not seen in years. For our sleeping comfort they gave us a lovely room with a big bed, down pillows and comforters, and a soft mattress. We had grown accustomed to different sleeping arrangements, however, and all this luxury was too much for us. After the door to our room closed we took our bedding and put it on the floor. The hard surface made us feel much more at home.

The next morning was Sunday, and the family invited us to join them in church. Having heard so many anti-Semitic remarks from the boys, we were afraid to tell them we were Jewish. Instead we successfully pretended to be too tired to accompany them.

Our experience with this family made us realize even more vividly that, while these young men had been incarcerated, they at least had not lost their loved ones and their homes. In contrast we did not know who in our families, other than mother, had survived. And we did know that we had been forced to abandon our homes and our possessions and that there would be no luxurious bedding or delicious food spreads—let alone a roof over our heads—waiting for us upon our return. The fear of facing the devastation that awaited us became very real.

Later that day we boarded—or rather mounted—the first train going south. This time we hopped onto a passenger car, riding on its roof. What an adventure! Traveling was free, and since we had nothing with us, the trip was easy. Our fear about what would face us when we arrived in Krakow was the difficult part of this leg of the trip.

Mother and Luna, Krakow, 1946

Chapter Twelve
Returning to Poland

S tepping off the train with Mala onto the familiar soil and surroundings of my beloved city filled me with irrepressible joy that bounced out of my worn body, but also with nervousness, anticipation, fear, and a spectrum of other emotions I could not identify. The illusion of re-entering life where I had left off four years earlier gave me a warm and secure feeling.

Immediately Mala and I were struck by the lack of war scars in Krakow. The Germans had made it their base of operations in the area, preserving completely its centuries-old beauty. While we had aged in the camps, time on the buildings and streets of Krakow had stood still. The Planty was blooming in the beautiful May sunshine, and little children were playing hide-and-seek, winding their way around park paths. All seemed—well, normal—as I made my way back to the family homestead at 13 Wielopole Street.

It was there that my illusions were shattered.

When I walked onto my home street I encountered many of the same storeowners I had known throughout my life, though they now offered only meager wares. But missing—entirely absent—were any of the Jewish storeowners. I meandered my way down the block to our apartment house, which from its exterior, like all of Krakow, appeared unchanged. Even the prewar janitor had maintained her job. She greeted me with a caustic remark, reflecting resentment that I had survived and returned. Christian tenants, who had rented apartments in this building that had been built by my grandfather on grounds that had belonged to our family for generations, were still there. The apartments that had belonged to our family members had been taken over by non-Jewish strangers, however, who had no intention of welcoming us back to the space they now called "home."

I knew exactly where I would find mother: in the apartment of the Zaczeks—the family who had been tenants since the day grandfather had constructed the apartment building. At the risk of their own lives the Zaczeks had sneaked sundry items to us when we were living in the ghetto, helping us in our fight for survival. I learned when I arrived at their apartment that Mr. Zaczek, a burly, gray-haired man, had passed away during the war, before I had an opportunity to thank him for his kindness. But energetic little Mrs. Zaczek was still alive and giving shelter to mother. She opened her arms and her apartment to Mala and me the day we stepped foot again in 13 Wielopole Street.

By then mother had already been waiting for us two whole days. Because of our inability to communicate—there were no phones or wire services available—she had imagined the worst. The longer the delay in my arrival, the more panicked she had become. The joy and relief we both felt when I stood at the door of Mrs. Zaczek's apartment were immeasurable.

Our positive feelings lasted as long as the telling of the events that had occurred during our brief parting. They dissipated soon thereafter, when I learned that in contrast to the warmth that Mrs. Zaczek had showered upon us, her niece—to whom we had given our apartment at the time of our deportation—would not allow us to re-enter.

When we were forced to leave we had the option of allowing the Germans to repossess it, a decision that would have allowed us to reclaim it after the war. Of course in 1939 we could not have anticipated future legal consequences. Mrs. Zaczek's niece, her husband, and her children had been homeless refugees from western Poland. My parents, feeling compassion for them, had handed them a key to our apartment. Now there were no duplicates being chiseled for us despite our homelessness. The ownership of our property and the furniture within it were denied us.

Their attitude was not unique. While some Christians, like Mrs. Zaczek, were extremely welcoming, many others resented the return of the Jews, often expressing their feelings in overt and hostile tones. While some maintained that if the Holocaust were to be repeated they would provide shelter for us, the concept of helping us restart our lives post-Holocaust was not on the agenda of a lot of people.

In any event, our former apartment was, by virtue of newly enacted law, too large for mother and me. With the huge shortage of living quarters that characterized post-war Poland, the government had issued a decree that each person could occupy no more than a predetermined, limited amount of square footage. Had we fought to reclaim the apartment, we would have had to share it with the present occupants, replete with their animosity and anti-Semitism. Mrs. Zaczek's niece stated adamantly that she would not share an apartment with "strangers." The prospect of living in such an adverse environment was more than we could cope with, and we were too tired to get involved in legal proceedings.

For several days mother and I stayed at Mrs. Zaczek's apartment, taking stock of the ramifications of the war and the Holocaust. While we tried to comprehend the myriad ways in which our world in Krakow had drastically changed despite its physical appearance of sameness, our thoughts were chiefly directed to learning what had become of father and Niusia. The last information we had received had been in Leipzig from the women who had seen my sister in Auschwitz in the spring of 1945. We had great hopes of finding her alive. We had heard nothing about father.

Every day we ran anxiously to the city center to wait for the trucks carrying camp survivors. We were convinced that one day father and Niusia—as well as other family members—would be in the group of passengers. Frequently we found old friends who were sick, tired, hungry, and searching for their families. It gave us great joy to help them reunite with loved ones.

Meantime, we needed to take charge of our lives, a challenge that required, as a first step, finding more long-term living quarters. So many homeless people were returning from the camps that long lines formed daily in front of the city housing department, which was assigning apartments. We joined the crowd.

At first they gave us a temporary assignment in a room of a building that had been erected just before the war to accommodate the Jewish aged. The room was cheerful with a nice view facing the river, even if it had only army cots and a primitive table. Twenty people lived in several rooms on the floor, sharing one bathroom and draining the electrical capacity. I became a master in constructing fuses from rolled up paper and pieces of wire. I had no idea that my invention created a terrible fire hazard. I should have had a clue, since nobody else followed my lead. Rather, in my absence they sat in the dark, awaiting the return of the literal giver of light.

Whatever the shortcomings of our accommodations and the outrage of our inability to return home, our temporary quarters were luxurious in comparison to the ways in which we had all lived over the past number of years. Additionally the companionship of friendly people returning from the camps compensated for inconveniences. We were intoxicated with freedom.

Although we had temporary shelter, food and clothing were at a premium. The American Jewish Joint Distribution Committee distributed these subsidies, but many of us felt humiliated by having to stand in line for such basic needs.; A handout, no matter how generous, was something we did not want to face. Almost as essential as food and water was our need to restore our dignity. For us an earned spoonful of food tasted much better than the most delicious charity meal. Soon after mother and I were situated in our apartment, we began working as seamstresses in a cooperative shop at a local railroad uniform factory. The job offered no salary, but a day's work was exchanged for daily meals.

With time the cooperative began to pay us minimal compensation. Once they even gave us a gift of herrings to take home. The rare treat coincided with my nineteenth birthday, and I decided to bring the herrings to the party my friends were throwing for me. Stowing the newspaper-wrapped fish under my arm, I boarded the streetcar. I had already informed my guests of the delicacy we would be sharing, and they greeted me enthusiastically when I entered the party. I proceeded to unwrap the package, and to everybody's amused horror we discovered that the slippery fish must have found its way to the streetcar floor during the trip. One of my friends, an artist, produced a comic strip to commemorate the event. The incident remains a subject of jokes amongst us even today.

In June 1945, a month after we had returned to Krakow, mother and I received a bank notice informing us that $100 had been wired to anyone who survived from Marek Fuss's family. The senders were seven children of father's eldest brother Avram, who had emigrated to Belgium during WWI. Their parents—my uncle and aunt—had died between the wars. When the Germans approached during World War II, the seven children had escaped with their families to Cuba, eventually making their way to New York. They had spent their youth growing up with father, and they were very fond of him. They understood that any survivors of their beloved uncle's family would need assistance.

In addition to being caring and generous, the family was well established in America. By postwar Polish standards, the $100 was a fortune (in comparison, the combined monthly income of mother and me was $10 a month), and at first we felt blessed. Ultimately, however, bureaucratic red tape kept us from obtaining it. The authorities insisted the only person who could receive it was the addressee, my father, Marek Fuss, whose whereabouts were still painfully unknown.

Even had we accomplished the impossible and figured out a way to convince the government officials to give us the money, we would have lost it to the bank exchange rate, which amounted to something in the range of five cents on a dollar. Our needs notwithstanding, the simple fact that there were people in the world who cared about us gave us an incentive to push forward.

What a joy it was to find father's large family! We immediately wrote them a letter, filling them in on what had happened to mother and me and explaining the anxiety caused us by the lack of any information about father and Niusia. A continuing correspondence with cousins Dora Bar and Joel Fuss followed.

Aware of our inability to gain access to the cash when it was wired, Cousin Dora began to send us letters every four weeks or so, hiding 10- or 20-dollar bills between pages. She also sent large packages of food and clothing. We managed to exchange the dollars on the black market, doubling our earned income. The cans of sardines and bars of chocolate were too valuable for our consumption. On the black market they commanded a generous price, which further increased our income and the amount of food that graced our table

Shortly after our correspondence with father's American family began, we received a letter informing us that their friend, a journalist, would be coming to Poland. They requested that I be his guide since he did not speak Polish. He was an elderly gentleman whose family had escaped Germany and spent the war years in Spain. My limited German-language proficiency qualified me to be his guide and translator.

Before the journalist and I embarked on our journey, he handed mother an envelope containing the $100 in cash that we hadn't been able to obtain from the bank. Exchanging it on the black market, we were handed a truly staggering amount of currency, a large portion of which we used to start proceedings to reclaim the house on 13 Wielopole Street. The law stipulated that only individuals living in Poland at that time had the right to make a claim for property. Consequently, the claim was filed on behalf of three family members then in Poland: Esther Wolf, her brother Ralph Horowitz, and mother. We knew that taxes and a loan dating from before the war had encumbered the property.

I do not remember the name of the journalist or that of his employer. These details were concealed by the very nature of his trip and what he was to cover. In any case he asked me to accompany him to Auschwitz, only two months after the war.

So in July 1945 I found myself in Auschwitz, the camp where the women from Krakow who had arrived on a transport to Leipzig in April—just four months before—had told mother and me they had last seen my sister Niusia.

In sharp contradiction to my previous experiences, the journalist and I entered the silent, empty camp—already partially turned museum—of our own free will. I lingered in all the rooms where the exhibits were displayed, facing them (to the extent possible) as an objective onlooker despite the fact that the eyes in the photos belonged to the collective me. Here in front of me was the documentation of my past, the remnants proving that my Holocaust experience had not been just a bad dream. Here I faced the reality.

In one area was a showcase of objects that had been made by prisoners. Among the collection of drawings was a watercolor that made a lasting impression on me because it symbolized my own feelings during the years of incarceration. The painting depicted a silhouette of a prisoner bent over a spade in front of barbed wire, looking longingly to the other side of the fence where a singing bird sat on a tree, the sun of a new day rising over the landscape. This artist had captured the longing for freedom that all of us inmates had experienced in the camps. It immediately brought to mind the morning in Plaszow when Commandant Ghett had entered the barracks, requiring me to report to him the number of inmates present. It had been a spring day, and I had been conscious of the outdoor sound of a bird freely chirping its song, oblivious to the human slavery endured nearby.

As we meandered through Auschwitz that day the journalist asked me questions about my experiences, shocked at the horrors I revealed. Neither his intellect nor his imagination had prepared him to comprehend the wartime existence we inmates had known. He seemed incredulous that the mountains of valises inscribed with Jewish names that were on display had been thrown into their piles by Jews so the Germans could redistribute their contents at home. He was speechless when he witnessed the hills of shoes, glasses, and braids that had been confiscated from prisoners. Each time we came across new evidence of inhumane cruelty, he attempted to verify its validity. The truth was almost impossible to comprehend.

In summer 1945 the realities on display at Auschwitz were recorded not only in the photographs and other pieces of evidence strung across the museum walls. Death was still fresh in this brutal murdering ground. Though sanitized, everything tangible in Auschwitz still bore traces of the inmates' presence. I could feel the breath of the people whose shoes, shaving brushes, pots and pans, and other items were displayed in large crates. The stench of the crematoria lingered, polluting the air and the ashen ground with executed human remains.

Shocked and numb, I approached the crate piled with hair that had been cut from the heads of the victims, saved by the Germans to use for stuffing mattresses. I stared at the contents, scanning the mess for blond braids that might have belonged to my sister. I turned and confronted a crate housing eyewear, and I stood for an interminable period searching in vain for father's glasses.

Facing these objects, despite the absence of knowledge about the fate that had befallen father and Niusia, I realized in a more concrete way, for the first time, that mother and I might never see them again. My own wounds were too fresh to evoke additional emotion. I simply felt overcome by an all-encompassing sadness. At the same time I needed to find the strength to put this experience behind me, and return to mother with a smile on my face. We were so fragile, and she had suffered enough. I could not undermine the delicate balance she tried so hard to maintain. Privately we both mourned; publicly, we continued to support each other as we began to carve out new lives.

Despite the difficulties presented by daily life, we had survived years of torture, and this postwar Krakow chapter felt like a great adventure. Placing great weight on our sense of humor, we embraced our newly found freedom with gusto. On the more superficial levels, it appeared that life was starting to take some shape.

But those who know freedom understand the responsibilities that accompany this great value, sometimes trapping its beneficiaries into a different form of imprisonment. My new road was paved with many obstacles. The wounds on mother's feet reopened, requiring hospitalization for many weeks. Left alone, I was totally unprepared to take charge of managing my life. After all, I had not been experienced in this regard; I had lost my freedom at the age of 12. Eventually the old-age home in which we resided was reclaimed by the city, and we had to leave. Our apartment assignment had not materialized yet, and mother was still in the hospital. The red tape was very hard to overcome. Nothing happened quickly. I did not let anybody know of my predicament. Although people were very ready to share whatever they had, my need to grasp independence prevented me from taking advantage of their generosity. Too proud to ask friends for space, at one point I slept on a park bench.

The despondency was heightened by the continuing absence of father and Niusia. Our hope started dwindling after a few weeks of impatiently running to the town center expecting to recognize their faces among the crowds of survivors returning to Krakow. The days wore on. Mother was hospitalized, and I was forced to focus on my own daily survival. Still no sign of father or Niusia. The trucks bringing survivors to Krakow were coming at greater intervals. On an individual basis, a few stragglers wandered into town, giving us a ray of hope that our loved ones would still be alive and somehow find their way back.

And some did. At 13 Wielopole Street news intermittently buzzed about several of our relatives. Some had arrived in Krakow before us, among them my cousin Ralph Horowitz, the son of mother's eldest sister. A survivor of concentration camps, Ralph had obtained employment with the Jewish Agency upon his return. His two brothers, Moshe and Smil, had also survived. Living in Vilna, Lithuania, before the war, they had escaped eastward across Russia to China, where they had spent the war in the Shanghai ghetto. Ralph, Moshe, Smil, and their older sister Ester—who was only five years younger than mother—were the only ones of their 12 siblings who survived.

We appreciated each communique relating happy news about the survival of family members as much as we cherished each reunion.

But the one reunion about which mother and I had dreamed through the darkest nights of our incarceration, the one fantasy that kept us alive as we struggled to overcome the terror defining our daily existence in the concentration camps—that long-awaited, desperately clinging family hug with father and Niusia—never happened. Father and Niusia did not return to Krakow.

As the days wore on without them, the realization that they had likely not survived grew inside me like a malignant tumor. It slowly became clear that never again would I hear father's romantic stories, or look to him for advice on pranks or feel wrapped in his security and love. My wonderful, witty father—the student who had traveled through Czechoslovakia by bicycle, the young man who had enlisted in the Austrian army, the Russian prisoner of war, the Krakow immigrant, the papa who had set up shop in our apartment building so he could see Niusia and me when we returned from school each day—existed now only in my young-girl memories.

As did Niusia. What had happened to her beautiful blond braids, I wondered? Where had she gone after her escape from Auschwitz? And who had fed her with sustenance through the years of torture and deprivation? How had she endured the cruelty without mother or father? Had she survived by the strength of the same dreams mother and I shared, envisioning a family reunion one day? And, I kept thinking, how terribly tragic to have come so close to surviving the war's end, if the account of the Krakowian women who had seen her in Auschwitz before they were deported to Leipzig in April, was correct.

The thoughts and images raced through my mind like an endless film loop, taunting and haunting me, making my nights restless and my days dreary. At last I gave up hope of a reunion with father and Niusia. Forever internally ripped apart at the tragic loss of a daughter and husband, mother nonetheless exhibited strength and dignity whenever she looked at me. Somehow, she knew, we had to move from the present into the future.

After a few months, a friend of my father came to Krakow and told us that father and Niusia had been deported to Auschwitz in1943 and that father had been immediately sent to the crematorium. In a conflicting account, someone else later told us that he had seen father in the Matthausen concentration camp in Germany. As a result I am not sure when, where, and how my father perished. I haven't the courage to investigate.

But years later we learned definitively of Niusia's fate. In 1982 a childhood friend from Krakow named Ilona Werdiger came to our New Jersey home. She explained that she and Niusia had been together in Auschwitz, where my cousin from Belgium had also been imprisoned. My cousin from Belgium had been assigned to work in the kitchen and had been able to supply the girls with extra food. Toward the end of the war, Niusia, our cousin Ecka who had owned the fashionable millinery salon, and Klara Bigeleisen, the sister of Niusia's boyfriend from the ghetto, had been sent together to Stutthof, one of the most terrible camps. As the Allies were closing in toward the end of the war, the German soldiers loaded the Stutthof inmates on ships and then sank them in the Baltic Sea. Rescuers on Swedish boats who fished them out from the water saved a small number of women. Ilona had been among them, but my sister, Ecka, and Klara were not.

Mala did not find even one member of her family, and she could not bear to remain in town with her vivid prewar memories and the postwar environment of hostility. With mother in the hospital and my own lack of living quarters, I did not have a place to offer her to stay. After three months in Krakow she departed. I later learned she had gone to a displaced persons camp in Bindermiehl, Austria. I felt guilty that I had not been able to help her, and I missed her terribly. Other than mother, Mala had been a key anchor helping me to survive the most awful moments of the preceding years. It was hard to imagine moving forward without her reassuring presence.

After a few weeks mother was released from the hospital, and she dedicated herself to helping me take positive, future-oriented steps. Our assignment for an apartment finally came through: located off the courtyard of a large apartment house on 18 Gertrudy Street in the beautiful center of town near the royal castle, our new home was a tiny room overlooking a rat-infested courtyard with no interior plumbing and hence, of course, no hot running water. We had to share the outhouse with a local bar and were afraid to use it at night when drunks frequented the area. The square footage of this little space was the maximum allocated for two people. Mother and I resigned ourselves to the poor quarters, since we expected to emigrate from Poland at the first opportunity. In the meantime it offered a place to rest our heads without having to share our space with hostile roommates.

Actually, we did more than resign ourselves. We furnished the tiny apartment and gave it a pleasant, homelike character that it had probably never known before. At the time of our initial deportation from 13 Wielopole Street, we had placed our furniture in the house of the Zaczeks' daughter, who had come to Krakow from western Poland after the German invasion. Nela and her family had found a large but unfurnished apartment. Rather then leaving to the Germans the dining room furniture that had been designed by mother for her 1923 trousseau, the grand piano, and a large tapestry that mother had embroidered in 1935 framed in a guilded, beautifully hand carved frame, we had given all these items for safekeeping to Nela.

When mother and I moved into our tiny apartment, the noble woman returned our belongings. We immediately sold the piano for a paltry sum, which nevertheless put a substantial amount of food on our table. The beautiful dining room pieces and the framed tapestry made the apartment appear almost stately. For "entertainment" we watched the rats play in the garbage outside our windows. We ignored as best we could the miserable conditions that characterized our new home.

In July 1946, while I was still working in the uniform factory, a young Polish Jewish boy named Olek Kahane, who sported a dashing British uniform given to him by the liberating soldiers, arrived in Krakow to create a students' home. He was bent on rallying students around the tenets and implementation of Marxism. Having just arrived from the Displaced Persons' Camp in the British zone, Olek was busy spreading stories about rich and selfish capitalists devoid of culture. As he saw it, the answer to Poland's postwar problems was communism, under the reign of which everyone— Jews included—would be "equal." In a communist system, Olek believed, the government would provide for all the needs of the people and exploitation would cease.

Somehow Olek got my name when he arrived in Krakow, and he enlisted my assistance in his effort to organize dormitories for students on Esterka Street near Kazimierz, the old Jewish section of town. There was a constant influx of youth without parents who were seeking education, and this was to be a facility where food and lodging would be provided for students enrolled in tuition-free education offered by the government. Not much of a political activist, I nonetheless was inspired by this dynamic demagogue who even offered an English class. I enjoyed the new adventure as well as the exposure to new ideas, optimism, and young people.

I enrolled in Olek's English class. But I attended it only once—on a day when fortunately I met a young man named Alex Kaufman, who was also there with his best friend, Eddie Szubin. When the class ended, Alex escorted me home, delivering a long-winded and animated lecture on the evils of communism. He had just come from Russia, where he had spent some of the war years. He was the sole survivor of his family; not even one distant relative was still alive. In contrast to Olek's opinions, Alex believed the benefits of democracy and capitalism as practiced in the West far outweighed anything communism had to offer. He insisted that any sensible person living in Poland ought to attempt to emigrate as soon as possible.

Alex's wise eyes and the colorful visions with which he painted his future in the Western world struck me. He was only a year older than me, but his wisdom far surpassed his chronological age. His arguments were persuasive, and his presence made me feel very secure. At a time when most of us were looking for fun, he was looking forward to a future. During the three months he was in Krakow, he and I kept constant company.

The dormitories were a central gathering place for students, and we spent many evenings there embroiled in passionate political debates. Elected president of the dorms, Alex ruled with a sense of authority, which impressed me very much. He formulated rules for the house which gave guidance to the unruly crowd, and despite the restrictions he imposed, he was well-respected. Among his demands was a requirement to attend classes, though he himself was not too conscientious about attendance. He also imposed penalties for swearing, but not without a good sense of humor.

During that period I enrolled in a high-school equivalency program, and shortly thereafter I was admitted into the Jagiellonian University and a music conservatory.

The borders surrounding Poland at that time were closed for legal emigration, but many people escaped en masse through the "green border," i.e., by bribing border guards and walking for miles through the woods. When the opportunity arose Alex found his way out via this route, but I could not go with him. I would not have been deterred by the limit on personal possessions this kind of traveling would permit, but mother was too sick to undertake the trip. Moreover, mother and I had experienced one march, and escape was too frightening a prospect for me. Engaging in illegal activity held no appeal for me. If caught we could have landed in jail, and the idea of losing our freedom yet again was anything but attractive. Even if we could have succeeded in our imagined escapade, mother's wounded feet were still raw, and I lacked an education and employable skills if we reached a destination. We were likely to go no further than a displaced persons' camp. Moving to another camp, even under different and better conditions than those we had known during the Holocaust, was not something we could face.

So Alex and I parted with heavy hearts, uncertain whether we would ever see one another again, and if so, when and how. Under new laws forming an "Iron Curtain" that barred emigration from Eastern European countries and made communication with the outside world very difficult, even letters sometimes took several weeks to arrive. But Alex and I were not discouraged; we wrote to one another several times a week. A year after we parted, he sent a beautiful letter to mother requesting my hand in marriage. Although Alex had developed a special relationship with mother and she was very fond of him, still the formality of his request took us aback. Clueless as to how his plan could be carried out, mother nonetheless replied immediately with enthusiasm. So at the age of 20, I was involved in a committed relationship.

My first year at Jagiellonian University presented a difficult challenge, since I still worked at the uniform factory and my scholastic workload combined assignments from three programs: the high school equivalency, the university, and the conservatory. I had no piano on which I could practice, so I used one at a local Jewish community center established in the aftermath of the war. The room where the piano was located was not heated, and at times I practiced wearing gloves and a coat. I did not complain. It felt delightful just to have the opportunity to play piano again.

The financial supplement that Cousin Dora continued to send eventually permitted me to stop working and devote myself solely to scholastic pursuits with the intention of obtaining a degree in musicology. Although I was attracted by other fields of study—particularly science and architecture—my formal education had ended at the age of 12, when I had finished sixth grade. In a hurry to make up for the lost years of schooling, I could not afford to begin a new field of study. In comparison I had played the piano since I was six years old and felt grounded in that area.

At the end of my first year at the conservatory, just before my final exam in piano, a letter arrived from cousin Dora containing 20 dollars—enough to purchase an upright piano. Now I felt equipped with the right tools.

The growing movement of Zionism with its dream of returning to the ancient Jewish homeland of Israel filled us Jewish youth with pride and purpose. My friends and I joined a Zionist organization called *Poalei Zion,* through which we received training in martial arts and spent many hours in classes devoted to Jewish education. Our group was vibrant and dedicated.

In spring 1947 *Poalei Zion* organized a free month-long vacation for students in the mountains of southern Poland. A large group of friends and I took advantage of the opportunity. I looked forward to my first experience spending time on my own in the company of handsome boys, although I pledged not to attach myself to any of them because I looked forward to being reunited with Alex. With great excitement we packed our belongings. Intent on exhibiting my beautiful though sparse wardrobe, I brought all the contents of the valise that had been given to us by the Russian doctor mother and I had met before and fled from Olganitz, the town where we were liberated, and headed back to Poland.

The trains traveling to the mountains were terribly crowded, and the only place we could find a seat was on the floor in the corridors. We traveled through the night, sleeping very soundly. When we arrived at our destination in Ludwikowice, I picked up my valise, noticing how light it seemed to have become. I opened it to find that all of its contents had been stolen.

Every day for a month, therefore, I wore the same green dress with the white-lace collar that I had worn when I had initially boarded the train, washing my only pair of underwear daily. I was so sorry that I would never have a chance to wear my beautiful chiffon dress with its multicolor sweet-pea design. The inconvenience never hampered my fun, however. I had just spent four years in one dress of a different kind, without washing facilities. I figured I had come to the mountains for fun and company, not for a fashion show.

Mother, who had attained a position as an accountant at the uniform factory, was delighted to see me when I returned after the month in the country. My time away had been our longest separation since the war had begun. Smiling, I explained to her that I had come home, but my clothes had not. When I explained what had happened, we shared a hearty laugh.

For us, material possessions had become so unimportant that we did not waste time worrying about them. Mother was simply happy that I had returned home rested, in great spirits, and with a lovely suntan that made me feel good.

The monthly packages from Cousin Dora continued to arrive, bringing a bonus of beautiful clothing that ensured I would be the best-dressed young woman in school. I did not feel lacking in the clothing department. She even sent leather pocketbooks to match my winter coats: the epitome of elegance. As a seamstress I sometimes combined two dresses into one, designing very original styles.

My Jagiellonian schoolmates were not Jewish. While we became close and studied for exams together, our social lives were totally separate. Three million Polish Catholics had been killed during the war, as had three million Polish Jews. But before the war there had been 30 million Catholics in Poland compared to three and a half million Jews. So while the Poles had lost 10 percent of their population, they still had families and elegant prewar homes. In contrast we had lost 90 percent of our population. I felt like a nomad (albeit with nice clothes), reduced to living in a rat-infested apartment and eating at the dormitory.

The students' dormitory that I had helped Olek Kahane organize attracted Jewish students who had fled to Russia during the war and had returned to Poland afterwards. Surviving there with their families, they had been able to continue their education. The level of intellectual discourse they brought with them was stimulating. I learned as much from listening to them as I did in my classrooms. They also provided necessary support in difficult moments when life felt particularly tough or the university lessons were too complicated for the comprehension of those of us who had missed high school.

In 1947 I traveled one more time to Auschwitz. The trip took place over our summer vacation when a producer of a movie called *Ostatni Etap* ("The Last Stage") came to the university looking for extras to be cast in a movie about the Auschwitz death camp. A group of Jewish students decided to make some spending money.

We found ourselves in Auschwitz housed in the barracks, on the same bunk beds where the prisoners had slept during the war just three short years ago. We spent a week in the killing camp of Birkenau, filming over and over every night for seven nights a scene depicting the arrival of a transport. To convey an accurate image the director loaded us into cattle cars that exactly replicated those that had transported inmates during the war. The first night of the filming was chilly, and the rain drizzled quietly as we sat inside the train. Suddenly the doors flew open, and we were subjected to the barking order of German soldier-actors. Being confronted by those uniforms, even on the bodies of our friends, caused tremendous emotional shock that we were not prepared for.

The film was produced on a shoestring budget, and I believe the hundreds of prison uniforms came from the Auschwitz warehouses themselves. In the end we did not even receive the promised compensation. The production had evidently run out of funds. We went home with a few little black and white photographs (for which we had to pay!) intended to be mementos of the experience! The movie, incidentally, received an award at the Cannes Film Festival, and my picture wound up on posters all over town.

In May 1948 the establishment of the Jewish homeland in Israel became a reality which we welcomed with great joy. For the first time since the outbreak of the war, we had a sense of rootedness. The Iron Curtain opened to let the Jews emigrate to our new land. Like many others at the time mother and I concluded that we had waited long enough in Poland for surviving family members to return. The chances of finding others from whom we had not heard three years after the war had ended were too slim for us to continue to wait. Almost the entire family of father had disappeared without a trace. Of mother's huge family, she was the only survivor of her generation.

The time had come to legally leave Poland and reunite with family members in Israel who had preceded us and fought for the nation's freedom. And although by then Alex had completed his studies at the Stuttgart Polytechnic Institute in Germany and had emigrated to the United States, I knew that the prospects for our marriage would significantly increase upon our immigration to the democratic country of Israel. It had been almost five years since I had last seen him.

When I finally left Poland in 1950, I managed, despite all the missed years of education in my youth, to bear diplomas from the university and conservatory in my hand. Indeed, my commencement exercises were held in the very same magnificent hall where my cousin Aron, the son of father's brother Sender, had graduated from law school in 1939. Although a degree in musicology did not later prove to be very beneficial in terms of related employment, I never regretted my choice of academic study. As one proverb states, "A mind once stretched never shrinks to previous dimensions."

Luna and Alex's wedding, Tel Aviv, September 6, 1951

Chapter Thirteen
Israel

While Poland had been the country of our ancestors since the Spanish Inquisition, our attachment to it gave way to ambivalence, ultimately yielding to a resolute desire to leave. Alhough we did have some wonderful Catholic Polish friends, postwar anti-Semitic sentiment was strong. The majority of Poles saw Jews as outsiders and resented our return. We longed for a home where we would feel like welcomed members of society.

Our decision to emigrate to Israel was made easier by the fact that family members who had preceded us were impatiently awaiting our arrival. Cousin Jozek Hilfstein had gotten married and had moved to Haifa, where he was employed by the railroad. Esther Wolf had settled in the outskirts of Tel Aviv in a small village called Tel-Arish.

Two of father's nephews, Tulek and Oskar Fuss, the sons of father's brother Sender, also by now lived in Israel. Tulek had survived the war by carrying documents claiming he was Christian, and Oskar—together with his wife and daughter—had survived the war in Russia and then moved to a village called Sachne on the outskirts of Jaffa.

As frightened as we were to venture into unknown territory, we were reassured by the knowledge that a large family, by postwar standards, awaited us in Israel.

Emigration from Poland, however, was no easy matter. The bureaucratic requirements of the Communist regime were strict, and the likelihood that an applicant would obtain the requested visa was unpredictable. Refusal spelled jeopardy in the devastating form of job loss and blacklisting.

Moreover, since I was a member of the first graduating class at the university since the war's end, my plan to leave the country was not looked upon kindly. I had been given a free education, and even though musicology was not essential to the country's economy, the government had expected a return on its investment. When I was two exams shy of obtaining my diploma, I realized that receiving it would greatly hinder the chances of my emigration application being accepted.

This problem was solved by a professor of mine, Zdzislaw Jachimecki. An esteemed musicology scholar, Professor Jachimecki concocted a scheme that both gave me my degree and simultaneously made it appear as if I had not graduated. Interrupting his summer vacation outside Krakow to return to the city, he administered the missing exams to me at his home (a procedure unheard of at that time). This ploy ensured that there would not be a record of my graduation at the time of my departure. After I had safely left the country he filed my grade results, and the diploma was forwarded to me in Israel.

A few days before our departure we met Olek Kahane in the city. To mother's horror he delivered a fiery lecture to us, accusing us of disloyalty. He ranted about how we were abandoning the country that had given me a free education. How dare we take advantage of the privileges that had been bestowed upon us and carry the fruits to the capitalistic world abroad? he angrily demanded.

Mother was terrified that he might report us to the authorities as traitors, which would prevent us from emigrating—and likely ensure that we would be blacklisted. Fortunately for us he seemed to have maintained a spark of human decency. He did nothing to stand in the way of our emigration.

Years later I learned that Olek, who became a recognized poet, was not treated so kindly by his beloved Communists. In 1968 when the government expelled from the country what they believed to be the remainder of the Jews in Poland, Olek found himself a refugee in Germany, living under great hardship.

The anxiety created by the applications mother and I had filed was relieved when our permits were granted, allowing us three months to liquidate all our possessions and get out of the country. We were given a precise list of articles we would be allowed to bring with us, which included seven dresses apiece and a limited number of pairs of underwear, shoes, and household articles. Even handkerchiefs were counted. Valuables, furniture, and jewelry—if we had owned any—were out of the question.

We knew that since the Jewish state had just been created, few goods were available and jobs were in short supply. Consequently our belongings were the only tangible assets we could sell to support ourselves. But we felt that we had earned the meager possessions we had accumulated in the four years after the war. They were important to us, and prized despite their lack of monetary value. The challenge of selecting only a few meaningful, useful, and allowable items seemed formidable.

Among the quota of dresses I insisted that my prison uniform be included. For a reason I could not explain I was not able to part with this tangible, personal connection to the concentration camp. I took it as the only tangible proof that I had spent that time in the camp. The experience had begun to seem unreal.

The other significant object mother and I managed to bring with us was the large needlework mother had embroidered in 1935, which the Zaczeks' daughter had returned to us with our dining room furniture and piano. The needlework was one of the last links to our family home. Since emigrants could not take works of art with them we removed it from its beautiful, hand-carved gold frame. We sold the frame to a church. Since the number of dresses was very limited, I used the picture to smuggle fabric for a dress by lining it with green silk, which I intended for making a dress once in Israel.

Selling the upright piano we had bought for $20 provided us with enough money to purchase a few salamis, which we wanted to bring as gifts to the family in Israel since meat was almost nonexistent there. At that time sausages produced in Israel were made from fish fillet dyed red.

The item mother and I found most difficult to part with was our dining room furniture designed for mother's trousseau in 1923. The beautifully crafted black-oak furniture decorated with carved fruit baskets filled us with wonderful memories of our gracious salon, where all important family functions had taken place and where I had practiced piano for hours daily. At this table we had celebrated the wedding of Uncle Solomon; around this table my male cousins had gathered during the war to play cards before we were expelled from our house. But we could find no solution for the dining room set like the one we had found for the needlepoint, so we sold it to acquaintances of the Zaczek family.

Emigration laws prohibited us from carrying any cash abroad, but of course we knew we would need money to survive in Israel. With great sadness mother decided to sell her share of the family house on Wielopole, consisting of 15 apartments and three stores. After our grandparents had died the house belonged to all of their descendants. Although the family was large, postwar Polish law dictated that the only people who could claim ownership were those present in the country at that time, i.e., mother, her niece Esther Wolf, and Esther's brother Ralf Horowitz. After they claimed the property Esther and Ralf left Poland, making them ineligible to sell their property even with a power of attorney. Mother established their ownership of two of the three shares with the hope that one day they would be able to reclaim their interests. She then sold our one-third ownership rights.

After we purchased two sets of embroidered bed linens and three sets of custom-made embroidered silk lingerie (hoping we would be able to turn these valuable items into cash in Israel), all that remained was $200. We were afraid to carry the proceeds from the sale in cash because it was an offense that was punishable by a jail sentence.

The cash created a dilemma: How do we transport it? A sheet-metal worker named Victor Traubman, who had been employed by my grandfather during the construction of our house, crafted a truly creative solution. He built a double bottom in a thermos bottle, inserting the money between the layers and filling the thermos with tea.

Mother and I had packed two crates of goods to be sent ahead of our departure. Polish law required that exported goods pass a customs inspection. Particularly questioned was the needlework-turned-bedspread adorned with three embroidered ladies descending an elaborate staircase in a garden. Holding back his laughter, the young customs inspector asked, "What kind of a bedspread is this?" to which I innocently replied, "People have many different tastes." Since he obviously recognized my attempt to get around the regulations, we struck a deal: I would be allowed to take the needlepoint if he could take me to a movie. The agreement was not much of a sacrifice: he was young and handsome, and the new release of *Hamlet* had just arrived from England. The tickets were impossible to obtain by the public; they were available only to government officials.

I agreed to the deal, again causing mother some consternation. The inspector, however, was a perfect gentleman. After a lovely evening out I arrived home in a great mood—and carrying a permit allowing most of our crated items to be shipped. The only casualties were an oil painting without much material value given to me by a fellow art student and a sparkling—albeit chipped and therefore worthless—piece of Czechoslovakian crystal, a gift from a former boyfriend, with which I had no trouble parting. A 300-year-old quartz crystal bottle from grandfather's antique collection appeared worthless to the uneducated eye of the customs officer, so we were permitted to take it with us.

Finally the time came to depart. A special, sealed train was assigned to Jews leaving the country. On a rainy and dreary October evening, mother and I were accompanied to the railroad station by Zosia Rogowska—my dear friend from university and conservatory—and her mother. It was a very sad farewell.

The Iron Curtain separating Eastern Europe from the rest of the world had firmly closed. Traveling for tourism was impossible. Zosia and I thought our parting would be the last time we would ever see each other. Long before we knew that television existed (let alone could have imagined the invention of the fax), we fantasized that one day we would be able to write a letter that would instantly appear at the home of the addressee or that telephones would have screens that would allow us to see each other while we talked.

Needless to say the moment fax machines came on the market I bought one despite the fact that there was nobody I could communicate with.

The train took mother and me from Krakow to the border, where customs officers meticulously sorted through our possessions. The item that caused us the most anxiety was the thermos carrying the cash in its double bottom. As we were about to step off the train for an inspection by customs agents, we noticed that the glass insert had broken. Expecting to endure a very thorough search, we knew that our insistence on bringing a broken thermos would be too suspicious to the wary border officials.

Fortunately a stranger we had traveled with on the train had the same thermos, and without asking questions, offered to give us the glass insert. Hands trembling, we replaced the broken glass, snapping it into place without a minute to spare.

After undergoing hours of inspection we were allowed to board a sealed international train to Venice, where a ship bound for Israel was to be waiting for us. We were now officially stateless, deprived of passports, and heading for the unknown. We felt scared about our lack of national status as well as the Arab hostility we had heard awaited us. But we were free, and our relief was reflected in the heartwarming camaraderie among the passengers.

The train took three days to reach its destination, and I spent much of the time walking up and down the aisles, talking with other emigres. On one of my jaunts, after we had passed by Vienna, I met a friend I had known in the ghetto. Dressed in pajamas, he was very distraught and explained to me that he had just tried to escape from the train. He said his father and sister—the only survivors of his family, who had left Poland immediately after the war via the "green" (illegal) border while he was in a sanitarium recovering from tuberculosis contracted in the camps—had been awaiting him in Austria. The guards had caught him in his attempted flight, however, and to prevent further tries, his clothes were taken away and replaced with pajamas. Now he was heading for Israel without money or profession, lacking both good health and anyone who would await his arrival.

Our main objective was to leave Poland regardless of the destination, and at the time, Israel— swamped with new immigrants—provided the only open door and welcome mat.

As morning dawned, our train wound its way over the snow-capped Alps. Momentarily forgetting that we were traveling without passports in a sealed train to a potentially frightening future, we were encouraged by the sight of the awesome and legendary mountains, blanketed in white snow and bathed in brilliant sunlight.

When the train arrived in Venice, mother and I (and many of our fellow passengers) were mesmerized, feeling as though we had just stepped into a wonderland filled with our most wonderful fantasies. While we were guarded and not permitted to go beyond a limited area, sites I had just studied in art history classes spread before my eyes. Under the warm and blue Italian sky stood the breathtaking St. Mark's Square and the canals filled with gondolas.

But it would be a while before we left behind the political propaganda of the country from which we had just come. When we were offered Coca-Cola we thought that drinking it would cause holes in our stomachs. One member our group even spilled the contents of a bottle on the pavement to demonstrate the damage it did to the tar. We were convinced. In any event our questions about the toxicity of the drink were academic. The meager contents of our wallets did not yield extra change for such frivolities.

In Venice we were greeted by friendly Israeli officials dressed in casual uniforms. Their appearance took us off guard. With no gold buttons, shining boots, or ties, a military uniform (we suddenly learned) did not have to signify oppression. Our fears melted. Nothing more would harm us. We were going home.

We had come to the last leg of our trip: crossing the Mediterranean. We boarded a dilapidated cargo boat, which we affectionately named the "washtub," manned by young, handsome Jewish boys, well trained as sailors and effusive in their welcome. The sweet taste of freedom and pride in our cultural heritage permeated the atmosphere despite sailing in a vessel that resembled a ship from before World War I. Its sleeping quarters were crowded and smelly, and the main food staple was herring, the smell of which was revolting.

Mother and I spent most of the three-day voyage on the deck, being charmed by the courageous and intelligent young sailors and focusing on the land to which we were joyfully being whisked away. Discomforts no longer mattered. We were free at last, en route to the Promised Land.

On the third day after we departed from Venice our rickety ship glided toward northern Israel. Before us was spread a magnificent and tranquil panorama: the bright green Carmel Mountains, emerging from the dark turquoise waters of the Mediterranean Sea and soaring high against a brilliant blue sky. Scattered throughout the mountains were flat-roofed, Oriental-style white houses and majestic palm trees. Golden domes appeared regal on the horizon, and there were no signs of the recent War of Independence that had been fought on this site just a year and a half before.

As our boat docked we were greeted with blue-and-white flags, each adorned with a large Star of David, waving proudly in the breeze, and the emotional voices of Israeli citizens and public officials waiting in the harbor bellowed out the Israeli national anthem, *HaTikvah* ("The Hope"): "To be a free nation in our land, in the land of Zion, in Jerusalem." Tears of joy flowed in abundance. We had finally reached the port of Haifa. We had finally come home.

The dock was filled with hundreds of people eagerly awaiting the arrival of their family members and friends. With no customs, barriers, or emigration officers, the crowds came right up to the ship. What a difference from the police state we just left behind.

Each of us eagerly scanned the crowds in search of familiar faces. Mother and I first spotted my childhood companion and cousin Josek Hilfstein, followed by Esther Wolf and Esther's daughter-in-law, Moniek's wife Gusta, who proudly raised her two-year-old son above the heads of the crowds for us to see. The child named Haki was the first child born to the family after the war, brought into the world in a detention camp in Cyprus, where Moniek had received military training in preparation for the Israeli War of Independence during the time the family was awaiting admission to the Promised Land.

The concentration camps, the sufferings, the deprivations we had endured over the years—none of these realities seemed to matter any more. We felt ecstatic. The fear that had defined our daily existence for so many years seemed simply to vanish. True, we had been so conditioned by despotic regimes that we found ourselves looking over our shoulders each time we made anti-Communist jokes that, just weeks before, would have cost us interrogation if not imprisonment. But then, realizing that our paranoia had needlessly traveled with us, we broke into giddy laughter at these episodes. We felt drunk with freedom.

The camp was surrounded by barbed wire to contain us, but neither the new immigrants nor their Israeli friends and families took the forced separation very seriously. Our family members crawled through holes in the fence to visit us, and we ventured through the same holes to visit them.

On our first Shabbat in Israel Jozek Hilfsten led us out of the camp via the fence holes to his home for the weekend. It was a great joy to visit with him and meet his wife Hanka and newborn son Yaki. Their apartment was in a tiny white-washed old house with large windows and sunlight streaming in most of the hours of the day—a very welcome contrast to the dim apartment in Krakow that mother and I had left behind. Their residence was shared with another family of four. Each family occupied one small room, and the tiny kitchen area served both families.

Hanka served an elegant Shabbat dinner on a beautifully set table. She prepared inventive dishes for us, including frozen fish disguised as meatballs. Food was scarce and cooking facilities were limited to a small gasoline burner on which she even managed to bake a delicious cake. There was no electricity for cooking, nor was there refrigeration, and food rationing allowed no more than one egg per person each week. For mother and me, however, the incon-veniences—including sharing one room with Jozek, Hanka, and Yaki—were drowned out by the luxury of being together with beloved family in a free land.

We were greeted with a surprise when we returned to the camp on Saturday night. The escape hole in the fence had been closed, and friendly Israeli police awaited our return. The policemen were young boys from *kibbutzim* (collective farms) and new immigrants from all corners of the world who spoke many languages. They arrested us, apologetically sending us to spend the night in prison.

When we entered our cell I started laughing uncontrollably. Our "punishment" was to sleep for a night in a private room furnished with two comfortable beds with real mattresses and pillows rather than a tent for 50 crowded with army cots! Recognizing the absurdity of the situation, the policemen shared our laughter.

After several days we were assigned to a new immigrant camp in Hadera midway between the cities of Haifa and Tel Aviv. The camp contained many long barracks, each housing about 20 army cots lining the walls side by side. For privacy blankets were strung up between the beds. The fledgling country could not provide housing for the thousands that were arriving daily. The government counted on families to help new immigrants make the transition.

During the days we often planted trees on the old highway that ran from Haifa to Tel Aviv. Their leaves provided welcome shade for travelers.

I spent my 24th birthday in Hadera. Someone told us of a vineyard nearby, and we hiked there, bringing back a bottle of wine. Everyone in the barracks celebrated with me. No wine ever tasted better.

Mother's family members visited us frequently, trekking to Hadera on buses despite long lines at the stations. Public transportation was very overcrowded. One time Esther's son Joel Wolf showed up sporting a beautiful suntan that made his brilliant blue eyes shine brightly. His tall, trim figure dressed in a khaki military uniform exuded patriotism.

Until that point we had not yet seen the branch of father's family that had made their way to Israel. But after we moved to Hadera, Tulek Fuss, the son of father's brother Sender and the brother of Jagiellonian law-student Aron, greeted us with his pregnant wife, Klara, and their baby, Alex.

When I had met Tulek—10 years my senior— in 1939 at the graduation of Aron, he had paid little attention to me. Now the ties binding families were the most prominent factor defining relationships. Tulek was as handsome as I had remembered him. He and his lovely wife Klara welcomed us with opened arms.

Like other family members and many other Israelis the Fusses lived in an old house that had been abandoned by Arab families when Israel's independence was declared. Their home was spacious and even had the luxury of electricity. Residing in a village called Sahne, past Jaffa and far away from any transportation, my industrious cousin Tulek built a motorized bicycle. He was the only member of our family who had any form of transportation, and he frequently treated me to rides from Tel Aviv to his home on the bumpy, unpaved road lined with cacti. We often accepted their hospitality.

Mother and I did not stay long in Hadera. We accepted the offer of Esther Wolf and her widowed daughter-in-law, Gusta, to share their tiny home in the village of Tel-Arish. From the last bus stop in Holon the Wolfs' house was a long walk across a sandy desert with orange groves. At night our walk was accompanied by the howling of jackals.

Knowing that I was awaiting the arrival of Alex, with whom mother and I planned to emigrate to the United States, we did not want to take an assignment to an apartment so essential for people who intended to stay permanently.

The moment I arrived in the free world Alex started applying for papers to travel to Israel so we could marry. Few visitors from America came to Israel at that time, and even fewer people believed that he was really coming. Since talking about his impending arrival gave me the reputation of tale-spinner, I stopped doing so.

True to his promise Alex came just six months after mother and I had arrived. He looked very gaunt. Until I saw him I had not known that he had lived on little more than baked beans from the Horn & Hardart Automat so he could save enough money for the trip. But his hands were filled with gifts befitting a wealthy person: he brought me beautiful lingerie and a suitcase full of extravagances. Within a week of his arrival, we were married.

I had loved Alex since I had first met him in the streets of Krakow after the war. Over the mere three months of our courtship he had impressed me with his courage and his clear sense of self-direction. I felt that marriage to him would be the fulfillment of a dream. After all the years of terrible hardship my fortunes were reversing. For mother, too, the event was filled with deep emotion. Despite the sadness caused by the absence of father and Niusia—and the family of Alex, all of whom had been killed in the war—a wedding meant joy at the start of a new family. Our genealogical trees had been sliced, leaving only bare branches, but with our wedding Alex and I were rerooting our people and giving new hope to the Jewish future. In our small way we were reversing the Holocaust against the Jewish people that Hitler had spearheaded.

We were married on September 6, 1951—only one short week after Alex's arrival. I had not expected to have a new dress for the occasion. New immigrants received ration coupons allowing the purchase of necessary items for a minimal amount of money, and the only alternative was buying at exorbitant prices. Mother and I had neither enough coupons to buy a wedding dress nor enough cash to buy it at the black-market price. One night shortly before the wedding, however, while walking along bustling Allenby

Street in Tel Aviv, I saw in a storefront the kind of wedding dress I had always dreamed about. It was a powder-blue organza trimmed with satin ribbons. Unable to restrain my curiosity, I tried it on. How sad I felt when it fit perfectly and I could not afford it. Taking my leave, I thanked the shopkeeper, who asked why I did not want to purchase it. I explained my poor financial condition, and without hesitation, he kindly insisted I take the dress for the official and negligible price and he would supply the ration coupons. What a wonderful surprise it was for Alex to see me walk down the aisle in this beautiful dress!

Only Orthodox rabbis were given licenses to perform marriages. They required that brides-to-be take a ritual bath called a *mikvah* the night before the wedding and bring a certificate of compliance. Esther Wolf accompanied me to an adjoining town in the desert where the *mikvah* was available. The woman attending the dingy *mikvah* clipped my nails down to the skin in the preparation room, then supervised my three dunks in the filthy water. After she declared me "kosher," I requested a verification slip to give the rabbi, but the woman was illiterate. Always a problem-solver I wrote the slip myself, thinking that I could have written the slip at home and saved myself from this dirty adventure.

Since the wedding ceremony was performed in Hebrew, Alex did not understand a word! I served as the whispering translator to him. When he finally broke the glass signifying the end of the ceremony and the start of our married life, we were beside ourselves with joy.

Despite our legal status as a married couple there seemed to be no big hurry to furnish my emigration papers. The American authorities refused to extend Alex's visa beyond six months, requiring him to leave Israel without his new bride. As much as he felt committed to the future of the Jewish homeland Alex insisted that our future would have to be in America. While Alex had worked for a year in his cousin's garment-center factory, earning a total of only $1,800 to pay for the affidavit he needed to bring me to the United States he continued to nurture dreams of real financial success. The government of Israel demanded 51 percent control of every business, however, and this policy was unacceptable to my capitalist husband. Having shared his perceptive postwar judgments about Poland, which had stood in direct contradiction to the dogma of Olek Kahane, I had a great deal of faith in Alex, and I was inclined to follow his decisions, often without question.

Nonetheless, Alex was returning to America without a job. Breaking his promise to give Alex the needed affidavit, his cousin had ultimately refused. Resourceful Alex was able to obtain an affidavit from another cousin, but the altercation cost him his job.

For me the decision to leave Israel was not a happy one. For one thing I was frightened by the prospect of going to America. I had been fed by years of Communist propaganda depicting Americans as a greedy and selfish people. When Alex arrived in Israel in 1951 many of the people who disembarked from the ship with him seemed to fit the stereotype of wealthy, crude tourists sporting loud Hawaiian shirts and carrying wads of money. On the ground they expected services which we considered indulgent. I felt reluctant to live among such "barbarians."

Moreover, making *yiradah* (descent, in Hebrew) from Israel to the States felt like a national betrayal. Immediately upon my arrival on Israeli soil I had dreamed of serving in the army and making a significant contribution toward the creation of our new homeland. Now these dreams, like so many others I had previously entertained, were to be shattered.

More significantly, however, leaving Israel meant leaving all the relatives and friends who had survived the war with us. No one from our circles had emigrated to America. We knew that some members of the Fuss family from Belgium lived in the States—they had kindly sent us the wherewithal for our survival after the war when we had returned to Krakow—but I had never met them. They were total strangers to me.

The most heartbreaking consequence of our decision, however, was that leaving Israel meant being separated from mother for the first time in my life for an undetermined period and leaving her with very dim prospects for supporting herself. We realized that obtaining emigration papers for her would take several years since the Polish immigration quota to America was so limited, and there were thousands of applicants. (Ironically, the Germans were able to emigrate to the States very easily.) After losing half of our family, parting with mother was very traumatic. I worried about her future. While we had a number of relatives and close friends in Israel, her prospects of getting a job were slim, and Alex did not earn enough to help her in a significant way. Yet mother always had my interests in mind, and she urged me to go.

For a good part of our first year in Israel mother and I lived in the homes of the Fuss and Wolf families who generously shared with us their small quarters and limited food supplies as we waited to find available housing. During the period of Alex's stay in Israel, before his visa expired, a friend let us use his newly built *shikun*—an apartment assigned by the government— in a new development on the sands of Holon, a town outside Tel Aviv. Initially there was no electricity, and the narrow roads bordered by deep sand were a trap for traffic. None of these inconveniences fazed us very much; we had made do with far less than a lack of electricity, and few cars were expected to come our way.

When the two big wooden crates arrived from Poland carrying the meager possessions mother and I had been able to take out of the country, one fell off the truck en route to our apartment in Holon, causing it to split in half. This turned out to be fortunate: the wood had cracked into pieces that had just the right dimensions for two beds—and enough space to put clothes inside to serve as mattresses. The second crate provided enough wood to build a table and two benches. Despite our primitive carpentry and engineering skills, thanks to which we frequently landed under the table during meals, we felt proud to be in possession of a "furnished" apartment. Moreover, the stone floors and large windows and white-washed walls made the apartment feel spacious and cheerful. The big red enamel pot we had brought from Krakow for heating water served in Holon as an icebox. Every other day we awaited the sound of the iceman's bell in the neighborhood, and we raced across the sand to get blocks of ice from his truck.

Although I had submitted papers to emigrate to the United States there was still no sign of my application being granted when Alex's visa expired. So six months into married life Alex and I were again bidding each other a tearful farewell with the plan that I would follow him to the United States as soon as I could obtain a visa.

It was a year and a half before my visa was granted, and during that time I forged ahead with different aspects of my life: working, learning, and growing. Mother and I held a series of inconsequential jobs, including assisting a kindergarten teacher, assembling gold chains, and even making pull chains for toilet water tanks. We used all our skills to earn badly needed money.

The more upscale jobs in Israel required Hebrew-language fluency. While my skills improved daily, ultimately enabling me to become a salesperson in a gift shop, I chose not to enroll in an *Ulpan*—a three-month concentrated Hebrew course sponsored by the government—because it entailed boarding at a *kibbutz*. Given the temporary nature of my stay in Israel, I did not want to part with mother for this length of time. At the age of 59 mother was not a candidate for the *Ulpan*.

Instead of focusing on Hebrew I enrolled in a three-month English course at a Berlitz school. Unfortunately the teacher taught "the King's English," and the two-hour, twice weekly program did little to enhance the language skills I would need in New York. Consequently after a couple of years in Israel I spoke only enough Hebrew to get by in Israel and only enough English to get by in America. I had perfected my skills in neither language.

Public transportation was overloaded and expensive, so I spent much of my free time exploring the country by hitchhiking. I never hesitated to climb aboard a truck. People were friendly, and hitchhiking was a normal means of travel. The spirit of building a new country infused every moment with enthusiasm and a spirit of brotherhood. Everything was an adventure. We even had an abundance of lemons, which so delighted me that I used a half in every glass of tea, not even realizing their power to heal my gums that had been damaged by malnutrition in the camps.

On many weekends friends and I traveled north to a *kibbutz* in Tiberias called Ein Gev, located on the eastern side of the Sea of Galilee. Famous musicians were coming to Israel to perform, and the *kibbutz* hosted some marvelous concerts. The road to the *kibbutz* wound its way along the eastern shore of the lake, immediately below the Syrian border. Syrian soldiers often shot at the passing buses. I cannot pretend the episodes were not frightening. At the same time, however, the sound of guns was familiar to me and my friends, who had also survived concentration camps. And unlike our prior experiences we were now in the company of soldiers whose job was to protect—rather than harm—us. To avoid the bullets we traveled to the concerts on boats across the lake, which added a romantic touch to the adventure. Nothing bothered us. We would not have considered missing a chance to hear Yehudi Menuhin or someone of comparable musical excellence.

I spent many wonderful times with my friends in Israel, exploring our new homeland and opening ourselves up to new experiences. After so many years of living in fear I finally felt safe. Not even the occasional episodes of shooting derailed that feeling. Wherever we went we encountered sometimes familiar and other times unknown but warm faces, happy to greet us and make us feel at home. We had little in the way of material goods, but we enjoyed every moment of life. I wished that my two years in Israel could have lasted forever.

Luna with first car, West New York, 1953

Chapter Fourteen
Emigration

As the spouse of an American resident I had preferential status to obtain an American visa, but the process was nonetheless extensive, time-consuming, and humiliating. Although I was still trying to overcome the anti-American propaganda that had been stuffed into my head during the years of living in Communist Poland, my visits to the American embassy in Tel Aviv served only to reinforce my negative impressions. The receptionist, an Egyptian woman, was arrogant. Simply getting past her to go to the necessary office was a major feat. The authorities required me to undergo interviews that felt like interrogations of a crime suspect on trial. The more I dealt with the officials, the more I regretted my decision to emigrate. I wondered how I would possibly live happily in a country of such inhospitable people.

Alex tried every avenue to obtain a visa for me. The lawyers recommended to him were too costly—and only questionably effective. After a year without success, a cousin introduced Alex to Elliot Roosevelt, a relative of President Roosevelt who was running for office in Connecticut, and Alex appealed to him for help. The younger Roosevelt wrote one letter to the immigration authorities on behalf of Alex and me, and my documents were approved. On December 16, 1952, I received my visa to emigrate to the United States. At the same time, however, new legislation was enacted in the United States spearheaded by Senator McCarran requiring emigrants from the Communist block to undergo additional investigations. It seemed to me to defy logic to suspect as Communist sympathizers people who had fled from Communist regimes, but rationality had little application at this time of national hysteria created by Senator McCarthy and his hearings.

The new legislation, entitled the McCarran Act, was scheduled to take effect on midnight of December 23, one week after I had obtained my visa. Although there was nothing in my background to cause suspicion—after all, I had not only already been cleared by all of the investigations initially required and an additional search would have again revealed only the Krakow ghetto, concentration camps, and university/conservatory education as a Jew in the midst of a bare struggle for survival—another investigation would have created more interminable delays, particularly since I had come to Israel from Communist Poland. (Another friend in the same circumstances who did not act quickly had her visa revoked, ultimately causing divorce.) Consequently a frantic effort ensued to get me out before the new law's deadline.

Since returning from Israel Alex had resumed saving money for the purchase of my airline ticket. Recognizing the urgency necessitated by the McCarran Act, he borrowed additional money and bought a ticket in New York's Patra Travel Agency for a December 22 departure. Patra insisted on delivering the ticket directly to the airport rather than issuing it to me. Not suspecting any foul play, I was amenable to the plan.

When I arrived at the airport and received my ticket, which had just arrived, I realized it had been issued only to Paris, where I would have to disembark, travel to the Patra office there, and get a second ticket (already purchased) to the United States. In that moment I realized the game that had been played. While Patra had been paid in American dollars by Alex, the company had purchased from the airline only half the ticket in American dollars; it would purchase the second half from the airline in Paris using francs, which were valued much lower than dollars, thereby obtaining the benefit of the currency exchange. Had they sent the ticket directly to me, they would have run the risk of my recognizing the ploy in advance and putting a stop to it. Yet having only a day until the McCarran Act took effect, I had no alternative but to board the plane at that time and deal with the issue in France.

Mother and two of her childhood friends—a Professor Waldman and his wife, Gusta—accompanied me to the airport. Our emotional embraces were filled with great sadness as I mounted the steps of the plane, leaving mother on the ground surrounded by the black night, knowing it would be a long time before I would see her again (under American law, obtaining mother's visa first required me to become a citizen, and that process took a minimum of five years). At that moment she appeared so fragile, yet she stood strong and did not shed a tear in my presence. I am sure her pillow was quite wet that night. Exhausted by the chaotic preparations that had accompanied my departure, I was not yet able to face the emotional upheaval of our parting. Once aboard, I sank into my seat, letting the plane escort me to the next step on the strange path to my destiny.

The plane arrived in Paris too early in the morning for me to venture into town, but the flight to the States did not depart until that night, leaving me the entire day to reach the Patra office and obtain my ticket for the balance of the trip. A young man who had traveled with me on the flight from Tel Aviv suggested we sit down for a steak breakfast at an airport restaurant. Not having had the luxury for two years of tasting a juicy, rare piece of meat, I allowed the prospect to blot out the financial consequences. The delicious steak would have fed a family of six in Israel. I sank my teeth into it with gusto and munched the accompanying pile of crisp golden French fries and mayonnaise. Until the bill arrived, for $4, I allowed myself to forget my troubles. I had been carrying in my pocket a mere $10 in foreign currency—the maximum allowed by the Israeli government.

Armed with the remaining $6 and an Israeli passport that enabled me to go through passport control, I set out on my trip to the Patra office in the city center. I did not know a word of French, but through universal language and hand signals I managed to navigate the Metro subway system and find my way. I knew that my problem would not be easily resolved, and keeping a cool head better guaranteed success. Internally I felt guilty for leaving mother, my family, my friends, and my nation of Israel. I would not have felt terribly disappointed had the agency not been able to issue my ticket immediately, effectively forcing me back to Tel Aviv. Patra's office was decorated with colorful posters enticing potential clients to visit fascinating places, but the promises made inside the offices were shaded in gray. I was informed that all the planes had been booked because of the Christmas vacation, and my flight would have to wait until the holiday rush had subsided. Submitting to their insistence would have meant the application of the McCarran Act to my immigration status, which would have required the reopening of my files and created long delays—if not refusal—for entry to the United States.

In desperation I stood next to the counter, and when customers entered I loudly proclaimed that Patra had stolen money from me by not issuing me a direct ticket to New York; that they had acted illegally at my expense. I alternated the language of my rightful protest between German and English, depending upon which I thought would be understood by most customers present when I spoke. After several hours seeking to avoid a scandal, they managed to find a seat for me on the plane.

Now armed with my valid ticket, I believed—incorrectly!—that I had one major hurdle left. Collecting the few cents I still had to get myself to the airport on time (the plane's departure time was drawing near), I purchased a ticket for the Metro and, feeling exhausted and oblivious to my surroundings, dropped into the nearest seat I could find. When the conductor made his rounds I absentmindedly presented him with my ticket. I had not realized that I had made the faux pas of sitting in a first-class seat with my second-class ticket, and he demanded a fee for the car upgrade. My pockets were empty, and my face must have appeared both dumbfounded and panicked—the latter as I realized that my successful ploy to obtain the ticket was on the verge of being foiled thanks to my own ignorance. As I scrambled to figure a way out of the dilemma a kind gentleman who overheard the confrontation offered to pay the fee. Another obstacle had thus been overcome on the path to the plane I wished I was not taking.

Yet the hurdles had not yet run their course, and I had not finished finding ways of defeating them.

Patra's deceit continued to spin its web. Israeli law allowed departing passengers to carry 20 pounds more in baggage than French law permitted. Since I had gotten a new ticket issued in Paris the French limitation applied to my luggage, requiring me to pay for the overage with money I did not have. I had left most of my few possessions in Israel. Sending them was too expensive, and most of the linen and clothing I owned were valuable to friends and family in Israel and more easily replaced in America. All the worldly possessions that were important to me were therefore contained in my two valises. In my 25 years I had been forced countless times to leave behind my most important belongings, and I was not about to part with them again.

My argument to the airlines that my husband would pay for the extra weight when we arrived in New York went nowhere. Desperate, I resorted to a tactic like the one I had employed in the airline ticket office: I protested in a loud voice using the little English I knew. While the scheme did not deter the position taken by the airline, a group of Japanese students overheard the conversation. They were traveling to New York for the holidays and offered to have some of my bags assigned to them since their loads were light.

I had made it to Paris, eaten a steak, gone downtown and obtained the correct ticket for the flight to New York, gotten myself back to the airport without enough money for the trip, and checked all my bags despite the fact that their collective weight violated regulations. Exhausted, I boarded the bouncy propeller plane heading to New York on a 22-hour journey, and I melted into the seat.

It was not long before the next encumbrance presented itself. An announcement was made that passengers were required to pay for their meals. I exchanged glances with the companion with whom I had shared a steak dinner. Although neither of us had a penny left to our names, food—though enjoyable—seemed far from necessary. Another day without food would be equivalent to no more than a Yom Kippur fast, and that was a minor inconvenience compared to the years of starvation to which I had once been accustomed. Fortunately, however, kindness followed us. An elegant Israeli book merchant who had heard the conversation between Steak Dinner Companion and me paid for our meals.

The plane made several refueling stops. In Greenland the pilot had to land a distance from the airport, and passengers were asked to disembark and go to the airport—in a howling snowstorm. Not having anticipated this detour, of course, I had taken off my shoes to be more comfortable during the long flight. When the time came to climb down the steps, my swollen feet did not fit into the flimsy shoes. Having spent the past few years in Israel where cold days were few, I had neither boots nor a decent winter coat, both of which I had planned to buy in the United States. But again fortune took care of me. The book merchant held my arm and helped me to navigate in the blizzard. In the airport he even bought a postcard for me to send to mother.

With only an hour before the plane would reach the long-awaited destination at Idlewild (now John F. Kennedy) Airport in New York, my mind was fixated on the reunion I was about to have with my husband. I imagined his eager face as he searched the crowds exiting from customs and his warm arms waiting to sweep me into their embrace. For five years we had been divided by an Iron Curtain, and for another year and a half— except for only a brief six-month interlude—we had been separated by the immigration policies of the "friendly" United States. Now only one hour separated us.

Or so I thought.

Idlewild Airport at the time consisted of one long building. Immigration procedures were extensive, requiring even an examination of medical reports at the arrival terminal. I had packed my documentation in my luggage, which could not gain access to until the immigration procedures were completed. As a result I was the last passenger to be processed. A fee was required for which I had to direct them to Alex; my wallet had long since been emptied.

From Alex's anxious perspective seeing all the passengers exit except me imposed yet another complication: since I had gotten my ticket at the last minute, my name did not appear on the passenger list. He frantically searched for me in the airport for an extensive time. Finally the immigration authorities found him in order to obtain the requisite fee—and that is how he learned that I had arrived.

I fell into Alex's arms, and all of the stumbling blocks—both physical and emotional—on my journey to the United States disappeared. In that moment I knew this was where I belonged. I looked forward to our life together, and I felt secure with Alex as the partner with whom I could establish a family.

Yet the reunion also had a bittersweet taste because I knew it would be at least five years before I would again see mother. At the age of 25 five years seemed like an eternity.

I had finally reached the end of the sometimes torturous, sometimes tedious course I had run for seven years: the United States of America. But this country that I had been so apprehensive about emigrating to—this land that everyone else had tried to convince me harbored friendly folks—had achieved what the Nazis had not. It had forced me to choose between being with a man I loved and leaving mother alone in Israel without the means to support herself.

I had made my choice. There was only one solution to justify my decision: set out to make the best of the rest of my life.

Bernice, Luna and Haja Wolf, New York, 1956

Chapter Fifteen
New York

My first impressions of life in America confirmed all my fears.

I had not grown up as a farm girl, but life in cosmopolitan Krakow had not prepared me for the massiveness and anonymity of New York. I felt lost in the sea of people. As happy as I was to be reunited with Alex, I felt totally nonessential to anything or anybody around me. In Israel I had felt a sense of purpose. I was making a contribution toward the building of this—my—

struggling country, which I had now abandoned. And for what? What difference did my existence make in this gigantic world? I felt like a grain of sand lost in a desert.

Reminiscent of Poland, the gloomy winter skies made everything look even more dark and dreary. The weather was in great contrast to the sunshine-filled streets of Israel lined with palm trees and beautiful geometric white houses no higher than three stories. The gigantic, gray buildings of New York felt like a canyon constantly on the verge of swallowing me whole. People in the streets rushed by. I recognized no one, and no one greeted me. Was this the reality of living in the States?

In an effort to house me in style, Alex rented what was considered a luxurious corner room in a large building on Broadway and 96th street. We shared the apartment, painted in dark blue, with a number of other people. Our bedroom, crowded with furniture and knickknacks, was dominated by a large bed covered with a flowered bedspread according to the fashion of the 1950's. After the sunny and sparsely furnished apartments in Israel where everything had been new and modern I found our "deluxe" accommodations depressing.

Our friends, all Jewish emigrants from Poland, congregated among themselves on the Upper West Side of Manhattan within a few blocks of our apartment. They spoke Polish, lived in isolation, and resisted change. Emotionally they were still in Europe, critical of everything American. They glorified the life they had left behind, forgetting the misery that had brought them to these shores.

To worsen my feelings of depression on the day of my arrival Alex and his coworkers at a firm called Hatco were served with an ultimatum: accept a cut in salary or look for another job (the company was undergoing financial difficulty). In light of our outstanding financial obligations, particularly the debt incurred by our travels, Alex faced a difficult decision. Filled with confidence in his boss's ability and the future of the company, he opted to stay.

The consequence, however, was that I needed to get work immediately to supplement our income. Equipped with only marginal English and few marketable skills, I did not have many options. I found two opportunities: bank clerk or seamstress.

My sewing skills had saved me time and again during the war; the job was clearly one in which I knew I would feel comfortable. However, working in the garment district would have placed me in a crowded, noisy room resembling a sweatshop, where I would be required to sit at a sewing machine for countless hours, forever working to produce my daily quota. I would have been among immigrants without an opportunity to speak and improve my English. Moreover, Alex's experience in the garment district—where he had exhausted himself for a year in his cousins' shop in order to obtain immigration affidavits ultimately denied him—had left us feeling negative about working there.

I therefore accepted a bank job offered by a family friend of Alex, even though it paid only $30 per week compared to the $100 weekly salary offered in the garment factory. Since the bank office was at Fifth Avenue and 17th Street, I knew I would have a chance to meet educated people from the mainstream of New York life and thus be able to learn more about this new country that was now my home.

During my interview I falsely told my prospective employer that I knew how to type. I accepted the offer with its limited income that, combined with Alex's $55 weekly earnings, was barely enough to meet our needs. Several days for security clearance intervened between the offer and the first day of work. Over that period I rented a typewriter, bought a manual, and learned to touch-type. While most other nontypists would likely have seen the job requirement as an impenetrable impediment, there were few obstacles I could not imagine finding ways to conquer.

Three days later, I reported to work in the bank as a typist.

One of the greatest benefits of the job, which I had not anticipated, was that it thrust me into the midst of a multiethnic work environment. Coming from Poland, where Jews were the only significant minority, and Israel, where Jews were the majority population, I had not been accustomed to dealing with these differences. I welcomed the opportunity.

Our department of five people was headed by Ann Javitz, a statuesque, elegant Jewish lady who, I had heard, was the first female vice-president in the banking industry. Lena, a dowdy unmarried woman from Brooklyn, was our immediate supervisor. There were also Ethel, a distinguished black lady from Harlem, and Gloria, a chic young Puerto Rican girl, closest in age to me. They all welcomed me and helped with my training, teaching me not only about the new job, but also about assimilating into American society.

Miss Javitz was a good role model for a corporate wife, which at the time I aspired to one day become. Her melodic voice and linguistic eloquence sharpened my language skills. She also coached me in American social graces. Coming from a very informal environment, I did not know customs such as issuing dinner invitations well in advance, arranging for dinner parties, making calls to announce my visit, or the American custom of writing thank-you notes. Getting educated in those matters saved me a lot of future embarrassment.

Lena, with her Brooklyn accent and unrefined manners, gave me valuable lessons in stretching my meager budget. A woman in her fifties, she was adept at finding bargains and budgeting money, skills she had developed as the only breadwinner supporting her aging mother. Though she appeared gruff to those who did not know her, under that exterior was a caring and kind woman. She seemed to have given up hope of marrying and having a family, and she neglected her appearance. Her wrinkled clothes and home-dyed reddish-brown unkempt hair did not present a sense of fashion worth emulating.

For that I turned to Gloria, a petite Hispanic young woman with a cultivated sense of style despite our meager resources. Gloria took pleasure in guiding me to street merchants and helping me add sparkle to my wardrobe. (I still have a beautiful necklace I bought with her for one dollar; I recently learned it was made of real coral and mother of pearl.) In contrast to the other three women in my department, Gloria was very flirtatious and fun-loving.

Ethel was a mature black lady, immaculately dressed in conservative dark clothes. She went quietly about her tasks, always ready to bail me out of difficult predicaments. Often trustees of the bank would call, expecting (impossibly) to be recognized without identifying themselves. Upon my troubled signal to Ethel, she would intercept the call and save my job. But her most valuable contribution to my American education was the introduction she gave me to African-American culture. She regaled me with information about life in Harlem and black musical culture, and she brought me delicious fragrant cornbread and other Southern delicacies.

I never heard Ethel address the issue of segregation or prejudice. Considering the harmonious coexistence in our department, I was naively unaware of its existence. In retrospect I realize that not everything was so smooth. When Lena went on vacation a few months after my arrival she asked me, rather than my coworkers, to take charge of the department. Since the other women were more qualified, I suspect this decision was prompted by prejudice. Nobody objected to Lena's decision, however, and in my innocence at the time I did not either.

The substance of the bank job was also beneficial for me. I worked in the loan department, which gave me insight into handling credit, a totally foreign concept in both Eastern Europe and Israel. The training served as a good background for managing our marital finances.

Our meager budget never interfered with my happiness. I prided myself in my decent dress styles. Long lunch hours and short working days permitted time for bargain-hunting, and my sewing skills came in handy. Alex's extended working hours did not leave much time to throw money into entertainment, and my careful budgeting permitted us to live quite decently. Used to scrounging every penny in Poland, we considered our life quite luxurious. We also had the fortunate attitude of being content with whatever we had. We managed to pay our debts, and I even squirreled a few dollars into our savings account so we could send some money to mother.

Mother, Luna, Bernice and twins in the carriage, 1957

Chapter Sixteen
West New York

After three months in a crowded apartment the excitement of living in Manhattan wore off. The conditions were unacceptable: Alex and I had to share the kitchen with five strangers. Being able to use just a corner of a refrigerator shelf and waiting for our turn at the stove were not my idea of the American dream. Yet there were no other New York City options. With all the postwar newlywed couples looking for apartments, housing was scarce. When a landlord advertised available apartments, people lined up at the building as early as 5 a.m.

I wanted to get out of the city and to live in a place where people were friendly in a neighborly way. I was also eager to get out of what I called the "Polish ghetto" and move into a multicultural American locale.

The logical choice was New Jersey, where Alex worked, just on the other side of the Lincoln Tunnel. The neighborhood offered us the possibility of moving into an attractive residence within our means. We knew the change would require a commute for me, but not a much longer ride than the one on the crowded subway I had used to commute from the Upper West Side. We decided to take the chance.

Our first move did not make us much happier than we had felt in the Manhattan apartment. We moved to a furnished but shabby one-bedroom apartment in Union City. The bedroom was only slightly bigger than the bed, and the walls—two maroon and two gray—were very depressing. The large but windowless kitchen enabled us to invite friends for dinner, but not even extensive scrubbing could erase the musty odor.

To make things worse we had not realized that we had moved next door to a burlesque hall! Alex often worked long hours and sometimes I came home late at night and was not terribly pleased to walk past the adjoining bars filled with excited men leaving the performances. We lasted there only a few months, using the time to search for a better alternative.

In desperation and being a little nervy at a time when people bribed building superintendents to get housing priorities, we placed an ad in a newspaper stating that a young, childless working couple was looking for an apartment. Our friends laughed at our *chutzpah*.

The laughter ceased, however, when we received a reply from a wonderful couple. Armenian carpet dealers, the Kedershas owned a three family house in which they occupied one apartment. They were now moving out, but they did not want to hassle with the mobs they knew would respond to an advertisement. They offered us a four-room corner apartment within our budget. It was located in West New York, just across from Manhattan and one block from the Hudson River.

In contrast to the dungeons we had just left the rooms were painted a beautiful light tan, brightened even further by the sun streaming through large windows. With its white, enamel American kitchen cabinets, white washable wallpaper decorated with green ivy trellises, and all new appliances (including a large refrigerator), the kitchen became the envy of all our friends. For the first time since I had come to this country I felt the beginnings of the American dream taking root.

We furnished the apartment with traditional pieces inherited from mother's 94-year-old aunt Fanny Spira, who was liquidating her apartment and moving to an old-age home. This regal lady, the only surviving sibling of grandfather Schneider, had moved to America with her brother and sister in the late 1800's. Though childless she had lived in great comfort with her husband who had developed a substantial fur business. I met her when I first arrived in the United States, and I found her to be an amazing lady. Aunt Fanny gave me a number of family photographs, including a picture postcard sent to her in 1903 by Aunt Sala and Uncles Salek and Henry. The postcard was addressed to her apartment at Fifth Avenue and 118th Street. Aunt Fanny liked sharing stories about the farms that surrounded the apartment buildings. She had an opinion on every issue, including politics. She read the newspapers religiously and was particularly fond of following the anti-Communist proceedings of Senator Joe McCarthy, with whom she strongly disagreed.

We shared the upper floor of the apartment building with an Italian American couple our age, who were our guiding lights into American life. Jo and Frank Ripa came from large families, and we promptly became great friends.

I was traveling to New York City daily, and many evenings while Alex worked I went to movie theaters where I improved my language skills as well as enjoyed the entertainment. The apartment was a close commute to New York,, and Alex had only a 20-minute ride to the Hatco plant where he worked. He commuted in style in our beautiful blue Pontiac, which we had bought shortly after moving to New Jersey. So the living arrangement worked out fine—until the day the Hatco plant burned down. The factory moved to Fords, New Jersey, located 30 miles away. Alex did not complain about the longer drive, and I was too happy in West New York to consider moving.

After two years in the United States I felt eager to start a family. Following the war each new baby was greeted as a miracle, and after all the experiences Alex and I had undergone we felt a strong need to contribute to Jewish—as well as our own familial—continuity. Admittedly the thought of an infant frightened me. I had never held a baby in my arms, and I knew nothing about rearing a child. Moreover, the separation from mother became particularly painful. Since I had applied for citizenship the law did not permit mother to get even a visitor's visa. It was hard to resign ourselves to the prospect that for a still undetermined amount of time, she would not be able to see or hold her first grandchild. But we were committed to moving ahead in life. There was no point in waiting.

Jo Ripa and I were pregnant at the same time, sharing our simultaneous apprehension and joy as well as all the new information we could gather. I maintained my job throughout my pregnancy, commuting to New York and climbing 13 flights of stairs a day. Three months ahead of me Jo delivered a girl, beginning right away to teach me by word and example about a baby's needs and desires.

On June 20, 1955, we were blessed with a beautiful little girl. This tiny bundle with big brown eyes and dainty hands immediately became the focus of our lives. After I gave birth I left my job, and Bernice, named after Alex's mother and my sister, filled my days with awe. She was a delightful, easygoing child. I could not have imagined myself as a mother but she captivated me totally. She was widely adored. Our New York friends were frequent visitors, treating their treks to New Jersey as excursions into the country.

At the same time as I was enjoying the experience of new motherhood, however, I found becoming a housewife difficult. I did not feel comfortable using money I had not earned despite the fact that Alex was very generous. At times the days felt very long. Other than my deep friendship with Jo living in West New York did not offer many opportunities for social involvement.

My citizenship was still two years away. To compensate for the impenetrable bureaucracy preventing mother from joining her first grandchild we sent a constant stream of photographs. They were a poor substitute for the hugs and kisses of a baby, of course, but mother never complained.

Alex was making great progress on the job. Typically calculating the possibilities of progress he switched from working in the laboratory to the production end where he believed the possibilities for promotion were much greater. His foresight brought forth fruit, and he became well-positioned in the company.

Some time thereafter the Ripas had another child, cramping their space in the one bedroom apartment and causing them to move. We were very sad the day they vacated their apartment. Their absence left us lonely for friends similarly situated. The new tenants were a young, childless couple. Though they were very lovely people no one could replace the Ripas for us.

Soon after their move I became pregnant again. I was thrilled. We had wanted more children, and I believed that raising kids close in age would encourage a special emotional bond. My opinion, of course, was rooted in the memory of my sister Niusia who was only 15 months older than me, and I wished to provide my children with the chance to have a similar relationship. I had cherished Niusia, and I missed her so much.

In 1957 with my citizenship approaching, the opportunity to obtain a permanent visa for mother loomed on the American horizon. Our experience with the immigration authorities had taught us the benefit of turning to politicians for help, so with my bulging belly and an infant in my arms I journeyed to the local office of Congressman Tumulty, who had a powerful position in Washington. When he saw me pregnant he promised to do his best to assist us.

On a crisp February morning in 1957 Alex and I—with 18-month-old Bernice in tow—ventured to Idlewild Airport, anxiously awaiting mother's flight. We watched for the plane in the brisk air on the observation deck. The bright sunshine made everything that moved through the skies acutely visible. From far away on the horizon we spotted a big white metal bird carrying our precious cargo. The plane seemed to take forever to touch the ground.

As the steps were pulled up to the airplane exit and people started to descend, a familiar figure appeared in the doorway. Dressed in a beautifully tailored black coat with a halo of white hair crowning an elegant silhouette, mother walked very slowly and deliberately, as if cherishing each step that brought her closer to us. Almost instinctively Bernice stretched out her little arms to mother. Bernice's gesture and the sight of my tremendous belly promising another arrival brought tears of joy to mother's eyes.

We only later learned that mother's slow gait had reflected the pain of terrible back problems. In Israel she had boarded from a wheelchair, but not wanting to upset us she had valiantly descended in Idlewild without showing any signs of discomfort.

Just as our large family had welcomed me with open arms when I had arrived, so now they were eager to offer mother their hospitality.

We had also planned to buy furniture for the new apartment into which we had planned to move in the summer. We needed larger quarters with four now in the immediate family and an addition on its way, and we preferred to relocate closer to Alex's worksite. The long commute and working hours cut too deeply into the time he could spend with the family.

But all the plans had to be scrapped. The last few months of my pregnancy were very difficult. I felt surprisingly tired, and other than going to New York to find a physical-therapy program to help mother's back problems, we could no longer indulge in the escapades there that had given us such pleasure. Much to our surprise, three weeks after mother's arrival—on March 8 to be exact—I gave birth to twins. We were all thrilled, especially me, since I had wanted eventually to have more than two children and had been dreading another pregnancy.

On March 8, 1957, the twins were born in St. Mary's Hospital in Hoboken, New Jersey in a small nursery with only 11 other babies. Mark Isidore was named after our fathers and Irene after Alex's sister, therefore utilizing all the names of our lost family. They were eight weeks premature, requiring a one-month incubation period during which they received care from the nuns that we could not have given them at home. The nuns adored the infants and spent countless hours with them. They never calculated overtime. While the twins stayed in the hospital I had a chance to recover and spend some quiet time with Bernice and mother before the happy madness started.

A month later when Mark and Irene finally reached five pounds each we brought them home to the seeming delight of Bernice. Only 21 months old she greeted the two bundles, one in pink and one in blue, by singing "Rock-a-bye Baby." Judging by their size and appearance—Mark with his shock of black hair and robust looking tiny body and Irene with her creamy complexion, enormous blue eyes, and beautiful golden locks—they resembled dolls more than babies. For Bernice they were the equivalent of toys, and she appeared to compensate for the diversion of attention away from her by participating in her new siblings' care: she handed me diapers, brought me bottles, and helped rock them to sleep.

We enjoyed the benefit of a wonderful system of support. Mrs. Kedersha, who initially had rented us the apartment because we were a childless working couple, three years later found four additional tenants in the same apartment, including three children. Undaunted she visited me in the hospital, bringing a great bucket of flowers, and graciously permitted us to install a washing machine, which was a great luxury in the days of cloth diapers.

By the time we brought the twins home mother's back pain was largely on the mend. Together we faced the challenge of preparing 24 bottles at a time and doing mountains of laundry. Having mother's help—in her own, quiet way—was invaluable. The love I had always felt for her was now multiplied by so many people, and we were grateful to share our happiness with her. The new lives in the forms of Bernice, Mark, and Irene filled the voids that had been created by the losses she and I had suffered. Despite months of sleepless nights we were elated that no amount of work seemed to be too much.

Now we were together with no threat of separation and nothing could have dimmed our happiness. Perhaps if our daily lives had not been so chaotic mother would have felt lonely. She had few friends, and she lacked the ability to communicate since she had come to the United States at the age of 65, too late in her life to learn English. Although she missed the family she had left behind in Israel she felt that what she gained by living with us more than compensated for the loss.

There was no longer anything keeping us in West New York. Not even the allure of Manhattan with its theaters and cultural life had any sway at this stage in our lives filled with diapers and bottles. I welcomed the opportunity to move to a new location and a new apartment.

Mark & Irene, Franklin Township, 1959

Chapter Seventeen
Franklin Township

For Alex proximity to work grew more critical as our family grew larger. His 60-mile round-trip commute was taking its toll on time the family. The children needed friends, schools, and a place to play outdoors. Mother needed a place where she could be surrounded by people and would not be imprisoned without transportation. I needed a community of stimulating adults with goals. With three infants in the picture it was difficult to accommodate all these requirements.

An avid search uncovered cooperative garden apartments under construction in Franklin Township, New Jersey—just a few miles away from

Hatco—which fulfilled all the criteria, and we signed up for the first available unit. By the summer of 1957 the six of us had become the first tenants in a lovely, newly constructed three-bedroom apartment.

The development attracted many intellectuals and activists because of the proximity of Rutgers University and sophisticated industries situated nearby. Being surrounded by educated contemporaries opened new vistas and provided opportunities to make friends. Proper facilities for children were of prime interest to the residents, most of whom, like us, were young couples with small children.

I took the cooperative concept very seriously, volunteering *kibbutz*-style (as had been done on Israeli collective farms) for various assignments. I led the effort to furnish a child-safe playground where a rubberized surface promised to cushion falls and prevent scraped knees. The addition of colorful playground equipment, rare in those days, created an appealing gathering place for children. Shortly after the playground was built a cooperative nursery was formed where the parents, led by highly trained teacher, volunteered on rotating basis. There were weekly lectures and discussions about child rearing. A novice on the subject, I imbibed all the information and experiences at the same time as I reached out to form new friendships with other young parents. It was a joyous time.

The happiness did not last long, however. Just when we thought we had settled into a secure American life a new cloud appeared on the horizon. After six years on the job in Hatco, the chemical company where Alex had progressed from laboratory technician to plant manager, he was fired on the spot for refusing to work on the Jewish High Holidays. The ultimatum was presented to him in no uncertain terms: If he did not come to work on Yom Kippur, he would lose his job. The problem sprang from nowhere, since up to that point Alex's Jewishness was never an issue.

We were shocked and alarmed. In the country that had claimed to be a bastion of tolerance this event was a very painful blow. In addition to confronting the disappointment that rang frightening internal warning bells, concrete realities lurked: we had three infants, had lived in our new apartment for only two months, still owed a debt for mother's ticket from Israel, and had only $700 to our name.

Nonetheless, we had already paid a dear price for the "crime" of being Jewish. It had stolen our youth, and it had stolen the lives of father, Niusia, and Alex's entire family. No punishment could ever match the cost that hatred had already exacted from us. We were determined to wage this new battle successfully.

Three months later when our bank account had reached bottom and tempers had cooled, Alex and his boss reconciled. Alex after all had always loved his job and anticipated a future for himself in it. He had made his point; now it was time to move on. However, as had occurred during his recuperation from the accident two years before, some of his coworkers felt they were able to do Alex's job in his absence and considered his rehiring a barrier to their promotional track. They made his return very difficult. The employer therefore created a new position for him as marketing director, through which he again rode the path to success, contributing greatly to the growth of the company.

Our next hurdle was obtaining mother's permanent visa. Her visitor's visa was to expire in the fall, just two months short of my obtaining the citizenship that would entitle me to apply for mother's permanent visa. Our original request for an extension of mother's visa was denied, devastating us. Forcing mother to leave the country would certainly have meant another agonizing separation, which could have lasted years. In a last attempt I visited the Immigration and Naturalization Service (INS) office in Newark, New Jersey, hoping that a personal appeal could accomplish what a written application had not.

I approached the INS agent using reverse psychology. I told him of mother's desire to leave our madhouse of three crying infants and return to Israel where she had a lovely apartment and many friends. I pleaded with him to help me retain her for another few months since her assistance was so important to me and the children. I explained that if he gave her an extension she would be too embarrassed to leave me taking care of three infants by myself.

The fatherly man listened carefully. He was touched by my plight, and he generously added six months to her visa. I returned home triumphant, much to the disbelief of the family. Six months, I knew, would be enough time for me to obtain my citizenship papers.

In January 1958 I became a citizen and we immediately applied for mother's permanent visa. When we received it after six years of anxiety about possible additional forced separations, our joy was indescribable. From that moment on, mother would stay permanently with us. Our entire community in Franklin Township celebrated.

Along with my citizenship came the right to vote, a responsibility I took seriously since I had witnessed first hand the consequences of the electorate's voting to bestow evil power upon Adolf Hitler. Our Franklin Township neighbors organized a candidates' night, inviting everybody to attend. For the first time I felt like a participating member of society.

The candidates' night filled me with a sense of privilege and awe. I realized that sitting in a room with people competing for the right to run our country was witnessing democracy in action. That night I decided I would forever more be an active participant in the democratic process of the United States of America.

As a new immigrant I felt deeply grateful for the acceptance, inclusion, and friendship offered me by my Franklin Township neighbors. We were a great ethnic and religious mixture, of which I cherished being a part. Even Alex's temporary dismissal from Hatco for failure to go to work on a Jewish holiday was motivated more by a personal power struggle than by the vicious anti-Semitism we had known in Europe. In Franklin Township I finally experienced the feeling of being included in a society that celebrated differences. In retrospect I view the time I spent there as a pilot project for my future.

Nonetheless, after living in Franklin Township for three years I sadly realized that this home was to be only another stepping stone toward a permanent residence. With our growing family the time had come to buy a house.

I took the challenge of finding the right place to live seriously. Coming from a Krakow home where my family had lived since the seventeenth century, I looked for a spot where we could put down our roots, spend the rest of our lives, and establish ourselves as members of a community. The image of "wandering Jew," which had characterized Jewish life for hundreds of years, no longer felt suitable for our family. We felt the time had come to plant permanent family roots, enroll our children in a consistent school setting, and join a Jewish congregation.

First day of school, 1962

Chapter Eighteen
Watchung

For a year and a half I scouted many areas but I could find nothing that felt like home. At one point the real estate agent even brought me to a converted funeral home that looked like a fortress. I was incapable of communicating to the agent what I was looking for: a place where I could transplant the tradition of my family who had lived for generations in Krakow. I could not compromise.

Once during the war, in the Leipzig concentration camp, when Mala and I found a rare moment to rest on our bunk beds, I had shared one of my fantasies with her. I told her I imagined that the war would end and we would be separated. No thoroughness of search would produce results. Years would pass and I would live in a gray stone house on a hill, surrounded by flowers and trees. One day I would sit in a square room with big windows, playing a piano, and she would pass in the nearby woods riding a horse. This was how we would find each other.

Shortly after returning to Krakow, when Mala discovered that nobody from her family was alive, she disappeared from Krakow without a trace. No amount of searching produced results.

I told the real estate man the story, and while he did not understand it he nevertheless eventually found the kind of place I had been seeking. One drizzly day in spring 1960 he brought me to the rural village of Watchung, New Jersey. Since he had no key to the house we were able to look at it only from outside, in the garden. Even so, I felt the blood begin to race throughout my body. This was exactly the house of my dreams! The gray stone ranch house stood majestically on two acres of land atop a hill, surrounded by the most lavish, multicolored azaleas. A large flower bed full of three-foot-high purple and yellow irises filled the garden. The property was edged by scores of pink dogwoods, and the orchard in the backyard emitted the sweet fragrance of apple, pear, and cherry trees. The rain enhanced the bright green of the velvety lawn. One walk around the exterior, and I knew the internal layout did not matter. This could be a home for my family, not just a house.

The next day Alex and I toured the interior. The spacious rooms had large picture windows, and while the wallpaper was gray, the coloring did not dampen the cheerful feeling of the house. Though there was not enough space as it was then laid out to accommodate our family of six, we felt as if we belonged there.

The seller, a Dutch lady who had loved living there, interviewed us to decide whether we were suitable to occupy her home. After we passed her scrutiny we purchased the property in 15 minutes, during Alex's lunch break!

Moving to this spectacular dream house was exciting, yet leaving Franklin Township was emotionally difficult. In the three years we had lived there I had become deeply involved in the town's social, political, and academic life, and the children had made many friends. The majority of the tenants had been young couples, most of whom were connected to Rutgers University or to local industries. The sense of belonging and contributing to a community gave me great satisfaction. I felt that I was becoming a well accepted, well respected, and useful member of my new society.

Our new neighbors were much older than we were, and there was little in the experiential language they spoke with which we could identify. They were part of the old American establishment. We rarely saw them, since our houses were too far apart from one another. The isolation was difficult for us all. I missed my friends and the way of life we had shared.

Every destination was a driving distance, and I was the only driver during the day. mother was totally dependent on me to take her places. There were no people in the vicinity with whom she could associate. This fact, added to the language barrier she had already faced, made the move to Watchung particularly difficult for her.

The task of maintaining a large house on our very slim budget was daunting. We had bought the house with an inflated financial statement since our earnings would not have supported the size of the mortgage we needed. We had never lived in the country and had no idea how to maintain a garden, yet we had no money to hire help. The first year Alex tended to the garden. With his long working days this was a formidable task. I rolled up my sleeves and made curtains for the whole house, adding many decorative touches.

It did not take long for us to realize we had made a sound investment, and having a permanent home base fulfilled my dreams. The children never again knew another school district. We no longer had to search for a new location no matter how much further Alex was promoted. The house was suitable for private and company parties. Having a gracious home was the best investment we could make, even if the first years required some sacrifices.

The fulfillment of my Leipzig fantasy had been almost complete. The missing puzzle piece, of course, was the presence of Mala. I had not seen her since she had left Krakow three months after the war, and none of our countless inquiries had borne fruit.

One day in the 1960s, we attended a ball of Krakow Society. As soon As I entered the room I was suddenly enveloped in a warm and loving embrace. It was Mala! She had come to the party with her husband, Henry. She did not arrive on a horse as I had imagined in Leipzig, but there she was, in the flesh. She and Henry had been looking for me over the years, obtaining no better results than we had in our search for her. Amazingly I learned that for several years before our reunion she had been living only 15 minutes away from us in Clark, New Jersey. She had arrived in the States in 1949 with her husband and an infant son named Jack.

I was afraid to call mother, who was babysitting that night. Mala had been like another daughter to her throughout the war. As I had anticipated, when I finally broke the news, mother's elation was hardly containable.

I felt fortunate to have rediscovered my cherished and loyal friend, with whom I had shared the depths of hell. Despite our diverse paths in life, the past had created a link stronger than any blood line.

It seemed to me that purchasing our dream house had produced wonderful benefits. Interestingly Mala and I realized that we had both attended the same party in the same location a year before, but we had not seen each other.

Twins Bar-Bat Mitzvah, Watchung, 1970

Chapter Nineteen
New Life

While awestruck by the beauty of the new home in Watchung that had figuratively called out to me, for some time I wore its address as uncomfortably as an untailored suit. It did not take long for me to understand the expression about living in an ivory tower. Our house, situated on two acres and surrounded by beautiful gardens, was gracious indeed, but its very nature resulted in total isolation. The tall, graceful trees peeking through the windows blocked views of our neighbors, who seemed almost nonexistent. I yearned for the friendships we had left behind. With Alex working long hours I spent my days at home with mother and the three children our only companions.

Moreover, growing up in a city was poor preparation for becoming a country squire. In our youngest days my sister Niusia and I had roamed the parks, shops, and streets of Krakow, often with our older cousins. We had rarely known the feeling of being alone.

Unlike my youthful experiences my three children had few companions other than one another. Fortunately, however, they seemed to enjoy each other's company from the outset. At the ages of five and three when we moved to Watchung they frolicked together like little elves in the garden and the house.

Never one to be controlled by my feelings I reasoned that since so many people in my new culture were striving for this kind of life, it must be filled with some kind of hidden merit, and I put my mind to the task of finding it.

The process began with the garden, which I immediately noticed was growing at the same pace as the children and with many analogous attention-seeking needs. With no time or money to get an education in gardening I launched into the task with pruning shears, common sense, and a trial-and-error tactic. Whether I was blessed with a "green thumb" or had inherited the genes of the land-owning Fuss family, the garden must have been treated right. It flourished.

A few weeks after moving in, while I was still experimenting in the garden, Bernice started school. She marched resolutely to kindergarten to meet the challenge. School was a very happy experience for her. She was always mature for her age, plunging into new situations with zest. At the end of her first day I waited on the corner for the bus to drop off my little girl, but for a long time Bernice was nowhere to be seen. Finally the bus arrived carrying only Bernice on board, though in the morning the same vehicle had been crowded with children. As she descended the steps with dignity and strutted toward the house, she informed me that the bus driver had forgotten to stop for her on the first route and had to return to deliver her to the appropriate location. Questioned whether she had been scared, she looked at me with amazement, stating calmly, "If he picked me up, he had to bring me home." I was reassured—elated, in fact—to realize how secure she felt even after such a short time in a new town.

The twins attended nursery school a few days a week, as finances would permit. The most accessible child-care center was located at the local Protestant church. Since the program was nondenominational Alex and I felt it would be good preparation for our children, who were immersed in Jewish culture at home, to become acquainted with kids from different religious backgrounds.

The decision to enroll the children in that nursery school was a good one for our values. One day Bernice, who also attended occasionally after school, came home relating with pride that the pastor had told the kids that Jesus was a Jew. While this statement was apparently not unusual in Watchung Christian circles, I later learned, the experience shocked me in a most positive way. In the stringently Catholic Poland where I had been raised and to which I had returned after the war, no one—let alone a member of the clergy—would have dared to make such a statement. Its utterance confirmed for me the intelligence and open-mindedness of the minister and the community he served.

This event was particularly significant since, having survived the Holocaust and having moved to a Christian town, I wore my Jewish identity with some degree of discomfort. I remember, for instance, the High Holidays arriving a month after we had moved to Watchung, and I had absentmindedly permitted the children to invite a Christian playmate to join us for supper. When I realized I would be preparing a traditional Rosh Hashanah holiday dinner and we would be celebrating this religious occasion, I instinctively revoked the invitation, feeling uneasy about sharing the table with someone who was not Jewish. Years later, after many positive experiences with my American Christian friends, I regretted that I had deprived the child of a lovely experience.

Before a local election only two months after we had moved to Watchung, a candidates' night was sponsored by the local chapter of the League of Women Voters, or LWV. One of the candidates for City Council belonged to a clique of people who had served in office for a number of years. An irresponsible alcoholic, the councilman enjoyed a post that had been well-greased and well-assured. His opponent presented himself as a bright man with good ideas and a lot of energy. I related to Alex the information I had collected about the competitors, and he in turn conveyed it to his boss, who also lived in town. In the end, the incumbent lost by two votes, and the opposition gained a seat on the council. It was the first time I had witnessed democracy in action, and it stood in marked contrast to the prejudice against the American way of life that had been fed to me by the Communists. In big cities perhaps one vote seemed like a grain of sand. But here we lived in a fish bowl, and we saw firsthand the difference that one vote can make. The experience provided a strong incentive for me to play an active role in the work of the LWV.

In cosmopolitan Watchung people of many backgrounds resided. Though there were very few Jews and I believe Alex and I were the only Holocaust survivors in town, we felt accepted without any reservations. There was a pervading sense of mutual respect and pride in heritage among our fellow townspeople.

Our traditional Jewish observance of holidays at home made our children strongly aware of their Jewish background. One incident particularly filled me with pride. When Mark's first-grade teacher asked the class to write a letter to Santa Claus, he wrote, "Dear Santa Claus: Thank you; I have already received my gifts for Hanukkah, but how is your wife?"

While someone else might have felt angry about the teacher's infusion of the Christian Santa into a public school, for me the emphasis lay elsewhere. As a child in Krakow I too had attended public school, yet in my school catechism was taught and there was an altar where my classmates prayed to Mary and Jesus—all taking place during the school day. Admittedly the Catholic-lesson period was my favorite time of day. When the priest—a jolly, rotund, and friendly man with a ready smile—would enter our classroom, I would chat with him about schoolwork and current events, after which I and the other Jewish girls were excused to go to other classes. Rather than feeling slighted for having to leave my classroom during catechism lessons, I looked forward to spending the hour in higher grade and learning advance subjects. I considered the requirement a privilege. Jewish children did not receive religious education. Nonetheless, compared with my children's Watchung experience, religious icons and expressions within my public school environment were ever-present, and Mark's assigned letter to Santa—which glowed with comfortable consciousness about his Jewish heritage—was far from threatening. I felt that the children's admiration of Christmas trees and other people's observances would not endanger their commitment to Judaism. Instead, it enriched their lives and prepared them to live in a world of diversity.

The passing seasons, as we settled comfortably into our Watchung home, were marked by the physical development of the children, the expansion of the minds of all six of us, and the changing images of nature that appeared outside our windows. In the spring we would wake up to dense pink dogwood trees, multicolored azaleas, and the fragrance of jasmine and lilacs saturating the house. Tranquil and luscious greenery blanketed the grounds in the summer, and in the fall every hour produced such a different shade of gold that washing the dishes in front of the kitchen window facing a mountain became a treat. The winter produced further visual excitement. The snowcapped evergreens cast a fairy-tale picture, which following freezing rain resembled an enchanted crystal forest in which ice-encased branches sparkled like diamonds when the sun shone. For three years there was no covering on the windows, allegedly to prevent the loss of even a single moment of this exquisite view. This was as good a justification as any, considering that our budget did not allow an investment in curtains; better to put the blame on nature than bemoan our lack of funds. As soon as we could afford the many yards of fabric needed to cover the large windows, I embarked on the job of sewing curtains, enjoying the creativity and ignoring the fact that buying cloth rather than the finished product was still dictated by limited finances. The circumstances did not faze me in the least. I had so many times throughout my concentration camp internment been saved from death by my creativity and handiness that I had learned to find in them a source of satisfaction and comfort.

When the children were settled in their school lives I ventured into involvements outside the home. The LWV gave me an opportunity to meet and work with thoughtful and smart women. The League opened new vistas for me, fueling my enthusiasm, which in turn was followed by an invitation to join its executive board. While some of my fellow Leaguers had lived in town for generations they did not shut the organization's doors to newcomers or to people of different nationalities. I viewed the League's acceptance of an immigrant relatively unfamiliar with the American political system as a fine example of the society's values. It was clear to me that in America if you were willing to roll up your sleeves and pitch in you would encounter many open doors behind which lay endless opportunities. I was determined to step through these portals.

The members of the League taught me about this country, but they were also interested in learning about my past, which I saw as integrally related to the crucial role of this organization. I believed it was vitally important to use the atrocities through which I had lived as a warning and an education, particularly in the context of a democratic society.

The issue of welfare was the one topic of vocal disagreement between me and other members of the League. I felt bothered that society would essentially write off a segment of the population by giving handouts. I had witnessed the negative effects such a policy had wreaked in the displaced persons' camps in Germany after the war, observing how the process had produced many black marketeers. I advocated instead for job-training programs and assistance in self-help as ultimately more humane and productive.

My years of work with the League provided a priceless education as well as long-lasting and wonderful friendships. One year I was even elected as a delegate to the League's national convention in Atlantic City. My involvement caused me to feel like a truly integral member of this country, of which I had initially felt so suspicious.

Now America was my nation.

Another organization that offered me a chance to participate was the Girl Scouts of America, with which I got involved when Bernice was seven years old. The group was in need of parental leaders and I quickly volunteered. That I shared the role with an Italian Catholic woman gave us an opportunity to teach the girls in the troop about both Christian and Jewish holidays. Again, although there were surely silent dissenters who disagreed with the teaching of religious customs in the context of a semipublic organization like the Girl Scouts, I was happy to give Christian girls the opportunity to enjoy matzo on Passover and to teach them the Hanukkah story. Likewise, Jewish girls learned about Christmas and Easter. If the troop learned one thing it learned about diversity and tolerance—the most important values in my book. Even Mark attended the troop's meetings as an honorary Girl Scout.

Word got around, and I was asked to teach some Jewish songs and dances for the Christmas pageant in the school the children attended. The event evoked great joy for me as I watched some of the dancing students perform the beautifully staged *hora* that I had taught them. Amazingly the vigorous movement brought the pioneering feeling of Israel to the stage of a Watchung public school as part of the Christmas pageant. How great it felt that despite the past during which I had suffered because of my religious identity, my children were living in harmony and mutual respect with many people from a spectrum of religious and cultural backgrounds.

After several years of volunteer leadership roles in Watchung the hesitation I had initially felt about moving to a non-Jewish neighborhood totally disappeared. It would have been inexcusable for me, with the past I had barely survived, to sit on the sidelines, so I embraced the challenge to be active. I learned to balance home life and voluntary activities without shortchanging anybody. Being a part of my children's developmental years was both an obligation and a joy. But being active helped me grow personally and simultaneously improve the world in small ways.

When the time came to prepare the children for *B'nai Mitzvah* (religious coming of age) our Eastern European background initially made us feel uneasy about joining a Reform Temple. With few exceptions the Jewish families I had known as a girl had belonged to their congregations for generations. In most of the synagogues the ideologies espoused were much more observant than the practices of their members. Despite the contradiction this was a tradition with which almost everyone felt comfortable. Only a handful were interested in attending congregations with more liberal religious philosophies.

It soon became obvious to us that the tenets of Conservative Judaism did not conform to our way of life or thinking. It felt hypocritical to eat nonkosher foods and then attend an institution that preached the observance of *kashrut* (Jewish dietary law). We shuddered at the dishonesty of people who parked around the corner from the synagogue on days when driving was traditionally prohibited, then walked into the building. We did not agree with teaching our children rules we did not practice and soon became determined to find a synagogue that matched our beliefs and manner of living.

We also had a disagreement with the Conservative rabbi of the synagogue about Bernice's Jewish education As a result of our Eastern European customs we had not thought about her *Bat Mitzvah* (Jewish girl's confirmation) and had not started her in the Hebrew school program until she was 12 years old, just one year before her *Bat Mitzvah*. For the Conservative rabbi this duration did not prepare her properly in the Hebrew school environment. Instead, he recommended a private tutor. To Alex and me, however, the most important aspect of Jewish education was the involvement and interaction with Jewish children and the development of friendships with classmates; so the rabbi's solution was not acceptable.

The other synagogue in town was Temple Sholom, which was Reform; the religious convictions of the vibrant and active membership accorded with our way of life. We were welcomed with open arms by the congregation's dynamic leader, Rabbi Sidney Nathanson. In exchange for Bernice's promise to continue her Hebrew school education an additional three years until her Confirmation in tenth grade, Rabbi Nathanson admitted her to a class preparing for the special occasion. We were happy about the compromise.

Staying in religious school during Bernice's teenage years in the tumultuous sixties compensated for the lack of a Jewish education in the public schools of Watchung.

Joining Temple Sholom enriched our family life. Attending services and celebrating holidays made us feel a part of an extended family circle. It compensated for the absence of relatives, the world mother and I had known in Krakow where family members had played such an important role. mother, still struggling with her English and reluctant to dismiss the prohibition against riding to temple on the High Holidays, nonetheless loved attending services. Despite the more lenient rules to which the community adhered, the old melodies provided her with the nostalgia she craved, and the warmth of the congregants made attendance very pleasurable. We all felt a sense of belonging at Temple Sholom.

In 1968 we celebrated Bernice's *Bat Mitzvah*, which was held on the Jewish harvest festival of Sukkot. Bernice chanted her prayers in a beautiful Hebrew. Poised on the *bima* (altar) she conducted the service with dignity and self-assurance. Mother, Alex, and I were almost frozen with pride as the ceremony progressed. We were celebrating our Jewish heritage with joy. Following the *Bat Mitzvah* service we had a small family celebratory lunch in the traditional *sukkah*—a hut with a woven roof overlaid with branches and leaves—that we had constructed at home for the occasion.

Our choice of synagogues proved wise. Not only did Bernice continue her Jewish education but later she joined the youth group, ultimately becoming its president. Indeed, several of Bernice's classmates became so interested in Jewish education that following their Confirmation, they requested that a class be formed on the topic of great Jewish philosophers. To conduct it we managed to find a young rabbinical student at the Reform Hebrew Union College named Josh Gordon, a charismatic intellectual who challenged the group in a very positive way, and the students attended his course with enthusiasm.

Two years after Bernice's *Bat Mitzvah* it was the turn of the twins to celebrate their joint *B'nai Mitzvah*. The Temple Sholom sanctuary at the time was a large brick space with few objects other than a bank of marbleized, pastel-colored windows resembling shower doors. While the environment contributed little to the atmosphere of a house of worship, our two small figures with angelic voices chanting ancient prayers infused the room with spirituality. Like their older sister two years before they stood at the pulpit ordinarily occupied by the rabbi and cantor, and they faced an adoring congregation of relatives and friends.

When the Saturday temple services had concluded the guests were invited to our home for a reception. On that May 23 1970 nature celebrated with us. After a week of rain the sun shone brilliantly, illuminating pink, purple, and white azaleas that opened their blossoms in a symphony of colors on cue for the occasion. The house stood majestically on top of the hill, presiding over the garden that bustled with those whom we had invited to share this meaningful moment in our lives. The wholesome picture reflected what we felt in our hearts.

The *Bar Mitzvah* ceremony, observed as is traditional on *Shabbat* (Saturday), made it impossible for our Orthodox family members who did not live nearby to attend. Their custom prohibited them from traveling on *Shabbat* and most Jewish holidays. Wanting them to be a part of the celebration and respecting their beliefs, we held a second reception on Sunday.

In a steadfast sentiment that dated back to our family life in Krakow, despite the diversity of religious observance in our extended family—from very liberal to extremely Orthodox—we all treated each other with great respect. Being familiar with the Jewish traditions and the dietary laws of *kashrut*, I considered it my duty to stay strictly within those rules as a hostess for our guests. No meat was mixed with dairy. Every food item was originally packed and stamped with a rabbinical seal attesting to the *kashrut*; and the only dishes used were paper with plastic utensils, all enclosed in their original wrapping to assure they had not been touched by nonkosher foods. My relatives were very comfortable and enjoyed the party because they trusted my adherence to the Jewish laws. The preparation gave my children an opportunity to learn some customs as well as respect for others' convictions.

A month after the twins' *B'nai Mitzvah* Rabbi Nathanson met me in the temple lobby and invited me to join the school board.

The Hebrew school met two afternoons per week and every Sunday. Although the curriculum was filled with a range of subjects from the Hebrew language to Jewish culture to biblical studies, the program needed improvement. The children were not interested in the materials, and the teachers were not providing stimulating instruction. I felt flattered to be asked to help revise the curriculum. Although I had been very involved with the youth group and had become a familiar figure at the temple, it surprised me that as a new member I was being given an opportunity to participate in decisions of significance involving youth education. I regarded this as a great responsibility.

I became an outspoken member of the committee and was greatly surprised and honored a year later when I was asked to take over the chairmanship of the school board even though I was its newest member. All my predecessors had been men and had occupied seats on the temple's board of directors before they had assumed the post which I was being offered—and which I accepted.

The time was the 1970's. It was difficult to reach students using traditional teaching methods, and more innovative ideas flourished. The school director I inherited was a devoted and hard- working man but too traditional and rigid for the children's mindset. The second year into my tenure I embarked on a search for someone more dynamic and communicative in a way to which students could relate. A young rabbinical student named Ron Kronish accepted the job. Ron was creative, and he recruited intelligent, young, and progressive teachers. He also involved the parents in working out his methodologies. Among other activities he held weekly breakfast round- table discussions under the guidance of skilled teachers in which children confronted their parents to discuss their differences. During a period when intergenerational communication was virtually nonexistent, this practice was welcomed. In the spring Ron organized camp-outs under the trees, replete with singing and learning. While some of the traditionalists in the congregation worried that we were bringing a revolution to the school, the increased attendance and interest of students was enough proof of the program's success.

That year Rabbi Nathanson suffered an aneurysm on his brain which left him incapacitated, and the board of directors was left to run the temple for a year. As president of the school board I felt like a remote-control operator since there were so many changes being implemented that needed instant attention, and yet I had to rely on intermediaries to deliver my messages and request action without having a vote on the board. In need of a direct line of communication I was appointed to be the first female member of the board of directors to represent a significant committee. This determination was soon followed by a decision of the progressive directors to invite the president of the youth group to have a voice on the board. It so happened that Bernice was appointed as the first voting youth representative.

It was a great pleasure to attend board meetings with Bernice. Only 16 years old at the time, she was treated with great respect by the men and encouraged to voice her opinions. With Rabbi Nathanson ill and deciding to retire in Florida, Bernice and I were both invited to be members of the pulpit committee assigned to select a new rabbi.

Toward the end of the year a problem developed in the Hebrew school involving a difficult student. One day he provoked his teacher, who lost his temper and gave the boy a swat. The teacher apologized, and we disciplined him for his action, but an internal battle ensued. The majority of the students praised their beloved teacher and threatened to leave the school if he was dismissed. They had learned a great deal from him. Although I strongly disapproved of the teacher's action I felt he was very valuable to the school, and I did not let him go. At the annual meeting, however, the parents of the boy demanded that I be removed from my position for refusing to dismiss the teacher.

Tempers were heated. At the same time, the ailing Rabbi Nathanson was being replaced by a young man, Rabbi Jerry Goldman, and it seemed to me to be counterproductive for him to take over a split congregation. To calm the situation I invited the parents of the boy to join the school board so that they

Bernice's graduation 1973 – Irene, Luna, Alex, Bernice, Mark and mother

could have policy-making input. My action, mirroring the reformation of the time and the need for sometimes radical solutions, surprised the other school board members.

Three weeks later that family had a *Bar Mitzvah* for the boy, and I was among the invited guests. In order to quell any lingering hostility Alex and I attended amid speculation that we would not do so. The incident was resolved peacefully. Afterwards the mother attended one school board meeting then dropped out because of personal problems she was confronting.

With Rabbi Nathanson ill, different board members took turns representing our temple in community meetings normally attended by rabbis.

Because of their gender bias some of the Conservative rabbis were not receptive to my participation. One resorted to addressing me through his colleagues to emphasize his point that traditional men do not deal with women in leadership roles. While the gesture was meant to intimidate me my ego was not crushed so easily. His actions neither deterred my attendance nor prevented me from expressing my opinions and taking part in decision making.

Indeed, my commitment was so intense that at year's end the congregation was forced to change the title of an annual award from "Man of the Year" to "Award of the Year." I was its first female recipient.

Rabbi-in-training Ron Kronish served only one year as school director, but he made significant and welcome changes. With the coming of Rabbi Goldman, Temple Sholom had a young scholar capable of guiding the school in new and exciting directions. With the school now in the hands of people with outstanding leadership qualities I knew the time had come for me to step down after four years. I rarely held any post for more than five years; there are too many other people who can offer their leadership and too many additional interesting opportunities to explore.

I was delighted when I discovered in 1995 that Rabbi Ron Kronish, living in Israel, had created a dearly needed organization for dialogue among Christians, Jews, and Muslims.

EAR van, 1973

Chapter Twenty

EAR

This was a time of many transitions for our family. In the early 1970's the Occupational Safety and Health Act, or OSHA, was passed. Its purpose was to protect workers from the injurious effects of the workplace, and one of the concerns addressed was hearing loss in noise-creating industries. The audiological testing envisaged as compulsory under the new legislation presented an opportunity to establish a meaningful and needed enterprise. As a side business, therefore, Alex and a group of three other men formed a partnership that created Environment Acoustical Resources, Inc. (EAR, Inc.), an industrial hearing-conservation company designed to accommodate anticipated requirements arising out of OSHA.

As a student of acoustics at the conservatory in Krakow I was very interested in the subject. EAR, Inc. projects gave me an opportunity to work in the field, while learning about the social consequences of deafness. Alex's three partners—all men—were experts: one was a prominent acoustical expert, another an audiologist, and Alex and the third partner were business people. They purchased one of the first vans equipped with audiological testing facilities.

To gain expertise in this field I got an audiometric technician's license. I then put my new-found learning into action. Believing in the importance of prevention I organized the conducting of hearing tests in schools to alert young people to the damaging effects caused by blasting music through earphones.

Other EAR, Inc. educational activities included promoting awareness about trauma connected with hearing loss and obtaining sponsorships through the Lions Club to offer public testing in communities. The press coverage we received—in part fueled by a newspaper reporter whose brother suffered from hearing loss—provided a lot of information on the subject to the public. While this branch of the business was socially beneficial and I felt we were delivering a useful service, it was not income-producing. I counted on the industrial aspects of the firm to cover the expenses.

Nonetheless, the faltering economy of the time altered political priorities, and the Carter administration did not enforce the OSHA programs. This neglect had a heavy impact on our business, threatening bankruptcy. The innovative programs that served the community could not compensate for the lost dollars.

The EAR, Inc. partners were businessmen, and bankruptcy would have been a terrible blow to their individual and collective credit ratings. I was determined to protect our family credit, which was tied to Alex. The board therefore elected me to assume the presidency, and it became my obligation to protect the credit and avoid any legal consequences in case of financial failure. The only solution I found was to sell the company without impairing the partners' credit. Amazingly I found a means to accomplish the task and even get off debt-free.

While proud, I noted with some disturbance how worthwhile volunteer activities, like the management of the religious school, were regarded as relatively unimportant while becoming the CEO of a commercial enterprise, however insolvent, commanded great admiration.

My work with EAR, Inc. took me away from the house daily, leaving mother with our lovely Polish housekeeper Genia, a welcome companion, though no adequate substitute for the family. I felt guilty that mother was confined to the house, but there was little I could do to alter the situation. In contrast to my extroverted personality, which mirrored my father's, mother had always been a quiet lady, preferring handiwork to community meetings. Joined by a birthright we were otherwise the two most unlikely individuals one could imagine to walk the path of life together. Yet, as was the case in the mutually respectful relationship between mother and father, we loved each other and accommodated each other's needs despite our differences. My responsibilities took me in different directions than she was inclined to follow, but she never clung to me; rather, she respected my guidance, accepting every step I took without criticism. Her only aspiration, silently manifested, was to share the life stream in which we both swam and which she could not navigate alone. I can imagine how difficult it was for her to hang onto the turbulent daily experiences that typified my life.

Mother's portraits, 1946-1974

Chapter Twenty-one
Mother

Mother had arrived in 1957, just in time to help me raise the children. As she had done during the war she accepted my leadership with great respect. She acknowledged the fact that this was my house, and she accepted my directions. She conveyed quiet wisdom and great love. The children adored her, and having one more generation to live with greatly contributed to their understanding of older people. The world did not revolve around them. They had to care for someone too and at times make concessions.

They passed the test with flying colors. In 1970 mother was left to take care of them while we were on a trip. She did it so well that she continued to do it quite often. Getting around Watchung without public transportation was a challenge they managed very well.

One time, however, her child-care abilities were put to the test. In the middle of the night mother had a heart attack. Bernice was 15 at the time, and the twins 13. They called an ambulance immediately, but could not locate us at our hotel. The girls went with mother to the hospital to translate for mother and the doctors, while Mark was left behind to serve as an information link. In a strange way it was fortunate that we were not home. Remembering the conditions in Polish hospitals, mother was very frightened to be admitted to one. It was out of consideration for the children she agreed to it immediately.

She spent a month in the hospital, and we had her for another four years.

In 1972 we decided to celebrate mother's 80 birthday by spending a month in Israel. We rented an apartment in the center of the city, and while mother enjoyed the warmth and attention of her loving family and friends I took the children to explore the country. We visited every corner of that wonderful nation. Our most exciting trip was to the newly acquired Negev desert. The travel agent warned us of the difficulties involved in this adventure, but our youth led us to embark upon it anyway. In the 120-degree weather the bus was not air-conditioned. There was no toilet on the bus—any rock served as one. But it was the arrival at the gates of the Santa Katarina monastery that really tested our patience. To enter one had to wear long pants and sleeves. A young group that traveled with us was not aware of the rule and two boys had only shorts. Utilizing my sewing skills we found a blue sheet and I hastily fashioned two pairs of pants just in time before the gates were closed for the night, saving the boys from having to sleep outside the gates in a bus. At 4 a.m. we were awakened to start our trek to Mount Sinai. First to greet us as we left the monastery was a field of camels led by Bedouins, bathed in blue moonlight. Its mysterious appearance made us believe that we were in biblical times. The long and arduous climb that followed gave us a lot of time to reflect on the hardships people endured in ancient times.

The trip ended in Sharm el-Sheikh, where the only escape from the blistering sun was an air-conditioned dining room that served the most horrible food. After this repast the group left for Tel Aviv while we awaited our flight to Eilat. Unaware that there was no airport we were stranded on the beach for five hours. When the time came to depart I asked for a taxi, to the amusement of local people. This was not Tel Aviv, and there was no transportation. Luckily a tourist bus came and the merciful driver took us to the airport. When we got to Eilat the hotel receptionist thought that a bunch of hobos had come from the beach, so unkempt were we after five days without a bath.

In Tel Aviv throngs of friends and relatives gathered every night in our apartment, eager to meet my family and reunite with old friends.

The year 1974 signaled a major change in our family life. The children were growing up, and the years of a full house bustling with activities were coming to an end. Bernice had left for college in 1972, and the twins were preparing to leave in the fall. Taking care of the family had been the focus of mother's life since the day she had first arrived on American soil, and the "empty nest" prospect frightened her.

As a senior in high school Mark took a job at a kennel where the owner doubled as a dogcatcher. One day Mark came home from work pleading the case of a Great Dane his boss had caught. The 150-pound dog had been abandoned by its owner and was facing destruction. It was just too difficult to keep him in a kennel. Sympathetic, Alex and I agreed to adopt him. Mark affectionately named him Toots, and the dog moved in with us.

Toots was an enormous and beautiful black and white harlequin whose height permitted him to lick my face while standing next to me. An oversized puppy that none of us in the family knew how to handle, Toots was very obedient to mother's orders. This little lady could command him in Polish better than any of us, no matter the language. Mother's relationship with our new family pet was ironic: Toots greatly resembled the dog owned by Amos Ghett, the brutal commandant of the Plaszow concentration camp. Three decades before, the sight of a Toots look-alike had projected shivers throughout the inmate population. Now, with Toots in our house, I came to realize that Ghett's dog had terrorized us by his sheer size; no one had been aware of the gentle character of the Great Dane breed. I found it amusing that this was the type of dog to which I would be giving shelter. Mother made no fuss about Toots's arrival, though she was puzzled as to why we decided to keep this monster!

Mala did not share my amusement. Since we had reunited at the dinner in New York we kept in close contact, and she visited our home often. But Mala retained vivid memories of Ghett's dog, and she felt traumatized by the presence of Toots. She would not enter the house unless we locked the dog in the basement.

At this time I came to realize I no longer actively carried the nightmares of my life in concentration camps. I had apparently moved on constructively with my life, to the point where I seemed actually free of the past trauma. I felt like a normal person taking in stride the antics of a boisterous pet.

The trauma of losing our family during the war made the anticipation of the children going away to college that much more painful for mother. Her busy mornings fussing over their breakfast and equally busy afternoons preparing evening meals were coming to an end. For years we had witnessed the sparkle in her eyes when she greeted the children returning from school. Its constant presence underscored for us the terrible loss we knew she would experience in adjusting to a relatively vacant house. The children had showered her with love, repaying with loving devotion the attention she had given them. Indeed, the children were so reluctant to leave mother alone—afraid that she would be lonely—that on Saturday nights when Alex and I returned home from various activities, we never knew how many children would be sleeping in the house. One evening we came back very late to find one of their Irish friends sitting alone in the recreation room. When asked why he was there, all alone, he explained that the group of kids who had gathered wanted to go out, but they were taking turns staying in our house to keep mother company. Despite the fact that she never felt comfortable enough to speak English, there was some unspoken communication between mother and the children's friends that created a strong bond. She was everybody's grandma.

Mother turned 82 in 1974, and her energy was diminishing. New ventures in which she could participate were not an option, particularly in the isolated area of Watchung. Even crocheting and embroidery were no longer able to keep mother occupied. Her tired hands could not create the beautiful works of art that had once filled her days and had left us with treasures. The household over which she had reigned for 19 years became too demanding physically for her deteriorating strength. Still, doubting her ability to be idle, I invented a slew of simple projects for her, the last of which was knitting cotton bandages for people affected with leprosy in Africa. Other than these distractions, she spent her days waiting for our return home.

The golden fall of 1974 gave us an opportunity to entertain many of our friends and family. My dear friend Mala had visited mother every week for years, and on a beautiful December day that year the two of them posed together for a special photograph. As I look back it seems as though all of her friends and family had visited the house within the last three months of her life, as if to say good-bye.

On December 11, over the eight-day Jewish holiday of Hanukkah, Alex was out of town, the children were busy, and Genia had gone home for the weekend. I realized this was a rare opportunity for mother and me to be alone. On Friday evening we went to temple, where the rabbi and members of the congregation greeted her very warmly. Despite her limited English she had developed close ties with the congregants.

That Sunday my son Mark, then a state youth group dance leader, was teaching Israeli dancing at the local Jewish Community Center's Hanukkah party, and we went to watch him. Although mother complained of not feeling well, she insisted on attending. The room was filled with people of all ages, following Mark's instructions with zest as they stepped to the beat of vibrant Israeli music. The pride in mother's eyes was evident as she admired her grandson so ably introducing the audience to national Jewish dances.

When night came and mother felt weaker, I summoned the doctor, who examined her but found no specific health problem. His diagnosis was supported by her deportment: the next day I came home early from my office at EAR, Inc. and cooked a supper that she ate with a hearty appetite, commenting that the meal was the best she had had in a long time.

Later that evening we realized that Mark, a member of the school's Russian club, needed to cook a dish for the club's party the next day. With an empty refrigerator on that dreary winter night, I offered to drive him to the store. Mother's companion decided to accompany us since she had spent the whole day inside the house. We knew that Irene was expected to arrive momentarily, so mother would be alone only briefly.

As we were about to leave, Mark said he did not want to leave mother by herself. My instincts confirmed his feelings, so I shut off the car and returned home.

After a few minutes I suddenly heard mother calling: "Lunia, Lunia, hold me; the room is spinning."

I raced to the room, followed by Irene, who had just arrived. Mother slipped into a coma in my arms as quietly as she had lived her life. Afraid to die alone she went quickly and in an undemanding fashion, asking only that I cradle her in the last minutes of her consciousness. As she had leaned on me since my teenage years in the ghetto, the camps, and life in the aftermath of the war, so in her dying moments did she expect my arms to offer her the peace she craved.

How rewarding it was to give her this last comfort! Mother and I had lived through so much together. Being able to hold her for her final farewell was one of the greatest gifts she had ever given me.

As her spirit moved rapidly along its path from life to death, Mark and Irene stood by her next to me. It was as if she had waited to say good-bye to everybody she loved except Bernice, who had just finished her final exams at the University of Michigan. For her first grandchild mother seemed to have waited long enough so she would not disturb her studies. Even in death she appeared to have considered the needs of the family first.

When I was 48 years old the part of my being from whom I had never separated thus suddenly departed, taking half of our shared experiences.

On a beautiful December Friday morning with the sun streaming into the sanctuary through the windows of the temple she had grown to love at the dusk of her life, a large crowd gathered for the funeral. Mother was eulogized by a Rabbi Goldman, whose language she could not understand but whom she had loved from their first encounter and who had responded to her in the same way. She was surrounded by family as well as old and new friends who had made her feel so at home in this land that had never ceased to feel strange to her. Our

Orthodox family traveled to New Jersey from Brooklyn even though the Sabbath was about to begin, with its Orthodox prohibition against driving. Our cousins had loved and respected mother so much that despite our different affiliations they took part in the Reform funeral and burial, even requesting to be pallbearers. This was a remarkable show of affection for which I was very grateful. Mother was the last of her generation, and the only one of that generation to survive the war. She was the matriarch of our whole, large family that had been rooted in Krakow for generations, and she was dearly beloved by everybody.

On Sunday while we were sitting *Shiva* (the seven days of mourning during which religious law prohibits immediate family members from leaving the house) the Orthodox family members visited from Brooklyn conducted a beautiful traditional service at our home. We spent hours reminiscing about the life of our family in Krakow and passing on to our children stories from the past. My cousins, many years my seniors, provided details that even I learned for the first time!

I was very grateful that the children were on vacation at that time, and I was not left alone. For days we talked about the compassion and warmth with which mother had blessed us. I felt it my responsibility to recall the turbulent years she and I had shared, from which we were somehow able to emerge strengthened by our scars, forging toward goals of a better life. Being surrounded by loved ones at that time made dealing with her death much easier.

Now I was the matriarch of the family, and I hoped to provide the same degree of sensible counsel with which she had always guided us. I constantly hear mother's voice, and it plays a big role in my decisions. She is eternally a part of me.

A few days after mother's death an account of the Jewish Center's Hanukkah party was printed in the newspaper. The accompanying photo showed mother lovingly watching her grandson as he choreographed the dancing. We were very glad to have this last memento.

Following mother's death I decided to pass on to my children the legacy she had left me; I wrote an ethical will to guide their decisions and behaviors after I am no longer here:

Ethical Will

December 20, 1974

Dear Children,

Now mother has passed away, and one day I will, too. Then the time will come for you to carry on the family tradition. To guide you on this task I would like to relay to you what the tradition has meant to me.

I was blessed with wonderful parents.

I inherited from my mother the love of the family she created. Even after the loss of my father, I felt the completeness of family in her presence. My strength to go on after the war resulted from the love and understanding with which she showered me despite the gaping hole in our lives engendered by the absence of those who were taken away.

My father taught me to love human beings, setting as an example the respect and love he showed for his father regardless of the callous treatment he had received as a young man. He taught me forgiveness, love, and optimism.

I hope you will remember me as someone who loved you very much and also loved many people around us.

While my past was rather difficult, I do not want you to feel sorry for me. I had a very fulfilling life. No life is free of tragedies, but do not let the negative episodes overshadow the rest of your life or become an excuse for not accomplishing your goals.

It is my greatest wish that most of all you will always love and support one another, both in joyous times and in the face of adversity. Do not be afraid to confront difficulties; eventually, your strength will make you victorious. Always forge ahead with positive thoughts, no matter what circumstances life brings you.

Bear in mind that you are not alone on this planet, and pay attention to the needs of others. Love your children unconditionally, and do not expect anything from them; the love will bear its fruits and will reward you beyond any expectations. Be a friend, and you will have friends. Find a purpose in life, and some of life's meanings will reward you with their clarity. Try to leave a legacy, no matter how large or small, that will affect future generations. Your impact is a component of something much greater. Just think: while one grain of sand does not seem very important, when multiplied, the granules compose a vast desert.

Do not hold grudges or anger; these feelings will only destroy your being without touching the objects of your scorn. Learn to ignore those who try to do you wrong; they will pay for their transgressions without your input.

And most of all: be positive.

Luna in Krakow, Wawel castle, 1991

Chapter Twenty-two
Poland Revisited

In the summer of 1975, after Bernice finished her second year of college, she decided to travel to Europe for eight weeks with two friends. In planning their itinerary, Bernice persuaded them that it would be an interesting addendum to visit some of the places in Eastern Europe where my family had originated. While part of me felt excited at the prospect of my daughter visiting my childhood sites, the Communism that raged in Poland at that time made me feel very uncomfortable about their going alone. With mother's death there was nothing keeping me back. Despite the strong restrictions on re-entry of Jewish emigrants who left Poland for Israel in the 1950's,

225

I volunteered to accompany them to Hungary, where family members still lived, and then to Poland.

I asked my son, Mark, to go to the Polish consulate in New York to apply for my visa. The clerk asked him where I had emigrated to when I had left Poland. When he told her I had gone to Israel she responded definitively, saying I could not get a visa.

A few weeks later I decided to try on my own. When the clerk opened my passport she indignantly informed me that she had already told my son I could not get a visa. I next asked a friend with connections at the consulate about the matter; his inquiry revealed that I had been blacklisted. He explained that the only way I would be able to obtain a visa would be to travel to the Polish consulate in Vienna, where they did not have access to the blacklists.

My friend's advice was good: I obtained my visa to Poland in the Austrian capital, where I met Bernice and her friends. But travel in Eastern Europe also entailed strict monetary rules. For a stay in Hungary we had to exchange $12 per day and had to spend all of it there; no local currency was permitted to leave the country. In Poland the amount was fixed at $9. The rules insured that visitors would not exchange currency on the black market, which would have provided 10 times the exchange rate. At the Polish consulate in Vienna I exchanged the money for our seven days' stay in Poland. I had already obtained the Hungarian visa and currency in New York without any problems.

The next morning, on a beautiful sunny day, we took a hydrofoil on the Danube for the trip to Budapest. The vistas that opened before our eyes— beautiful castles atop majestic mountains—were breathtaking. We were so lulled into the magic of the scenery that we forgot our destination: some of the most oppressed sites in Europe.

In Budapest we were greeted by Erica and her husband, Piszta. Erica is the granddaughter of mother's older sister Regina Kaner and her mother, Berta Bella, who had emigrated from Krakow to Budapest with her parents during World War I. Bernice and I were immediately struck by the extent to which Berta resembled mother. Seeing her only six months after mother's death prompted very warm feelings. Berta proudly showed us her family pictures, including a wedding photo of my parents. While I was sad that mother would never see it, the photo was a very welcome addition to my family album containing pictures dating back to 1903 collected from relatives and friends around the world.

Berta had survived the war with false papers identifying her as a Christian. Erica, born in 1944, was raised in the Christian faith. Even in the late 1970's, neither of them felt comfortable associating publicly with Jewish relatives. Their apartment was located across the street from the main synagogue of Budapest, the Dohany Synagogue. When we went there on Friday evening to attend services Erica departed from us around the corner. I was so sad to see that 30 years after the war she still did not feel comfortable with her Jewish roots, regardless of the religion she chose to practice.

After several days of sightseeing and dining on wonderful Hungarian food, it was time to depart for Poland. Although armed with my visa I still worried about my blacklisting. We decided to travel by train, hoping that word had not reached the railroad checkpoints. Late Friday night we boarded a train heading directly to Krakow.

The remaining challenge in our itinerary was the need for transit visas to present in countries through which the train passed, even if the passengers did not get off. At about midnight the train stopped at the Czechoslovakian border, where we had not planned to disembark. Not carrying Czechoslovakian visas, we were taken off the train and surrounded in the blackness of the night by border guards pointing machine guns at us. In panic we watched our train pull out. We were led to a one-room railroad station; our ignorance of the Hungarian language precluded our comprehending what would ensue. After approximately one hour the authorities brought in a railroad worker who spoke German, the language in which I had learned to communicate on a superficial level during my years in the concentration camps. He informed us that at 4 a.m. a train would take us back to Budapest.

Surprised to find American tourists in this tiny town, the translator badgered us with questions. Fatigued and anxious to be left alone, I responded succinctly and not fully truthfully, unconcerned about his impressions.

His key interest focused on the fact that all four of us were able to afford to travel so far away from home. I told him that the children had worked for five years to save the $50 each of them needed for this trip. He asked whether Bernice, Judy, and Danny were all my children. Thinking about nothing other than ending this uncomfortable conversation, I responded affirmatively. My hour of reckoning came when 4 a.m. approached and he insisted on buying our tickets since the cashier spoke only Hungarian. Fortunately a border guard had allowed me to keep some Hungarian money although we had been leaving the country (a forbidden offense). I gave the translator that leftover money and our passports, and when he opened the passports and saw the different surnames of the children, he became enraged that I had lied to him. My survivor instinct kicking in again, I told him that I had been married three times, a fib that amazingly seemed to pacify him. When the now eagerly awaited train pulled in, we were the only passengers to board.

Upon arriving in Budapest at 6 a.m. Saturday we called Erica who, about to depart for her country house, changed course and picked us up. As fate would have it she was working for a travel agency and was able to get us plane tickets on the next day's Budapest–Krakow flight, which departed from Hungary only twice a week. We had no other transportation choices at that point. There was no time to get the Czechoslovakian transit visas because our Hungarian visas were on the verge of expiring on Sunday.

Fortunately the blacklist containing my name had not found its way to the airport. As the rickety plane neared Krakow my heart started pounding. I could see from the air the familiar sites that I had left 25 years before and thought I would never see again. The old city, never touched by any war— including World War II—looked the same. But the police state that now ruled over it was much harsher even than the one from which mother and I had fled. Zosia Rogowska, my college friend whom I had not seen since the day I left Poland, awaited us at the airport. Our years of separation melted instantly as we fell into each other's arms. Despite only sporadic correspondence our friendship had survived the time and distance. Instantly it felt as if we had parted just the day before.

On the way to Zosia's home from the airport we passed the beloved university where Zosia and I had spent many academic hours studying musicology and many social hours trying to overcome the myriad of effects of war and growing from teenagers into young adults. We passed the large Krakow post office still located on the corner of the street where I had grown up as well as the rat-infested apartment house on Gertrudy Street which mother and I had called home immediately after the war. How far I felt from all the varied experiences of the past—both the happy moments and the problems. They even seemed unreal.

I had made arrangements to stay with Zosia. For the children we rented an apartment from Zosia's friend. Since we were staying with private citizens rather than in hotel rooms, we were required to spend half a day reporting our sleeping arrangements at City Hall.

Being exposed to Zosia's living conditions, I was shocked to realize that while my life had progressed dramatically since she and I had parted, hers had increased in hardship. While her smile never faded her disappointment with the oppressive regime that was strangling her was obvious. Living alone without a family, having to take care of a despotic father, experiencing constant shortages of food and clothing, and being unable to speak or travel freely made her life very difficult.

Of course I was the tour guide for Bernice and her friends in Krakow. My job was to introduce them to the city and my life and the history of a large Jewish community that had virtually perished. Among our stops were the family homestead at 13 Wielopole Street, where I had spent a wonderful childhood. Stefa Zaczek, one of the tenants who was now an old lady, still lived there and welcomed us very warmly. The visit to the Royal Castle with its ever-untouched charm was enchanting. I showed the children the spots where Zosia, Jurek Karolus, Andzej Gromczakiewicz, and I had spent days preparing for exams—an experience to which Bernice and her college student friends could relate despite the distant location and foreign culture. On Friday we bought a *challah* (traditional Jewish braided bread), which was still baked even without Jews in town. We tore apart the warm bread and devoured it while walking through the streets of the old city. For dinner we went to the famous Wencel Restaurant in the city's square. Elegant waiters dressed in purple medieval costumes offered us elaborate menus bound in leather. It took me half an hour to translate the marvelous delicacies. Choosing the meal was a very difficult task, but when the waiter came, he informed us that only veal stew was available. The selection, served on beautiful china, was very tasty, and the price was right: $10 for all four of us.

Before departing we met with Victor Traubman, a sheet-metal worker who had been employed by my grandfather when he was building the house on Wielopole and who had made the double-bottom thermos for mother and me to smuggle out $200 in cash when we had emigrated to Israel. Victor was overjoyed to see me and to meet Bernice. He took us to the Jewish cemetery to visit the graves of my grandparents. We located the plots on the plan, but we were not able to find the graves in the neglected cemetery. When I gave him a few dollars as we said goodbye he looked around to make sure nobody witnessed the transaction. Having foreign currency was severely punishable.

Our final—and enthusiastically anticipated—destination was Vienna. Again, I did not want to travel by plane for fear that my blacklisting would be discovered. While I initially thought I would be able to purchase train tickets at the railroad station in Krakow, I quickly discovered that they were available only in the capital city of Warsaw, an unanticipated stop approximately five hours north to which we would be required to travel.

First there was the matter of buying train tickets from Krakow to Warsaw. We embarked on the trip at 5 a.m., encountering horse-driven carts, hoofs clicking on the cobblestone streets, bringing produce to the open-air market. We heard the blaring of the trumpeter from the tower of St. Mary's Church, hourly revisiting the centuries-old warning of the guard that the Tartars were invading. Childhood memories of prancing along the streets with mother and father and Niusia and my cousins and friends came back to life.

We finally reached the window at the railroad station, but after an hour of standing in line, we learned that we would not be permitted to buy a round-trip ticket. The repressive bureaucracy was driving me crazy.

Prior to traveling to Warsaw I had notified Adam Feil, a Warsaw resident and the brother of Wanda, my friend who was selling my beadwork in Bronowice, about our trip. Adam and Wanda were the children of Dozia, mother's best friend since childhood. Adam, who had obtained Christian papers, had survived the war in hiding. He had never returned to his Jewish roots; indeed, he was careful to hide them. He had married a Christian woman and had forbidden his mother to visit them for fear of having his Jewish identity exposed. Wanda, who had become a prominent foreign reporter in Poland, was also fearful that her Jewish roots might be discovered. Ultimately she emigrated to Germany and settled in Frankfurt.

It would take another day to buy our train tickets from Krakow to Vienna; so Adam offered to rent us a place at what he claimed was his friend's home, insisting that I accompany him to the apartment to get the keys while the kids waited in the nearby park. When we arrived a man I did not know was waiting for me, requesting that I exchange my dollars for his zlotys. This black market exchange was illegal, and I wanted no part of it. He kept me there for about an hour trying to force me with his persuasiveness. He said he was going on a trip and needed foreign currency, contending that this was the only way to obtain it since no more than $10 could be legally exchanged. I was very angry that Adam was willing to put me in this dangerous situation for the sake of either doing someone a favor or making some money on the transaction. I refused to budge from my position. Finally I left, and when we closed the apartment door I noticed a sign announcing that the apartment had belonged to the secret police.

While I feared that a listening device had been planted in the apartment, all the hotels were booked, and the kids and I had no other place to stay.

None of us slept the whole night, though. My nightmares of a police state gave me good reason to be concerned.

The next morning we went to a travel agency to buy our railroad tickets from Krakow to Vienna, only to learn that the simple task was another all-day proposition. The tickets were sold at the snail's pace of one an hour, and the transaction was accompanied by harassment. The tickets we were finally given called for a departure a day later than we had planned.

Back in Krakow I attempted to call the States to let Alex, Mark, and Irene know of our delayed arrival time. I quickly learned, however, that one could not make calls from Poland to the United States without ordering the service several days in advance. Zosia, however, figured out a way around that. Since a call could be made to Germany without delay I called Wanda Feil, Adam's sister, who had sold my beadwork in Bronowice and now was living in Frankfurt. Wanda called Alex in the States, and he called us within minutes.

While waiting at the railroad station for our train to Vienna Bernice decided to take a picture of Zosia and me standing under the sign that read "Krakow." Instantly a young man in blue jeans sprang to his feet, ready to arrest her for the illegal act of taking photographs at the railroad station. I pretended that I did not speak Polish and begged him to let her go. My ploy was unsuccessful until I took the cartridge with the film out of the camera and bit it open to expose and ruin it. That was how we lost all our memories of that horrendous segment of the European trip.

Finally aboard the train heading for Western Europe we had not yet played out our last encounter with the country of my roots. When the train reached the border with Austria we heard a great commotion. Apparently an Australian man had been caught with $300 in zlotys, which he had been attempting illegally to bring into Austria. The man had no tolerance for nonsensical Polish rules concerning legalities, and he argued with the border guard who approached me to act as a translator for the heated argument. Still somewhat traumatized by the memories of my last departure 20 years before and the series of bureaucratic hurdles we had just overcome—as well as not wanting to get caught in the middle of the dispute—I told him that

Australian and American are two different languages. He bought my statement, and a woman who appeared to be more seasoned than I in these kinds of affairs volunteered to translate. Judging from what she told the border guard, she knew exactly what she was doing; her translation reflected nothing that the man said. While the train was held up for about an hour as a result of this argument, she managed to solve the problem. I don't know how.

When we finally reached Vienna I was ready to kiss the ground.

Luna with mascot, 1980

Chapter Twenty-three
Olympics

Reflecting on the past two decades raised a troublesome question: had my life begun to stagnate? I decided to infuse new zest into it.

One day I heard the famous surrealistic painter Salvador Dali talking about the high price of his paintings. He felt their value was reflected in the large sums people paid to purchase them. Dali's view affected me rather deeply. I began to wonder whether I had been placed in the numerous positions I had held because of my capabilities or because I offered to serve without compensation—as a volunteer. This question weighed on my mind as I became aware of the need to impose stronger direction on my future.

My first move in that direction entailed writing a curriculum vitae, more with the goal of taking stock of my life than with the intention of applying for a job. Staring at the balance sheet of my achievements on paper boosted my low morale; I realized what a long road I had already walked, filled with family and community accomplishments.

I also took very American steps to boost my self-image by presenting a more stylish appearance. Falling prey to contemporary ideas of "the perfect body," I joined a drastic weight loss program, which enabled me to shrink from a size 14 to a size 6, all the while recognizing the irony that a former concentration camp inmate who had survived years of starvation was now denying herself food to enhance her appearance! I paid a high price for the weight loss, as I developed a host of complications culminating in a blood clot on my lungs from which it took me six months to recover. Bedridden, with time to think about the path that lay ahead, I felt more obliged than ever before to make constructive use of my life.

One day while recuperating in my sickbed I saw a television advertisement seeking personnel for the 1980 Winter Olympics to be held in Lake Placid, New York, and I decided to seize the opportunity to embark on a new venture. I had always been an avid fan of the worldwide games and was enticed by the prospect of participating in the event as a "citizen of the world."

About six months later I stopped at the Olympics employment office in Lake Placid, where I applied for a salaried position. I then sought out lodging and met a dynamic real estate broker, a ski instructor from Stratton, who informed me that the only paying jobs were in the kitchen and doing general maintenance work—and those paid no more than the minimum wage. She explained that for the Olympics, the exciting jobs were volunteer positions.

The tangible benefits I could receive as a volunteer included two uniforms, limitless tickets for events, and marvelous contacts I could make with people from all over the world. Compared to these opportunities, I could not see myself sweeping rooms or cleaning tables to earn what amounted to a relatively few dollars. In this situation Dali's analysis, I realized, was inapplicable.

After an hour-long telephone interview with the person in charge of volunteers, I was offered the thrilling job of managing housing for the international press.

While enthusiastic about the upcoming opportunity I was simultaneously nervous about plunging into a situation in which I had no idea what to expect. Mark offered to accompany me on the long drive to Lake Placid to help me settle into the month-long job assignment.

With Mark and his sunny disposition in tow I reported for my assigned job. When I arrived I was asked to take an evening shift position in the Lake Placid Hotel, which housed the international Olympics committee. The assignment initially seemed disappointing; I had been looking forward to meeting a fascinating and vibrant group of young international journalists rather than what sounded like a group of stodgy officials. Always ready to plunge into new adventures, however, I accepted the responsibilities to which I had been assigned. I am a strong believer in "Luna's Law," which, in opposition to "Murphy's Law," claims that if something can go right, it will.

At the commissary I was issued an Olympics uniform. Seeing me clothed in it, Mark smiled and blurted out, "This is the second time in your life that you will be wearing a uniform!" (The first uniform, of course, was the one I was forced to wear in the concentration camp.) His witty sarcasm pricked the balloon of my passing gloom. The humorous comparison of the attire that signified global fraternity to the striped prison uniform of Leipzig made me realize the absurdity of my anxiety.

The work-schedule proved to be to my advantage. The closest international airport to Lake Placid was in Montreal, Canada, located a few hours away. Consequently most members of the International Olympics Committee who arrived during the week prior to the opening of the games checked into the hotel in the evening—during my shift. This fact, coupled with the lack of sophistication of the administration of Lake Placid Hotel, which was run by local residents, gave me the opportunity to become acquainted with the heads of all the winter sports. Contrary to my initial prejudice they were a fascinating and approachable group of people receptive to the development of new relationships. As it turned out in contrast to the opportunities I was experiencing, the volunteers who worked with the press corps in the position I had initially sought were housed out of town in isolated, windowless rooms, and their jobs involved arranging accommodations by telephone rather than in person.

Dealing with officials from the Eastern Bloc nations was particularly interesting. Suspicious of American spies, the delegation from the Soviet Union would not even provide us with their arrival schedules, apparently hoping to catch us off-guard. The first evening on the job I was confronted by Russians who marched in a day early looking like a group of bronze seals: They all sported the same brown fur coats and hats, but those higher up in rank had fur collars, and the top brass wore full fur coats. They marched only in groups.

Their sudden appearance created great havoc. Since we had not expected any arrivals at that time, the manager had left for the evening without allocating rooms, and in the pre-cellphone, pre-beeper days, it was impossible to reach her after hours. Since the delegation had not yet been expected the hotel management had decided to make good use of the available rooms by renting them to participants attending a local railroad convention. My first day on the job I knew very little about the facility (indeed, the apartment I had rented was located off the premises, across the lake), and I felt myself panicking. I am quite certain that my reaction was exacerbated by my previous encounters with Russians. While I could not fathom the specific reasoning behind the delegation's failing to inform us of their arrival time, I understood the Kafkaesque and authoritarian spirit in which this group might react.

Stuck within their own cultural gaps and stereotypical beliefs, the Russian committee attributed the situation to orders on the part of the U.S. government to harass Communists. I'm sure they didn't believe me when I explained that the government had nothing to do with the hotel facility—that it functioned under the jurisdiction of the Olympics committee. But my friendliness, which they had not expected, seemed to pacify them. The fact that I could understand Russian and could communicate with them to some degree also helped defuse their apprehension.

Close to midnight the day before the opening of the games, the Mongolian delegation arrived. While the hotel was able to accommodate their small delegation, the Mongolians encountered a much bigger problem: in that pre-fax era, their advance request for credentials giving them the right to compete had not yet reached the committee. Here they were on the figurative doorstep of the Olympics, speaking only very limited English, with an application deadline a few hours away and no one but me available to help at that late hour! I took their official papers and, at a stroke before midnight, slipped them under the room door of Lord Killanin, the president of the 1980 Olympics committee. The next day *The New York Times* reported that someone had saved the Mongolian delegation with no time to spare.

During the course of these Olympic games, the United States announced it would boycott the upcoming Moscow competitions to protest the military intervention of the former Soviet Union in Afghanistan. The decision caused pandemonium to break out. Fears about international incidents spread like wildfire, and the press swarmed the hotel.

Security access was denied in the hotel to police officers and FBI agents. It was granted only to the private firm of Pinkerton Security Services. I presumed this decision had been made to demonstrate independence from host countries. However, the relatively inexperienced young people who had been assigned by Pinkerton were unprepared to deal with large problems, let alone international conflicts. Since I was a mature individual with the access needed to observe activities in the hotel, I found myself being approached by the FBI to keep an eye on events happening inside the halls and rooms of the Lake Placid hotel.

At first I thought this was a joke. I had a foreign accent— an Eastern European one at that! Moreover, my security clearance was still pending since I had stepped into the job only upon arriving in Lake Placid. Confused, I approached a member of the White House Secret Service accompanying Secretary of Defense Cyrus Vance to inquire whether the solicitation of the FBI had been genuine. I had to make this contact outside the hotel since these officers were not allowed inside. In response, much to my surprise, the Secret Service also enlisted my cooperation.

The culminating competition was the famous USA-USSR hockey game. Even I, who had never before attended a hockey game, came out to cheer for our boys. The exhilarating victory by the USA became a symbol of American superiority.

The job entitled me to many privileges, not the least of which was a pass to all events. Indeed, I was even able to bring my children to the games. What a joy it was to parade them through town, introduce them to my new friends, and share these wonderful events in person with them. Sometimes the members of the International Olympic Committee, or IOC, who stayed at our hotel invited me to their VIP boxes containing the best views of the competitions. Explanations of exotic events like luge or ski jumps were included in the ticket price. I was able to attend all the skating events, including the speed skating performances of Eric Heiden that earned him five gold medals.

Another privilege was experiencing the camaraderie and inclusiveness of the participants. I never dined alone. No sooner would I enter a restaurant, than people from all nationalities—even the Russians after a brief cooling-off period—would invite me to join their tables. In preparation for the winter weather I had outfitted myself in a fluffy white-lynx fur coat and hat, which made me look like a familiar mascot on streets, at international parties, and even at a local disco with young people, where I was treated as a mother figure! We felt like one big family.

My work as a volunteer at the Olympics was a highlight of my life. In addition to feeling as though I was living in a winter fairyland, riding to work across the lake on a horse or on a dog-driven sled, I felt that I had a hand on the pulse of the world. The sense of harmony that reverberated inside me reinforced some of the faith in people that my wartime experiences had stolen.

Luna in hard hat, 1979

Chapter Twenty-four
Temple Sholom: Construction

One night at 10 p.m. I received a phone call from the president of Temple Sholom, Hy Tobi, offering me the position of vice president of the synagogue board, with the option to continue on afterwards as president—in total, a six year commitment.

While the timing seemed right in terms of my personal life and goals, the larger political context was contentious, making the potential challenge daunting.

I figured that I would be 56 when I finished my term as president, and the prospect seemed very frightening. I thought my life would be over by then! Still, it did not take me long to accept the offer.

The temple was located in the city of Plainfield, where Alex and I had initially looked for a house before we settled on the property in Watchung.

In 1960, when we had been in the housing market, the homes in Plainfield had not seemed affordable to us.

On the surface Plainfield appeared to be the quintessential idyllic American town with tree-lined streets and beautiful one-family homes surrounded by manicured gardens. Unlike many other New Jersey townships Plainfield was multiracial. For a while the city used this fact to create a deceptive image of harmony in the schools and in the elegant downtown business district crowded with shoppers of every race. But deeper scrutiny revealed fractures in this picture, as evidenced by disturbances that broke out in the 1960's in the city center.

The temple stood in the city center, and I remember once taking the children to Hebrew school while an army tank guarded the intersection. I was strongly against the temple's following the path of the Jewish former residents and the Jewish institutions that had abandoned the city. I believed that our staying power would provide some backbone to the suffering town. In America divisions along economic and racial lines were foreign and offensive to me, and I could not—would not—accept them.

The synagogue itself, moreover, had been rooted to this plot of land for 70 years. Congregants had celebrated and commemorated events and holidays in that space for seven decades. The strength of these feelings and traditions weighed heavily at the outset of the time of contention; nevertheless, following the riots, the temple and school enrollment held firm.

But as time wore on, the temple's location began to lose its attractiveness in the minds of a number of congregants. The prospect of raising money for badly needed construction at a site that was guarded at every event in the midst of a blighted city was shaky. Plainfield had developed a stigma. Many people, reluctant to invest in a future there, opted to move into the suburbs.

The political debate weighed heavily on me as I was faced with the decision whether to assume the temple's vice presidency followed by its presidency. I knew that an affirmative choice meant taking on a challenge whose divisiveness would resonate both in my personal Jewish community and in the larger outside world, and the divisive polemic left me nearly breathless.

I also weighed a number of other factors. On the positive side, assuming we were successful in agreeing to keep the temple in Plainfield, the building would require a massive physical restoration, including an expansion of the school wing. The opportunity to work with architects and contractors to create a lasting legacy would fulfill some of my dreams. I had always believed that had my education not been interrupted by the war, I would have become an architect. Working as the head of the temple's board during this period of renovation gave me a first-hand chance to find out whether the profession was as exciting as I had always imagined.

Another incentive was the prospect of working with three people for whom I had great respect: Rabbi Jerry Goldman, who was a scholarly and magnetic leader, and two presidential predecessors who would be my teammates in managing the construction project: Judge Bill Drier and lawyer Bill Ginden, who also later became a judge. I did not want to pass up the opportunity to learn from any of these people.

Balancing my fears against the potential benefits—and slightly intimidated by the realization that a positive decision would pave my personal path until the "old age" of 56!—I accepted the offer.

The first item on the new board's agenda was whether or not to move the building. Coming from Krakow, a city that has existed for hundreds of years, I was a strong proponent of maintaining the facility where it stood. It was heartbreaking for me to see that the Orthodox synagogue and the magnificent Jewish community center, both of which had served thousands of Jewish people for many years, had folded their operations. I could not accept the thought of abandoning the city without attempting to heal its differences. I advocated my opinions with great passion, though I believe the final decision— which accorded with my position— was based largely on financial rather than philosophical or political considerations.

After the decision had been made to maintain the temple's locale in Plainfield, the renovation project needed to be put into action. Although I had been led to believe that the plans were in process, when I finally got the opportunity to review them I was dismayed to discover a skimpy patchwork. To me a temple was a legacy for future generations, and it was essential to build it in a manner intended to last.

My first active board role was to look for an architect who could offer more attractive plans. After conducting a search for someone with good aesthetic sensibilities as well as a sensitivity to limited finances, synagogue treasurer Natalie Darwin and I came across James Gaspari, who had just completed a lovely addition to a temple in the New Jersey town of New Brunswick. With James's assistance we constructed a blueprint for a structure destined to cost five times more than we had originally allocated, but the scope of the work was correspondingly more impressive.

Once the new plans were presented for approval to the congregation's membership, accompanied by hours-long discussion, they were accepted and embraced. We received strong financial and moral support.

The first great hurdle in turning our plans into reality was fund-raising, a responsibility that was to be shouldered by the rabbi, Bill Ginden, and me. (As a judge, Bill Drier was prohibited from raising funds.) None of us had garnered the necessary experience prior to this project. When we sought guidance from the Union of American Hebrew Congregations (the umbrella organization of Reform temples), it was suggested to us that in addition to the new construction, we should also make improvements to enhance the existing facilities. The combination, we were rightly told, would give greater incentive to prospective donors.

The original design and construction of the temple had been quite spartan and lacked the splashes of color that give warmth. Most notable in this regard were the large, marbleized pastel-colored glass windows in the sanctuary that, to my mind, resembled shower doors. Having grown up in Krakow, a city where several large Catholic churches house some of the most beautiful stained-glass windows I had ever seen, I suggested we replace the original windows in Temple Sholom with ones in which rainbow tones cascade in Jewish themes. Such a color scheme, I reasoned, would supplement the existing blue window centered over the altar.

The congregation gave me free rein to pursue my ideas, and the artist who had originally created the blue window submitted a breathtaking design containing six massive ' panels depicting the 12 tribes of Israel as well as Jewish holidays. Though the price tag was substantial and at first met with objections in view of the expenses generated by the larger construction project, we decided to offer the windows as memorial dedications. Our idea was a success. Donations supplied 10 times the cost of the windows, leaving us with both a much more aesthetically pleasing sanctuary and many bills paid.

The plans were continually adjusted, and my daily presence and rapport with the contractors ensured a flexibility that effected substantial savings and permitted the recycling of old materials. For example, one day while demolishing a room paneled in wood, I prevailed upon the builder to save the wood, and we later used it to cover a main hallway that would otherwise have been finished in cinder blocks.

The process, involving decisions made by consensus, was truly a labor of love for all of us involved. After five months the construction was completed—just in time to start the new school year and at a cost within 5 percent over the estimate. What a joy it was to walk through space ample enough to accommodate our enrollment and divided into clean, bright rooms—some even with skylights. The sanctuary was also vastly enhanced; in addition to installing the stained glass windows, we put down rust-colored carpeting and enhanced the furniture on the altar.

At the dedication of the renovated building I received the congregation's appreciation in a unique form: a personalized hard-hat! The credit, however, did not rest with me alone. The two Bills, Rabbi Goldman, James Gaspari, and builder Louis Garlatti—himself a member of his church board and therefore very attuned to our finances—had been wonderful teammates. On a personal level, the experience confirmed my feelings that

I would have liked to be an architect had my life taken other turns at an earlier stage.

There was an added benefit to the renovation that was extremely important to me. Our congregation reaffirmed our faith in the racially tense city that had been home to it for close to a century. The construction infused vitality into the congregation, drawing new members from Jewish communities in surrounding towns committed to our values at the same time as it strengthened interfaith relations in the community. It was one of the most important achievements of my life up to that time.

Unveiling of Flame by Natan Rapoport,
April 23, 1985

Chapter Twenty-five
Temple Sholom: Presidency

Although the congregation had known I would be the incoming president, some congregants had a tough time dealing with the fact that a woman would be at the helm. I was the first female president in the temple's 70-year history.

I resented the characterization of my assumption of the presidency as being such noteworthy news simply because of my gender. I found offensive the local newspaper's headline: "First Woman President in Temple's 70-Year

History." Did the scrutinizing fascination with the issue imply that women are less capable and I was an oddity?

I am not a trailblazer. I do jobs that need to be accomplished without regard to gender. My style is more personal than revolutionary. I had probably learned that philosophy from mother, who, though a daughter of a wealthy man, chose to get a degree in accounting and (to my grandfather's dismay) take a job working for the railroad. Whenever I had feared a barrier based on gender, mother would ask, "Are you less able than the men?"

Before I was officially approved as president of the synagogue, every move I made was, though accepted, scrutinized.. The role I had played in the temple's construction gave me credibility, ultimately paving the way for my approval.

Once the issue of gender was resolved, I was able to confront the more challenging issues. The job proved to be much more demanding than I had anticipated. The financial obligations required a lot of attention. In 1978 I purchased a computer and asked Bernice to design a program similar to today's Quicken. With that program installed I loaded into it the whole previous year's budget, and I was ready for action

The most arduous challenge involved balancing the interests of congregants whose lifestyles fell across wide social, economic, and personal spectrums. The unstated job requirements included the ability to be a tightrope-walker, a master politician, and a mind-reader.

My aim was to create an environment in which all the members of the diverse congregation contributed, whether in the form of finances or skills, thereby ensuring that each member would feel proud of his or her contribution.

In 1981, as the last year of my presidency was approaching, I felt the responsibility to leave a meaningful legacy memorializing the Holocaust. Alex and I were the only survivors who were members of the temple. I developed a friendship with Natan Rapoport, the sculptor of the Warsaw Ghetto Monument that had been erected in Warsaw in 1948. We had met in New

York in 1962, and I had long been looking for an opportunity to erect a piece of his work.

It took 14 years for my wish to materialize. One day on the streets of New York I ran into Judit Sobel, a painter from Poland. She was in a hurry on the way to visit Natan Rapoport and invited me to join her. When I entered the one-room studio apartment on Columbus Avenue in New York City, I found myself standing face to face with the small, modest, and unassuming man who had radiated so much power. After that evening I commissioned Natan to make my portrait; the long conversations we shared over the several-month sitting deepened our relationship. The more I saw of the art and sculptures he had created, the more my admiration for him grew—and the more I was amazed at the extent to which he continued to struggle financially, remaining relatively unknown.

It became my goal to ensure that one of Rapoport's statues would be erected in a large space open to the masses where the story of the Holocaust would be told through the eyes of Natan: without tears, with empathy, and most significantly, certain to evoke pride, not victimization, in Jewish people everywhere.

My admiration for Rapoport's work prompted me to invite him to the Temple to consult with us about selecting one of his small statues as a memorial to the Holocaust that would sit in our temple lobby. This alone would have been a great honor for our congregation. I simply wanted him to choose the place and theme.

But he had a much grander idea. The walls of the sanctuary were 20 feet tall and constructed of brick, which did not create an inspiring atmosphere for congregants' spiritual experiences. For Natan, however, the brick resembled the surface of the chimneys of the Auschwitz crematoria, and he felt the walls would provide an excellent background for a bronze relief. His idea was to create a flame in which a column of Jewish people with Torah scrolls being consumed by fire would be depicted. The statue would be crowned by an image of a woman holding a child above the fire, like a bird emerging from the ashes to create a new life. Natan envisaged a work of art that would be nine feet tall.

I found Natan's idea extremely compelling both for its artistic and its educational merits. While presenting a powerful symbol of the destruction of the Jewish community, the emerging child represented a rebirth of Jewish life with which I identified very strongly.

The proposal, however, was on a much more costly than the temple community had anticipated. Cognizant of the restraints and eager to bring this work into existence, Natan quoted us a price that was modest for the project though still too large for the temple to absorb after it had just incurred the school restoration expenses. Yet neither Alex nor I felt we could let this opportunity pass. So we offered to sponsor the project in memory of our families, dedicating the sculpture to "THOSE WHO PERISHED AND THOSE WHO SURVIVED."

The board immediately approved the plan.

It took Natan seven months to create the sculpture, and in April 1982 we were presented with an exquisite work of art. When the sculpture was nearing completion we began to think about the dedication ceremony we would hold. We knew it would be a major event in the life of our temple and the Jewish community as a whole.

A classmate of mine from Krakow's Jagiellonian University, Eddi Halpern, had become a recognized Israeli composer and served as director of the national Israeli radio station *Kol Israel* (Voice of Israel). I contacted Eddi, who, as someone who had survived the war in the former Soviet Union, was empathetic toward my cause. I asked him to compose music for the occasion, and he responded with a new composition for four voices, percussion, and organ called *Akedat Yitzchak* (Isaac's Sacrifice). Eddi dedicated *Akedat Yitzchak* to me.

The ceremony was scheduled for April 1982. A new governor, Thomas H Kean, had taken over the reins of the state only four months earlier. I knew nothing about him, but I believed that his presence would attract a lot of attention. I was introduced to his advisor to the Jewish community, David Kotok, who agreed with my assessment and made arrangements for the governor's attendance.

The presence of the young Governor Thomas Kean prompted Jeffrey Maas, director of the New Jersey chapter of the Anti-Defamation League

(ADL), to use the occasion to present a Holocaust curriculum for schools that had been developed by the ADL though not yet implemented.

Sunday afternoon, April 25, 1982, was a historic moment in New Jersey Jewish history.

A large crowd gathered at the beautiful reception on the front lawn of the temple property. Our African-American neighbors joined in our celebration, restoring at least for that afternoon a sense of brotherhood in what had become a racially torn city. In addition to the presence of Governor Kean, Natan Rapoport, and the composer Edi Halpern, the occasion was attended by the Plainfield's mayor and state leaders of the Jewish Federation and Anti-Defamation League. The dedication had been transformed from a happy event in our temple's life to one that was significant in the larger Jewish, local, secular, and even statewide community.

Inside the building the sun streamed through the stained-glass windows, painting a rainbow on the white linen that was draped over the sculpture prior to its unveiling. Eddi's music resounding in the sanctuary created a very solemn mood. Everyone present could not help feeling that something significant was taking place. When the covering came down to reveal the emotionally monumental *Flame* sculpture, a hush fell upon the hundreds who had gathered. In that moment the need to teach Holocaust education reached our collective souls.

Later that day we learned that the young governor had attended our event not for political reasons but because of his personal interest in the Holocaust. His father, Robert Kean, had been a congressman during World War II and had tried unsuccessfully to pass legislation that would have helped halt the genocide against European Jewry. Governor Kean had committed himself to avenging his father's ideological defeat. To our surprise and delight he appropriately used the dedication as a forum to announce the creation of a Governor's Council on Holocaust Education.

On October 2 1982 at a ceremony held at Kean College Governor Kean formally created the Council On Holocaust Education, I was appointed as one of its charter members along with Sister Rose.

The important educational contribution to future generations that flowed from the installation of *Flame*, together with the string of positive events that flowed from its dedication ceremony, were the highlight of my tenure as president of Temple Sholom. They also made clear to me the extent to which I wanted to be involved in the transmission of education about the Holocaust.

A month after the dedication Rabbi Goldman led a trip of synagogue youth to Amsterdam to visit the house of Anne Frank; although he had initially contemplated having the group travel to Poland to visit the death camps, the Iron Curtain prevented that possibility. I accompanied the rabbi and students on the trip and served as a resource person.

It was heartbreaking when I learned in 2003 that Temple Sholom was folding its operations in Plainfield. All the hard work and money invested in the temple's restoration was going to waste. The members of the new administration had their own vision. The beautiful stained-glass windows commemorating loved ones were going to be abandoned.

My first thought was directed toward the Rapoport's sculpture, *Flame*, which had been installed 21 years before with so much love and care. At the time of its installation Alex asked me to write an agreement with the temple that in case of moving the sculpture would revert to us. Not having enough foresight I neglected to do it. Now I had to face the consequences.

From the moment the Museum of Jewish Heritage was built in Battery Park I have dreamed of having the sculpture there, and now the time had come to tackle the problem of getting it there.

I sought an introduction to the museum's director, David Marwell, and found him to be an intelligent man who understood the significance of Natan's work. But to my greatest surprise the museum was in a process of building a substantial addition. I arrived in the nick of time, just as they were framing the new building. He immediately delegated the curator, Ivy Barski, to inspect the sculpture, and upon her recommendation the room they chose for the piece was built to accommodate it. My joy had no bounds. Had I come a month later this would not have been possible, and I don't know what would have been the fate of this significant sculpture.

Natan, Major General Francis Gerard and Luna, Foundry, Peekskill, 1984

Chapter Twenty-six
Liberation Monument

In May 1982, shortly after the unveiling of the *Flame* in Temple Sholom, Governor Kean responded to Natan's invitation to visit his studio. Natan invited me to join them.

One of the sculptures in Natan's studio that made a great impression on me for its depiction of the strong helping the weak was a wax moquette portraying an American soldier carrying the limp body of a survivor. So closely were the two joined that it appeared as if they shared the beating of a single heart. The time was about a decade after the Vietnam War, when some people looked upon American soldiers with contempt. As a Holocaust survivor who owed my life to the Allied forces, I had a vastly different impression of America's military arm. I loved Natan's moquette of the liberation because it showed America's contribution toward saving humanity.

Originally the statue was to be commissioned by a small Westchester County town where it was to stand behind the city hall. In the end the town council chose not to allocate money for the project, and the moquette waited in Natan's studio. Anticipating the governor's visit and hoping this image would inspire him to head the project of casting the liberation in bronze, I suggested to Natan that he place the moquette in a prominent place.

My plan worked. When Governor Kean set his eyes on the moquette, he immediately agreed that a project be undertaken to erect it fittingly as a monument. Arlington National Cemetery near Washington was the first proposed site, to which Natan replied that he worked for the living, not for the dead, and that he would like to have the monument stand where children could visit it and learn about compassion. Furthermore, erecting an artistic structure in or near Washington, D.C., would have involved a lot of red tape, thereby consuming a particularly long time. The 71-year-old Natan wanted to proceed expeditiously lest he die mid-project. He also wanted to have the structure built during the administration and under the jurisdiction of Governor Kean.

As it happened Natan died exactly two years after the statue's completion.

Armed with our marching orders we ventured to a meeting at the Department of Defense where we encountered a room full of uniformed soldiers. Like many Eastern Europeans, including me, Natan was very intimidated and suspicious of people in uniforms. But it did not take long for him to be won over by the warm smile of General Francis Gerard. With his strong hand and loving heart he started things moving with military efficiency. His enthusiasm permeated all those who participated in the project.

Natan cherished his relation with General Gerard. It was the general who despite his busy schedule arrived in New York to celebrate with Natan when he received an award from the National Sculptors Society, one of the major awards he received. We all knew that without the general's commitment this statue would never have been erected.

Among the suggested locations were the Delaware Water Gap and Liberty State Park in Jersey City. While the proximity of Jersey City to New York was very appealing, both Natan and I were at first skeptical about the suitability of Liberty State Park. The newly established park was not very clean, and we worried that over the years the ground had been used more as a dump than as a park. When we ventured to the proposed site, however, we found a peninsula with a glorious vista of New York City and the Statue of Liberty, The experience convinced us that Natan's powerful monument needed to be erected on that spot.

I pointed a quivering finger at the suggested location, and shivers ran down my spine when I realized that the monument to liberty would stand there long after I would be gone.

Some years back Natan had proposed a 20-foot-high statue in New York City, *Scrolls of Fire*, depicting Jewish history beginning with the exodus from Egypt and culminating in the creation of Israel. The plan was to build the statue on Riverside Drive in Manhattan. The city, however, refused to proceed with the plan, maintaining that the subject was not appropriate for a public park. As Natan contemplated the view of New York from the vantage point of Liberty State Park, he exclaimed: "Although New York City did not want me, now I have the whole of Manhattan as a background for my work!"

Today the powerful *Scrolls of Fire* towers majestically over the Judean Hills in Jerusalem. Busloads of Israeli schoolchildren visit it as they learn the history of the Jewish people, and military schools use it as a background for swearing-in ceremonies.

Initially thinking that the peninsula we visited was the entire Liberty State Park, Natan suggested sculpting the statue no more than nine feet high. When we found out that the park occupied about 700 acres I beseeched him to make it as large as his artistic judgment dictated. To oversee the project and its dedication I asked the governor to appoint 100 prominent state residents, including representatives of different religions, the military, the arts, and industry. The three people he appointed at the helm were a Livingston resident, Marty Barber, who was to serve as treasurer; David Kotok off Cumberland; and myself.

The official announcement that the monument would be built took place at the New Jersey State Museum in April 1982, where director Leah Sloshberg mounted (on three months' notice) Natan's first, and unfortunately last, museum exhibit, occupying a whole wing.

As pragmatic businessmen, David and Marty opposed signing a contract that committed us to an astronomical amount of money with no identified resources. Being as impatient as Natan to have it started, however, I convinced them that we should move forward immediately. I was certain that no one would let us go bankrupt with a project as meaningful as this one. My reasoning prevailed, and we plunged headfirst, signing the contract with Natan. At the time we had great plans but not a penny in the treasury.

While we had very few substantial donors, the monument was built, as I had hoped, with the smaller contributions of thousands of supporters. Our initial budget was cut in half because a good amount of the professional work and supplies were contributed by individuals and companies, frequently amounting to thousands of dollars in value.

Marty Barber, for example, donated office space and equipment as well as stationery and printing. Jim Gaspari, the architect who had designed the temple renovation, provided the plans at no cost and recruited excavators, electricians, and others to donate materials and services. Lawyers worked pro bono. Even the last-minute printing of the dedication brochure containing a list of all the donors was donated by Jo Rubin, a printing contractor.

One of the most touching contributions came from the Sod Growers Association, an organization of hard-working farmers. The members all committed themselves to donating a certain amount of sod for the landscaping on which the unveiling ceremony would take place. They organized the transportation of the sod and delivered it in enough time to ensure a beautiful lawn.

Facing the task of the actual construction, I lacked the needed expertise, and the project was larger than I was able to undertake. I sought out a large construction company for advice and was introduced to one with which I was not familiar: Turner Construction. Not knowing how to start, I walked in with a few humble questions, and was overwhelmed when I walked out with an entire professional staff to manage the construction. Turner's CEO agreed to assume total responsibility for completion of the project, including assigning to it the company's job supervisor, John Urban, who dived in with enthusiasm and expertise. Turner built the base, soliciting their suppliers to donate marble and other fine materials.

Governor Kean designated officials to coordinate the unveiling ceremony, which took place on May 30, 1985, and drew a crowd in excess of 5,000 people. Echoing my feelings when I had spoken several years before at Monmouth Military Base, I was initially apprehensive about working with people who wore military uniforms. Natan, also a survivor for whom the military had once symbolized the most savage brutality, shared my preconceptions. Yet the gratitude we owed our saviors prevailed. Our misgivings were dispelled quickly when we began to work with General Gerard, a World War II flying ace. Following the lead established by General Gerard, who appointed Colonel Harold Nutt as project manager, the staff and the task force under Nutt's command put their hearts and unwavering support into the project. Natan developed a special rapport with the general. After 43 years Natan and I discovered in a deep and special way how much the American soldier is a friend of people.

Natan's *Liberation* statue, measuring over 15 feet high in its final incarnation, will for time immemorial retell the story to all who visit the park of the victims of the Holocaust and the great soldiers who rescued us. Even today I like to visit there on a nice day and watch hundreds of people from

*1987 Memorial Service for Natan Rapoport. Governor
Thomas Kean and Luna (Courtesy of Star Ledger)*

all over the world talk as they gather around the bronze history. For many, the lessons they learn in that spot about the evils of racism and the kindness of soldiers would never otherwise reach them.

On a dreary day in May 2005 the 20th anni-versary of the statue's unveiling, I organized a rededication ceremony. A substantial group of people paid their respects, that day, to American soldiers who still fight on foreign soil. It appears that the world has not learned, but we cannot stop trying.

Maneuvers of NJ National Guards, 1986

Chapter Twenty-seven
After the Liberation Monument

The dedication of the *Liberation* monument in 1985 marked the end of two of the most intense years of my life. The pressure-laden project had consumed most of my waking hours seven days a week.

I had become involved in the erection of the sculpture because of my driving commitment to educating about the Holocaust, particularly through the avenue of art in its various expressions. My dedication to the project had precluded any attention I should have paid to my personal life..

After the dedication of the *Liberation* monument and the acknowledgment that my marriage would no longer dominate decisions as to how I would live my life, I experienced a rush of freedom. For perhaps the first time in my life I felt I could choose my own course. Simultaneously I needed time to figure out the new direction in which my road would wind. Inspired by the title of a play in which Sammy Davis Jr. had starred, *Stop the World; I Want to Get Off!*, I decided to set out for a remote spot on the earth.

I bought an open ticket for the Pacific region of New Zealand and Australia and embarked on a trip without prearranged destinations or dates. The morning after Thanksgiving Day, when my whole family had celebrated my birthday with me, I announced that I would be taking off.

I felt like a citizen of the world, free as a bird. There were no appointments to keep and no deadlines to make. I had neither an itinerary nor an address. It was so delightful to walk into a hotel and get a room without making reservations or to book a flight to wherever I wanted the next destination to be whenever I was ready to move on. I floated from place to place without notifying anyone of my whereabouts.

New Zealand offered a tranquil refuge following the chaos of the preceding years. The easygoing nature of the people I met sharply contrasted with the lifestyle of New Yorkers. While often characterized as lethargic, New Zealanders, I found, enjoy partaking in daredevil adventures when they let loose, and on a few occasions I decided to adapt to this manner of living.

The first opportunity came as a fulfillment of my dream to ski during the summer season. Testing my courage, I signed up for "helicopter skiing," in which participants are dropped by helicopter onto an endless blanket of snow on New Zealand's Cadrona Mountain near Quinstown. I had not realized upon reading the advertisement that there would be only one guide, who would take off without looking back soon after we jumped from the aircraft! When I landed on the mountaintop, the frightening realities of what I had gotten myself into, including the possibility of encountering crevices almost impossible for an amateur to master his or her way around, suddenly became clear. At that point, however, there was no turning back. Mother's words rang in my ears: "If others can do it, so can you."

I did. I had a terrific feeling of satisfaction when I again saw the helicopter waiting to pick us up, though I am quite certain I would not repeat the stunt. I do believe that in doing it once I had proven my point to myself.

I was, however, eager to test myself in other ways. My next adventure took me to a river in a canyon where boats with jet engines run. As if the speed didn't furnish enough of a high, the excitement was enhanced by zigzagging through the canyon, coming within inches from the rocky walls. This definitely got my adrenaline going. At the end of the run there was an indescribable feeling of exhilaration.

On a physically less dangerous level, a third adventure involved meeting a former boyfriend I had known in Poland named Zyggi Frankel, who had emigrated to New Zealand in 1948, settling in Wellington.

I first met Zyggi three years after Alex had left Poland, when I did not know when—if ever—I would be able to reunite with Alex. Zyggi and I had fallen in love but had to part because he and his mother had received papers to emigrate to France. Our solution was to marry, but two personal obstacles (in addition to impending legal ones) stood in the way: Zyggi's mother was a very religious and difficult woman, and my mother was rooting for my union with Alex rather than Zyggi. We decided to keep our decision secret until after the wedding. Marriage license already in hand, we were heading for City Hall. On our way there, though, we stopped at my apartment, where as fate would have it a letter awaited me from Alex, expressing concern since he had not heard from me for quite some time (I had been formulating future plans with Zyggi!). His words were tender, instinctively stating how understandable it would be if I had gotten involved with someone else. Nonetheless, he asked me to at least let him know if I was okay. Zyggi—who did not know Alex—began to berate him, claiming that he was not suitable material for a husband for me and that I was doing the right thing in not waiting any longer for him. Still, I needed only one glance at the text of Alex's letter to scrap my plans to marry Zyggi.

Now, however, it was 37 years later, and I felt a desire to contact Zyggi. I even thought that perhaps we were destined to see each other again since six years earlier, in 1979, I had conversed on an airplane ride with a young Irish economist who happened to know Zyggi. Subsequent to our chance encounter, the economist had given both of us the appropriate contact information for each other!

Off I trekked to Wellington, where I was shocked to be met by a man who appeared homeless. Hunched over, dressed in shabby clothes, and looking much older than his age, Zyggi had virtually turned into a hermit. He had married a Christian New Zealander with whom he had three children, but he had left his wife several years before our meeting. Once upon a time Zyggi had been one of the most impressive intellectuals I had known, reading incessantly and mastering the game of chess. In Wellington, however, where access to the intellectual world was more limited, Zyggi had turned inward in a negative way.

Since his immigration, Zyggi's life had stood still; he had encountered few opportunities for personal growth. Confronted with his lifestyle, I realized again how blessed I had been to have emigrated to the States.

I spent three more weeks in Australia, and finally I found myself looking forward to returning to the world of opportunities, to my home, to the U.S.A.

On December 30, 1985 we celebrated the first of my children's weddings. Irene married Daniel Neiden, a wonderful man from Nebraska, ending 1985 on a high note.

But the new year began with a heartbreak. Bob Harrison, Bernice's boyfriend, was dying of cancer. Her commitment to him was remarkable, and the whole family felt this tragic loss of a 35-year- old man.

In June1987 Natan Rapoport died in New York of a heart attack. His daughter Nina flew into town from Paris, and I decided to accompany her to Israel, where he was being buried.

On the way back from the funeral I stopped in France to attend the groundbreaking ceremony for the museum commemorating the invasion of Normandy. I had been invited to be part of the American delegation because the chairman of the museum was considering a project to build a replica of the *Liberation* monument to stand on the shore of Omaha Beach. We were greeted with honors and fanfare: our private train was formally welcomed by the military band, we were received by the mayor, and the residents of Normandy rolled out a figurative red carpet. I could not stop thinking about what it would have meant to Natan, once a struggling artist in Paris, to have been a guest of honor of the French nation where he had lived as a refugee from Poland.

I had a deep need, at this point, for a spiritual connection. The first house of worship I encountered that Sunday morning was the Notre Dame Cathedral in Paris. When I entered, a Mass was in progress. I sat down and found the service with its beautiful music very soothing, momentarily quieting the internal turmoil I felt because of the seeming injustice of the lives death had taken in the past year and a half. While I am strongly rooted in my Jewish roots religiously and culturally, I think there are many roads to spirituality. I was grateful that a path had presented itself at a moment when I needed this kind of comfort.

*Frederic Douglass premiere, Irene, Mark, Luna,
Bernice, Newark, 1991*

Chapter Twenty-eight
Opera

In 1985 I looked for new avenues of creativity. I felt the need to spread my wings beyond my beautiful home in Watchung; while filled with memories, it had become empty and isolated. Nearby Manhattan, in contrast, held a rich cultural and social life into which I was ready to dive.

I acquired an apartment on the 33rd floor of a new building on the Upper East Side. The balcony gave me a view across the entire west side of the city, as far as the George Washington Bridge, which glimmered like a diamond necklace in the distance. The sight of a connecting link with New Jersey and the rest of the country sold me.

I considered purchasing the apartment an investment in my mental health. At the same time, however, I was determined not to part with the home in which the children had been raised through their happy childhood years. Coming from a Krakow family which dated back to 1700, I knew it was important for me to feel that my family was rooted.

I had formed tight bonds with a number of the people with whom I had worked on the Liberation Monument committee. Among them was the world-famous Metropolitan Opera singer Jerome Hines. This 6-foot 5-inch giant with a booming voice made me realize how much I missed my life in the music world.

Even though I had studied musicology at Jagiellonian University in Krakow and music had always been close to the inner core of my being, it actually had been decades since I had immersed myself in the culture of professional music. Strangely it was the experience in the concentration camps that cemented my devotion to the field.

I was twelve when World War II broke out. Like any child of a middle class family I had taken piano lessons since I was six and been otherwise exposed to cultural life. Of course with the beginning of the war all forms of education and public cultural life were halted. What did not stop, however, was the need for art and music on the part of both victims and victimizers in the midst of the violence and chaos. Even amongst the assailants, to whom barbaric treatment seemed to come so naturally, the arts played a significant role in communicating, lifting spirits, and expressing feelings.

One time in the Leipzig concentration camp several women collaborated on a musical play spoofing life of the personalities in the camp, using mythological and historical figures as the characters. The play was called Socrates, performed by the inmates in this farce. For some of the younger girls the production was a first "lesson" in the classics.

With the show ready for performance we all clamored for admission. Tickets were at a premium. We even gave up our meager portions of bread to be able to attend. A few flattering sketches about our guards gave us a little edge on security. Fed by curiosity and vanity the guards looked the other way, minimizing the risk of punishment for violating the prohibition against gathering. I still have friends today who remember and recite the lines of the production. They reminisce about this show as a highlight of their lives—a moment that brought smiles to their faces in the midst of hell.

I came to think about art as a form of conveying messages with the capacity to reach the most unreachable. I learned to appreciate its power. My decision to become a musicologist directly resulted from these experiences. So did my determination to expose my children to the arts at an early age.

When Bernice was eight and the twins were six I decided to introduce them to the opera. We spent many hours listening to *Aida* in anticipation of their first trip to its performance at the Metropolitan Opera. In the aftermath of the event, they talked enthusiastically about the gilded balconies, the red velvet upholstery, and the beautifully attired audience, all of which appeared to have left them with a more lasting impression than the music. It seemed that I had not succeeded in converting them into opera lovers, but at least they tasted its richness.

A year after the completion of *Liberation,* Jerry and Lucia Hines invited me to the New Jersey State Opera to see Gounod's *Faust* with Jerry starring in the role of Mephisto. I loved the performance, though I was disturbed by a tangential sociological phenomenon. Although the opera was performed in Newark, a mostly African-American community, the audience was predominantly white. Indeed, *Faust*, a story about the reincarnation of a Frenchman, had little relevance to the local community. Looking at the past repertory I noticed that all of the works performed were by European composers.

I felt disturbed that the African-American heritage had gone ignored. I was convinced that repertory must exist that would entice the local audience. If the opera company continued to devote its attention exclusively to the European heritage, I knew there would be no chance of introducing this powerful and worthwhile art form to the people of Newark.

At the end of the performance the president of the New Jersey State Opera asked me to join the board. With the children grown and experienced in business and networking, I no longer doubted my abilities. Nor did I continue to undervalue the jobs I was offered on boards of directors despite their failure to renumerate. I had come to realize that many organizations desiring to hire somebody with my abilities would not be able to afford the salary for someone with my skills.

Still, having been away from the field since my college days 37 years earlier, I was initially skeptical of my ability to contribute anything valuable to the world of opera. I did see it as an opportunity to create something meaningful that would encompass the various cultures among which we lived, though, and so I agreed to take the position on the board, hoping to test the waters.

At first I was asked to step in as treasurer. It seems that this initiation, like that of so many of the jobs I had previously undertaken, entailed mainly financial roles and responsibilities. The most expensive of all art forms, the opera was constantly plagued by financial difficulties.Yet as great as the problems were, so was the gratification. With time and with my business experience in EAR, Inc., I began to take over day-to-day management of the company. After only one year I was asked to assume the organization's presidency. Again I was destined to be the first woman to hold this position— and the first new president in 13 years. The honor was quite intimidating, but I could not resist the challenge.

There were many fascinating projects during my term in office. Among the achievements, we brought the performance of the rarely performed opera *Nabucco* by Verdi to distinguished Carnegie Hall in New York. What a glorious moment it was to sit in the center box of this magnificent house, packed to the rafters, listening to the music I had been involved in producing. While I was a student at the conservatory in Krakow, we had heard stories about performances at Carnegie Hall, but they seemed as legendary as the centuries-old tales of Queen Jadwiga in the Wawel Castle. Yet here I was, several decades later, a part of the legend. I could not help thinking in that moment about my musicology colleagues, including my friend Zosia, who were still struggling to make ends meet in Krakow, even further away that day from the dreams of Carnegie Hill than they had been as hopeful students years before. Yet fate had brought me into the world of this renowned institution.

The New Jersey State Opera began to diversify its repertory by expanding it beyond solely European composers and offering a variety of productions designed to reach new audiences. One of the most memorable —and meaningful to me—was what I believe to be the first performance by a professional company of the children's opera *Brundibar*, written by Hans Krasa, a Czech composer who perished in Aushwitz. The opera relates the story of two children seeking money to buy medication for their ill mother but prevented from their goal by an evil organ grinder. In the end, the children— working cooperatively with animals—prevail, demonstrating the power of unity.

The opera had originally been performed in the Therezienstadt concentration camp. Collaborating with the American Boys' Choir, we managed to obtain funding for the staging. Finding an appropriate venue for the performance became the next problem.

It was during this period that I was asked to speak about the Liberation Monument at the headquarters of the U.S. Army Communications-Electronics Command at Fort Monmouth, New Jersey. My speech was very well received, and the Chief of the Office of Equal Employment Opportunity, Susan Morris, asked whether I was involved in any other projects. Hesitantly but without any expectations, I told her about my effort to stage *Brundibar*. To my surprise she offered to have it performed on the base.

The premiere took place only three weeks after our original conversation, on May 3, 1988. In addition to offering the theater space, the Communications-Electronics Command assisted in the publicity. As a result, we performed the opera for hundreds of children who, through the powerful vehicle of art, learned about social justice, personal responsibility, and the power of unity that underlies *Brundibar*.

Another highlight of my experience at the New Jersey State Opera, however, was the organization and performance of the world premiere of

Frederick Douglass by Ullyses Kay, a New Jersey African-American composer. Finally the opera company was paying homage to the heritage of the culture that surrounded us. This time the local Newark community attended in droves, and I felt we had delivered a long-overdue project with relevance and meaning for Newark residents. I was deeply moved when a modestly dressed man approached the ticket window, requesting the best seats in the house. He had come to treat his wife to a night at the opera.

The performance was electric, and the wide-eyed audience was jubilant. The evaluator who had come from the National Council of the Arts expressed amazement at the multiethnic audience in attendance.

I spent five years on the job. Like the work in which I had previously been engaged, the presidency of the New Jersey State Opera was very demanding, requiring attention seven days a week and leaving me very little time for a personal life. The experience deepened my love for this form of musical art, though finally I felt the need to secure more time for myself.

Skiing in the Andes, Argentina, 1991

Chapter Twenty-nine
Around the World

One summer evening in 1991 a friend from Australia, Giza Frayman, called, suggesting we meet in Krakow. I immediately answered in the affirmative. Since I knew that the Communist regime had collapsed in Poland and that the country was beginning to rebuild, I did not fear confronting the same kinds of obstacles I had encountered on my 1974 trip with Bernice. Indeed, I felt a sense of excitement about returning to my native—and now democratic—land.

Three days later Giza called again, this time urging me to continue with her to Hong Kong, where her husband, Max, would meet us. I had known

Max since the war. He and I had worked together in the brush factory in the Krakow ghetto, and we had been part of a group of teenagers who had spent evenings after work parading on the ghetto streets. We had flirted and played as any teenagers would, watching beautiful sunsets through the barbed wires and trying to forget that we were encompassed by a war and enemies who hated us simply because we were Jewish.

In the factory Max had worked at the drilling machines producing boards for my job—stringing brushes.

As the war progressed Max and I were shipped to different concentration camps. Although we both managed to survive, we had lost contact. For many years we searched for each other without success. The road that led us to finding each other wound through the most unanticipated paths.

In 1987 two members of our temple, Natalie and Sidney Darwin, traveled to Manila, in the Philippines, where they met a man from Australia. During a supper conversation he told them he had originally been from Krakow, and he shared stories of his youth. Natalie innocently mentioned that there was a member of her Jewish congregation who was also from Krakow. Of course he would have had no reason to know my married surname, but my nickname Luna is unusual. He asked whether I have blue eyes and a mother who survived with me, and the affirmative responses made him—Max!—realize that he and the Darwins were referring to the same person. Both married with children, we began a correspondence, curious to find out how the different cultures to which we had relocated had shaped our lives.

Max seemed apprehensive about becoming reacquainted after a 40-year hiatus. He later confessed that he was afraid I might have become a *yenta* (the Yiddish name for a busybody)! Not wanting to be disappointed, however, he asked his son, Peter, to stop in New York to meet me on his way from Europe back to Australia. I seemed to have gained Peter's approval, and a few months later Max and his wife Giza, who was very supportive of our reconnection, arrived in New York. It was a great meeting. The common bond of the past had remained very strong despite the oceans and 40 years that had separated us. Like me, Max had made good use of his bonus years. We promised to make an effort to see each other every two or three years, health cooperating.

Giza Frayman's call could not have come at a better time. So I embarked on the trip, but not as my friend had initially envisioned it. To her itinerary I added a number of stops—and passengers. Since two of my children had never seen Krakow, Mark, Irene, and her husband, Daniel, joined me on the trip.

When I looked at the globe that Bernice had bought to make sure I knew where I would be trekking this time, the red string that traced my upcoming voyage made me realize I would be journeying up and down and around the world. The biggest joy was knowing that in every city I would visit, I would be welcomed by friends and have a chance to catch up with their lives. I had no idea how long I would be traveling. Equipped with an open ticket, I embarked on the trip.

Mark, Irene, Daniel, and I started the trip in Krakow, where I proudly showed them my magnificent city. The trio of artistic souls fully appreciated the medieval town full of history and antiquities. I wanted them to see the beauty that had characterized my childhood and to meet a few of the good friends I had left behind. I felt it was important that they become acquainted with the happy part of my past, not only the nightmares. I wanted to leave them with the legacy of having come from a fascinating family with a proud heritage.

My Krakow friends met us with great delight. Zosia Rogowska, my college friend, and Janusz Dolny, a pianist with whom I had attended conservatory, joined me in reminiscing about our youth. It was amazing how much older they appeared, as if they belonged to another generation. Spending time with them reminded me why I had never felt anti-Semitism in their midst.; They are truly open minded and unprejudiced people.

The greatest reward of the trip was finding the hand-carved black oak dining room furniture that had been designed by my mother for her trousseau in 1923. For years it had been Irene's greatest wish to retrieve the set, but I had never known how to find it. After a number of inquiries during our stay we lucked out: I found the person whose parents had bought it from us before mother and I had left Poland! It had been well preserved, and the owner agreed to sell it back to me. Today the furniture graces Irene's 150-year-old New York house as a piece of our family's heritage.

We left Krakow, with its rich memories, and proceeded to Moscow. Arriving late at night we found no water or food in the hotel or elsewhere. Suddenly no one was laughing at Irene's pre-trip insistence on bringing a valise of food for our Russian friends. We dove into the supplies and dined that night on crackers and peanut butter, appreciating every bite.

Moscow was overwhelming. After the intimacy of Krakow, we felt as though we were surveying this gigantic city through a magnifying glass. The massive, colorful buildings adorned in chipping paint spoke of past grandeur, like tattered clothes of nobility.

We visited the parents of Mark's friend ,Dina Zuckerman. Claudia and Boris, accomplished scientists, received us graciously on a beautifully set table in the formal manner of Russian hospitality. The meal they served consisted of bread and potatoes. Their "luxurious" apartment, which they were fortunate not to share with anyone else, consisted of two tiny rooms filled with books. Dina, their only daughter, had emigrated to the United States, and any contact with people connected with her brought them great joy. Among other tourist attractions, they took us to the Bolshoi Opera as well as a demolished church on the outskirts of the city. Several years later they managed to join Dina in New York. Now they all live in California.

Since the children had to return home after the Moscow leg of the trip, I proceeded to St. Petersburg by myself. The trip was fascinating, but the atmosphere in the city mirrored Moscow with its air of insecurity on the streets.

From Russia I went to Budapest to meet my cousin Erica. Budapest, known to some as the Paris of the East, felt very different than the Russian cities. After the revolution Hungary had blossomed out of its Communist clutches, taking the best from East and West. The elegant lifestyle of its citizens, somewhat curtailed by the country's struggling economy, created a very pleasant atmosphere. My cousin Erica, whom I had visited many years before on my trip with Bernice, was now the mother of a delightful young boy named Andrash. They were great tour guides and companions; their vivacity added spice to the trip.

From Budapest I went to Paris to meet Nina, Natan Rapoport's daughter. I felt very relieved to enter a city where people lived in comfort and freedom. I spent two wonderful weeks in Nina's Normandy house, refueling my energy for the trip still ahead.

The next stop was Frankfurt, where my cousin Peter Isenberg, his wife, Nita, and their six-month-old daughter Karolina—the newest addition to our family—lived. Peter was the grandson of my Aunt Sala from Bielsko with whom I had spent the last weeks before the outbreak of World War II. Peter's parents, Cyli and Fred, had lived in Warsaw during the war. A tall, blond, blue-eyed man whose first language was German, Fred had posed as a German officer while in actuality he had served as a contact for the Warsaw ghetto fighters. Their family had remained in Poland after the war, but when anti-Semitism grew unbearable there after the outbreak of the Six-Day War in Israel in 1968, Peter had emigrated to Germany with his family.

During the visit I was again reminded of my good fortune at having come to the United States. No matter how friendly, native Germans, unlike Americans, have always considered immigrants as outsiders. Dusseldorf and Cologne did not feel more comfortable than Frankfurt, except for the reunions I was able to celebrate with my wonderful friends.

Giza met me at the Zurich airport, where my Polish friends from the conservatory, Jurek Karolus and Janusz Dolny the pianist, who were vacationing in Switzerland, joined us for a few hours to reminisce about our student life at the Krakow Conservatory.

Max awaited us in Hong Kong, which surprisingly turned out to be the least exciting stop on my trip. To me this city resembled one giant shopping mall. Not being a shopper I found it had little to offer me.

I was glad to move on to Manila, where the Fraymans' linen factory was located. But Manila was a terribly sad place. This was my first encounter with cardboard shantytowns as well as with the contrast of such dire residential poverty with nearby luxurious hotels (our destination). Visiting Max's factory I admired the gifted artists who produced beautiful embroidery, but felt simultaneously sad that they lived in the cardboard boxes behind their workplace. According to Max they chose these residences rather than live in the outskirts of the city where the rents were more affordable. Although Max's business was one of the best paying enterprises in the area with workers earning almost double the local salaries, the people still made next to nothing by Western standards.

Next we went to the tax-free-zone where factories were being built. The area was swarming with workers like ants busily constructing buildings. To my shock and distress I did not see any heavy equipment; rather, all the work was done by hand. I was told that these workers were the highest paid, earning $5 a day. Their jobs were very hard to get. Machines would displace too many employment opportunities, it was rationalized, depriving the workers of a livelihood.

The realities of life in this part of the world were heartbreaking.

I was delighted to leave the Philippines, joining the Fraymans on their way home. I felt relieved to land in Australia.

In Melbourne I was very happy to see my cousin Oskar Hilfstein (who had lived with us in the ghetto), his wife, Jasia, their daughter, Julie, her husband, Norman, and a delightful granddaughter, Sally. Thanks to both the Fraymans and the Hilfsteins, I was very busy with social and cultural events.

At the time of my trip the New Jersey Performing Arts Center (NJPAC) in Newark was under construction. As an active member of the New Jersey arts community because of my immediate past affiliation with the state opera, I tried to visit a number of opera houses during the trip. My goal was to collect and bring to the attention of the administration information about different ways other companies around the world operated. The Hilfsteins took me to see several productions, and I admired how the Melbourne Opera had grown in the few short years since its inception. They placed a good deal of emphasis on giving opportunities to young local talent as well as presenting innovative, refreshing productions.

I then proceeded to Sydney, where I was equally warmly received by Genia and Martin Biggs. Martin, another friend from the Krakow brush factory in the ghetto, invited me to join him at a meeting of his B'nai B'rith chapter. I was amused that the Sydney chapter of this international Jewish organization more closely resembled an exclusive club than a group promoting brotherhood. Membership, I was told, required sponsorship by an existing member. For me to visit as a guest, the club had to be notified and given information about me in advance. What a difference from American open-door policies!

Again pursuing my NJPAC mission I decided to attend a performance at the Sydney Opera. In comparison to my impressions in Melbourne, this edifice did not strike me as people-friendly. Appearing from a distance as a beautiful sculpture perched on top of a mountain, in reality the opera house is not very accessible. With no parking lot adjacent to the building, the box office three flights up, performing spaces an even further ascent, and no elevators or escalators, the building was at the time virtually off-limits to elderly and disabled patrons.

From Sydney I took a long flight to Argentina, the next-to-last leg of my trip. This was a new world to me and was the most exciting. Alberto Alonzo, who had directed *Nabucco* for the New Jersey State Opera, greeted me in Buenos Aires. This majestic, sprawling city was confronting severe economic problems not obvious to visitors, who were generally escorted to well-stocked, elegant stores and luxurious restaurants, none of which the local working people—even those with high positions—could afford.

Alonzo took me to Opera Colon, the largest opera house in the world, which stood on a 450-foot-wide avenue. Its impressive gilded interior seated in excess of 4,000 people on five floors of boxes filled with red velvet armchairs.

He then took me on a tour of the three floors beneath the opera house, which housed the workshops. In contrast to the opulent performing space, this area reflected the actual state of the economy. The glamorous costumes, once sewn with luxurious fabrics, were stacked in piles where they had begun unraveling. The walls and floors, not maintained for years, were crumbling.

Eva Peron's spirit had not improved the life of the average Argentinean. Once again I encountered cardboard shantytowns. I wondered which poverty was worse: the kind I had encountered in Manila or the poverty that stared me in the face in Buenos Aires.

From the city I traveled to the very Germanic town of Bariloche, the luxurious ski resort in the Andes where poverty was not visible. My ski apparel awaited me in Bariloche, brought by a Slovenian ski instructor named Juri Hepner, who lived in my Vermont house during the winter and in the summer trained the Argentinean Olympic ski team.

The ski lift transported me to what seemed like the top of the world. The view of the endless mountain range appeared unreal. I had a hard time believing I was really skiing in the Andes, a place I had dreamed about for many years.

The trip lasted three and a half months and included visits to 10 countries and 19 cities. When I landed back on American soil I felt enriched by the many cultures to which I had been exposed. Even more significantly, however, I felt I had rekindled relationships with treasured friends and family members—the main agenda of the trip. I realized that the common bonds that tie so many of us together are much stronger than the interruptions in communication, some as long as 40 years, caused by our taking diverse roads through life.

Gov. Thomas H. Kean signing creation of Yom HaShoa, Trenton, 1982

Chapter Thirty
Holocaust Education

My belief in the critical importance of educating about the Holocaust as an essential tool in trying to prevent the recurrence of horrific genocides and atrocities had permeated the fibers of my being for years. While I had participated in Holocaust education in various ways over the years, these efforts picked up in 1982, when I was appointed by Governor Kean to the then newly formed Advisory Council on Holocaust Education.

Holocaust education bridges the past and the future. In studying the past we analyze the attitudes that produced the greatest devastation in human history, and the most valiant efforts of the victims to survive.

We learn how a progressive, highly educated society could be harnessed by diabolical leaders who would then enlist collaborators from occupied countries and lead them to destroy their own societies.

By closely examining these two opposed elements, the oppressors and the victims, we gain valuable insight into the functioning of a society. We realize the responsibility of participating actively and intelligently in the democratic process.

In 1977, accompanying Rabbi Goldman on a Hebrew school Confirmation class trip to Amsterdam, we visited the museum that had been built in the apartment where Holocaust teenage victim Anne Frank had hidden during the war. At the time, I recorded the following in a diary I carried with me:

4/11/77

Thirty-two years have passed since this chapter of my life closed, and today standing in Anne Frank's house the memories of the Holocaust started resurfacing from under the dense fog where they have been dormant for all that time.

No, they were never forgotten, but coping with the vastness of their impact took years. At first, too painful to unravel, they were stored safely in the bottom of my subconscious, allowing time to help dull the hurt. Life had to go on; the nightmares of the past could not be permitted to undermine the present of everyday life. There was no value that could have been achieved by rushing since a confused mind is likely to distort the past and destroy the present. My experiences during the war had to be evaluated from the proper perspective.

I feel that time has come, though I recognize that it will take many years of confronting the facts and finding ways to utilize the lessons derived from them.

How does one return to life after spending six years in hell?

* * * * * * *

The tiny model of the Frank house, although in Holland, had the same basic atmosphere as thousands of ghetto rooms all over Eastern Europe. Three years Anne's senior, as I traversed the spaces she had once called home I was transplanted into our Krakow ghetto room, and memories experienced as images intertwined with feelings began to flood my brain: five individuals living in the ghetto quarters; ghetto walls shrinking and apartment occupants increasing to 14; transfer to Plaszow concentration camp for those "privileged" to be able-bodied; deportation of neighbors and relatives to extermination camps; mothers following their infants into death and mothers with several children faced with deciding which child to follow (depending upon who needed them most); the sound of gunshots—constant gunshots— in the streets, all around us, toppling bodies, toppling acquaintances, toppling loved ones.

It sounds good today to say that we "wanted to live so we could carry on." It sounds so noble, but the truth is that in the face of death any reason disappeared. The desire to live was quite overrated since the cruelty of everyday living, wrapped in the constant, gnawing hunger and fear, did not induce a love of life. As I see it now, it seems to me that in the confusion and disbelief of everyday existence a suspense was created that resembled a bad dream, and the will to live was like a trance through which one shuffled along, hoping to awaken in a different world.

I survived, and I woke up. I am no longer bleeding. Enough blood has been spilled. Now I feel that I am holding in my brain a monumental curriculum that needs to be passed onto future generations, and I hope to have the wisdom to present it in the proper light, without bias or bitterness.

Let the truth speak for itself.

My first opportunity to teach about the Holocaust had presented itself to me in the early 1970's, when a high school teacher at Watchung Hills High School named Marsha Kestenbaum had asked me to talk to her class. At the time, even though I did not have an idea of how to present the issues, I felt obliged to comply with her request. I do not recollect how I handled the subject matter, but I walked away with a positive feeling about the experience.

Soon thereafter, Monica Maskie, the editor of the religion section of the Newark *Star-Ledger*, a major daily newspaper in New Jersey, asked me to be an interview subject at a seminar she was running for high-school editors. I was pleased to take part and was delighted by the astute questions and interest of the students.

During my tenure as president of Temple Sholom I had accompanied Rabbi Goldman and the Hebrew school Confirmation class on another trip to Amsterdam, further solidifying my interest—indeed, my need—to be involved in Holocaust education. After we returned I dived more intensely into this endeavor, and I felt particularly amazed and gratified by the extent to which non-Jews were interested in the subject. In my experience some of the first schools to embrace the education were private Christian schools. My lectures there were welcomed with great interest, and the children were well prepared to ask poignant questions with understanding and compassion.

On some level my lectures benefited me even more than my listeners. Experiencing the outstretched arms of members of the Christian community confirmed my belief that when people get to know each other in a personal way, prejudice disappears.

In the late 1970's we organized a Holocaust conference with the Reverend Franklin Lattel representing the Protestant church, Father John Pawlikowski representing the Catholic Church, and Rabbi Ichak Greenberg representing the Jewish community. It was a very dynamic trio who at this early date dealt with the issue of the Holocaust. We closed the conference with a seminar designed to prepare teachers to deal with the issue. The response was very encouraging—it appeared that there certainly was an interest in the issue.

Now I was not the lonely voice speaking on the subject!

An invitation to speak at the Monmouth Military base followed. The organizers of the event displayed my prison dress in a glass case alongside the American military uniform exhibit. In that powerful moment my prison dress became transformed from a symbol of slavery to a symbol of dignity.

Many speaking engagements followed. Once at a public school in a section of Newark which some people considered a war zone, the school administrators offered a guard for my car, maintaining that it was not safe to park in front of the school. It took me a little while to attract the attention of the students, but once captured, they were a wonderful audience. They repeatedly asked how I had emerged from this experience to lead a fruitful life. I felt qualified to discuss the pressure of prejudice, and I understood the importance of making contact with children who felt stigmatized. I talked about the difference between living in a country where discrimination was sanctioned and one with a Constitution promising civil rights. I expressed my agreement that those civil rights had to be implemented more forcefully, but explained that in this nation the population held the power to exercise this privilege. I told them to concentrate on improving themselves and not to hate, since hatred is like an acid, it spoils the container and everything in it. Some of the children—among them several who rarely opened a book, according to their teacher—asked me to publish an account of my experiences. While there is no way to measure the impact of such lessons, that day I knew my words had been heard.

Now we have so many signals alerting us to the intolerable conditions around the world, and yet we don't take action. It is my hope that talking about the Holocaust will prompt people to take action to meet the challenges they face—that we will learn to extend our arms to others and offer help that will embrace moral values as a guide for life.

I hope that we can teach the difference between Hitler and Roosevelt. Both men led their countries forcefully, but each used his power to a different end. The American moral values, of course, made the difference. And it is those values that I hope we can instill.

I have never stopped teaching. Whether my audience includes students at inner-city schools or universities or soldiers on military bases, my ultimate message is the same: I advocate in favor of unity, self-determination, and a system of values that permits people to live as equals regardless of differences. But most of all I urge my listeners to exercise their privilege to vote—to cast their ballots intelligently.

On July 19, 1995 I found myself on the very street corner where 52 years before I had stood with my mother during the liquidation of the Krakow ghetto. This time, instead of being driven out by Nazi soldiers with guns, I was leading a group of scholars and reporters on a trip to Polish Holocaust sites.

The brilliant sunshine that flooded the July sky reminded me of that day in the ghetto so long ago. The exterior of the apartment house where my family and others had lived—nine of us crowded into two tiny, shabby rooms inside the ghetto walls—was unchanged; the same scratches in the concrete that I had seen every day as a young girl continued to mar the building. No coat of paint or plaster had been applied to the structures that had constituted my ghetto world. But the Jewish inhabitants of these unchanged buildings, whose meager existence had been carved out of hopes and dreams and terrible suffering, had vanished. Those residents included my family and friends and thousands of others. For a brief moment my vision was clouded by the past, and I beheld Mrs. Podworska, our Christian neighbor in my early years, who during the "action" in the ghetto passed by in the streetcar, risking her own life to see what had become of us and whether we needed help.

As a stream of repressed misery unfolded in before my eyes, the clanking of a streetcar broke the silence and brought me back to the present. On that Krakow street in 1995, there were no cries or screams of deportees drowning out the noise of the trolley. There was no barbed-wire fence, and the uncrowded car rolled along an empty thoroughfare. The chaos of the past had been replaced by the serenity that engulfs a Krakow morning after the working people depart for their jobs.

Standing in this familiar place emptied of so many people whom I had loved, yet at the same time surrounded by political and educational leaders from the democratic country of the United States, which had become my home, I realized that my losses had not devastated me. Just the opposite: I was the victor.

As that thought came into my mind, along with it came the impression that I must be crazy. I had lost my father and my sister—half of my immediate family—along with my aunts, my uncles, my cousins, and my friends. I had endured years in Nazi concentration camps. The society in which I had grown up, the world I cherished, had been systematically destroyed. How could I possibly feel victorious?

My mind then traveled to the night before, which I had spent in an elegant Warsaw hotel. My children and grandchildren back in the States were going about their daily routines, living creative lives free from the burdens of religious intolerance. I was blessed to be matriarch to future generations who I knew would never permit the voices of their predecessors to be silenced. Despite the full-scale war on the Jews, I was standing in the company of scholars and dignitaries (among them ex-Governor Thomas Kean of New Jersey, now the president of Drew University), who were committed to teaching about the Holocaust so that the world would henceforth swear, "Never again."

Although my years of enslavement in labor and concentration camps had not taken me to Auschwitz, there were common elements to the experiences of inmates in all the Nazi facilities of death. One of these was the collective impression that no one in the world outside the electrically wired gates that imprisoned us cared about the inconceivable horrors that saturated our daily existence. In the hours and days and weeks and months and years that passed, we witnessed scores of people dying in the most brutal and inhumane ways, but no person or organization or government intervened to force an end to the madness. Details about our condition could be relayed only by the birds, it seemed, who flew freely over the gates of death but somehow, in their sweet songs, failed to make known our condition.

Forty years later, at the synagogue in New Jersey, I learned that my fellow inmates and I had been wrong. At least one prominent person in the world (Congressman Robert Kean) had cared about our fate and had tried to alter it, even though his call to arms fell on deaf ears.

I could hardly contain the emotion that consumed me when Tom Kean, the son of this man who would have been our hero had we known of his courage, used the occasion of the dedication of the *Flame* to announce the formation of a Governor's Council on Holocaust Education. I had been asked from time to time to speak at schools about my experiences during the

Holocaust, but I often felt that my accounts of horror had fallen upon ears that lacked the historical, political, and sociological context to understand my words in a meaningful way. The Council would guide the teaching of the teachers from whom future generations would learn; it would ensure that the experiences of those who confronted the flames of this terrible time in history would never be forgotten.

Governor Kean seemed transfixed by the *Flame* when it was unveiled. The Rapoport sculpture depicts a tower of human faces gasping for breath as they melt into a flare of fire. At its top a child emerges from the flame, a symbol of the continuity of Jewish life. During my days in the camps I was often drawn by the burden of tortured existence into a craving for death, yet I could never erase the feeling that the act of dying would have been an undignified surrender to the single-minded Nazi effort to annihilate the Jews. Living, however little of life remained within me, became my salvation and my creed. By living, I would defy my captors. By living, I would be victorious.

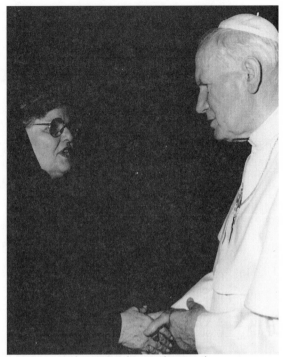

Luna with Pope John Paul II, Vatikan, 1994

Chapter Thirty-one
The Vatican

On April 8, 1994 I found myself in the most unlikely place for a Holocaust survivor.

The walls were covered with paintings of Raphael. The gilded chairs were upholstered in red velvet, and I occupied one. Our hosts wore the colorful vestments of the Catholic hierarchy.

Is this really me in this incredible place? I mused silently.

I thought that Monsignor John Oesterreicher's displaying my prison dress in the sanctuary of Seton Hall University's Chapel of the Immaculate Conception had been the pinnacle of my experiences in Jewish–Christian relations, but this surpassed any of my expectations. I was a Jew from Poland sitting in the most holy place in the world for Christians, awaiting the entrance of Karol Wojtyla, a man with whom I had attended the Jagiellonian University in Krakow and who had shared mutual friends with me.

Now Karol Wojtyla was Pope John Paul II, and I was waiting to be greeted warmly by his outstretched hands and hear him call the Jews "older brothers." Back in my college days I never would have dreamed of this man becoming a Pope or of our meeting in the sacred place I had learned about in art-history classes. I had traveled a long way from the concentration camps to the Vatican. I thought: "Maybe the world will change, after all."

I felt comfortable inside the Vatican, in the company of the Pope and many devout clergy members whom our group had been privileged to meet. That comfort level blossomed into an ardent personal quest: improving relations between Jews and Christians.

The seeds of my trip to the Vatican were sown on New Year's Day 1994. I had gone out for breakfast at a diner near my apartment and met old friends who invited me to join them at their table. As the lively conversation proceeded they mentioned they were soon leaving for a trip to the Vatican and asked if I would like to join them. In the excitement of the conversation they did not elaborate on the reasons for their visit, but my unquenchable curiosity did not permit me to pass up such an opportunity.

Ari and Sandra Brand-Weintraub submitted my name to the organizers of the trip scheduled for April. I initially knew nothing more. As the time approached more interesting aspects of the trip were revealed. I was to be a participant in a group of 100 survivors who were invited for the first concert of Holocaust music to be given in the Vatican. Apparently, on a visit to Krakow, the Holy Father had met a young American conductor named Gilbert Levine, who at the time was the director of the Krakow Philharmonic. Levine agreed to organize such a concert. It took two years of preparation to bring the idea to fruition.

In accordance with custom I dressed all in black and covered my head. Pope John Paul granted our group of about 100 individuals a personal audience. The emotions were overwhelming. His attention to each individual was so intense that each person felt like the only one in the room. His warmth and sincerity surpassed all expectations.

The next day the great audience hall was flooded by scores of scarlet-capped cardinals from all over the world and scores of others —a total of 4,000 people. Cardinal Jean-Marie Lustiger, the Archbishop of Paris—a Jew from Poland who had converted to Catholicism—welcomed us, speaking Yiddish. The Pope himself entered in the company of the chief rabbi of Rome and sat in the same row as the survivors, on a throne of equal height with the rabbi. When the *Kaddish*—the prayer of mourning, set to music by Leonard Bernstein and narrated by Richard Dreyfuss—resounded in the hall, there was not a dry eye. The balance of the concert, consisting of the Chichester Psalms by Bernstein, sung by a young boy with an angelic voice from New York's Metropolitan Opera, who was accompanied by the London Philharmonic Orchestra.

The following day our group attended services at the Orthodox synagogue in Rome. I did not cherish climbing the many flights of stairs to reach the balcony designated for women. Having lived as a Reform Jew, in a context where women had equal rights, I found it difficult to accept being relegated to the status of second-class citizen. Still, even though the traditional service was difficult to follow, being part of that religious experience was very valuable at a time when my emotions were surging. So I chose to participate.

I was delighted to proceed to Israel from Rome. It seemed like a fitting end to such a spiritually rich pilgrimage.

Several years later I was disheartened to read the extraordinary book by Father Edward Flannery, *The Anguish of the Jews*, which recounted the history of anti-Semitism in the context of centuries of love-hate relations between the various popes and the Jewish people. After reading the book I came to think of the relationship between Pope John Paul II and the Jews, as well as my own experience in the Vatican, as an interval of love through which humankind was fortunate to pass at that time, with no guarantee that such progress would outlast the passing of this great Catholic leader.

And yet, as I see it, we Jews need to cherish the opportunity of a hand stretched out to us with the ever-optimistic hope that accord will be everlasting.

This experience strengthened my resolve to work with Sister Rose at Seton Hall University. As soon as the Sister Rose Thering Endowment was created to further Jewish–Christian studies I joined the executive board.

I was brought up in a Catholic country. The public school I attended had an altar in the hallway where almost all my classmates prayed every day. Yet the religion of the majority of my classmates was never forced on me or the other three Jewish girls in my class. Always connected to my roots and strong in my identity as a Jew, I did not feel threatened by living in Christian surroundings. While I felt somewhat like an outsider, seeing others practice their religion enriched me.

In the 1960's Dana Rosamilia, the daughter of my co-leader when our children were in the same Brownie troop in Watchung—who was taking a class with a professor named Father John Morley—suggested that he ask me to speak to her college class about my wartime experiences. In her Brownie days Dana had been exposed to two religious traditions: Christianity by her mother, and Judaism by me. As a student at Seton Hall University, a Catholic school, her invitation gave me the chance to educate a classroom of college students about the Holocaust.

Following the lecture Monsignor John M. Oesterreicher and Father Morley invited me to participate in their first interreligious Holocaust observance. As part of the ceremony Monsignor Oesterreicher hung in the chapel sanctuary the prison dress I had salvaged from my days in the concentration camps. Before that moment I had always questioned my insistence on holding onto it, but after that event I realized it had become another essential part of history I was destined to teach.

This experience touched me very deeply. Remembering the anti-Semitism that had been so prevalent in Catholic circles where I was brought up, it was a revelation to meet Christian clergymen who stretched their hands out to Jews. In 1980 Father Morley presented me with a book he had written, *Vatican*

Diplomacy and the Jews During the Holocaust: 1939–1943. This cemented my desire to work at Seton Hall with the Catholic community there.

The 1974 Holocaust observance had also opened the door to my friendship with Sister Rose Thering. In the 1950's, while writing her doctoral thesis, Sister Rose had pointed out anti-Semitic content in Catholic religious teaching materials and advocated their removal by the Vatican. It took years for the Church authorities to take such action, but beginning in 1964 *Nostra Aetate*, a Vatican II council document, clarified the issue, formally repudiating the charge that Jews were singularly responsible for the death of Jesus. The document was adopted by a vote of the world's bishops and promulgated in 1965 by Pope Paul VI, in large measure due to her research, prayer, and persistence.

During the Liberation Monument period Sister Rose became very fond of Natan Rapoport. She was particularly touched by his aptly titled sculpture, *Reconciliation,* depicting two hands reaching toward each other, one bearing the stigmata from the Cross, the other a tattooed number from a concentration camp, symbolizing Jewish-Christian reconciliation. Sister Rose prompted Natan to propose erecting a copy of the sculpture in the gardens of the Vatican. Unfortunately because of Rapoport's untimely death, the project never materialized.

Recognizing the open-mindedness of the top levels of Church leadership to bridging the centuries-old gap in Jewish–Christian relations, educators at Seton Hall decided to focus on a more grassroots level, working with clergy members and teachers who had been instructed to implement the policies yet were not quite ready to accept them. Sister Rose set out to conquer the obstacles. In 1953 Monsignor Oesterreicher had established the Jewish–Christian studies department at Seton Hall with the purpose of teaching teachers about Jewish–Christian relations throughout history with a special emphasis on the Holocaust. Sister Rose joined him in 1968 as a coordinator for teachers' education.

I became a frequent speaker in this department. I had also taught scores of high-school students, and my personal history had been recorded on videotape in Watchung Regional High School, Kean University, Yale University, and as a participant in Steven Spielberg's *Shoah* project.

I was deeply gratified to realize that in instructing 40 teachers a year, each of whom then taught ultimately thousands of students, the Seton Hall program constituted a particularly valuable educational resource. Moreover, with survivors aging, I knew that schools would soon have to rely on recorded testimonies, and I felt it was critically important to devote my time to helping prepare the educational framework for teaching about the Holocaust in a postwitness period.

The teachers and students in the Jewish–Christian studies department consisted of people from many and widely different religious and ethnic backgrounds. It was very exciting to attend the opening of the school year and hear a Japanese teacher talk of her interest in studying Judaism.

Another moving moment came when an elderly Jewish man sitting across the table from a young African-American Muslim recognized the latter as his student. The Jewish gentleman had years before taught the man about the Holocaust. Now both of them were taking the course together with the intention of teaching the lessons of the Holocaust to future students, hoping to help reduce prejudice. It was not enough to remember the Holocaust, I felt; it was equally necessary to learn from this horrible experience and affirmatively to shape behavior.

Following her retirement from Seton Hall in 1989, Sister Rose became executive director of the National Christian Conference for Israel, annually leading Christian clergy on trips to Israel to foster understanding. But her activities did not end there. She also fought for the release of Jews from the former Soviet Union, and she lent a strong pro-Israel, Christian voice to American foreign policy.

My friendship with Sister Rose and her dedication to Israel's continuity and security prompted me to take two trips to Israel with her. The first one, in October 2000, was at the beginning of the Palestinian suicide-bombing rampage; we accompanied a United Jewish Communities fact-finding mission. The purpose of the trip was to demonstrate our solidarity with Israel. Though

Sister Rose was the only non-Jew in the group, this was her 53rd trip to Israel. Many top government officials greeted her as an old friend.

While we had heard stories before traveling to Israel about the desperate situation there, the hopelessness expressed by the Israelis surprised us. I had not witnessed such feelings even during the earliest days of the country's existence, in the first few years after the war. The accounts we heard about nightly shootings sharpened the reality; our hotel was located close enough to the targets for us to be awakened by the cruel—and once-familiar—sound of bullets. The mission leaders shuttled us from location to location to meet with officials from many branches of government who presented different perspectives.

One of the key points emphasized by almost every leader was the extent to which the foreign press had been biased against Israel, driven by a devious public relations campaign on the part of the Palestinians, who had banned from the territories any uncooperative reporter. The Israelis, on the other hand, were making little effort to counter the press attack. One time, for example, a photograph in worldwide newspapers showed a blood-covered boy. The caption indicated that he had been a Palestinian tortured by Israelis, but later it was revealed that the boy had been an American Yeshiva student being rescued by Israelis from an attack by Palestinians.

Reversing the religious make-up of the participants, on the next trip with Sister Rose to Israel in January 2002, I was the only Jew among 12 travelers. Most of the others were clergy members involved with the National Christian Leadership Conference for Israel. It was very encouraging to be in the presence of non-Jews who cared so much about Israel. Once again we were taken to meet with leaders, though this time the encounters included Israeli Christian heads of organizations playing a significant role in the country's future.

Jerusalem was deserted. The King David Hotel, which had for years been hopping with life year-round, was empty. Because there were so few guests the hotel needed to save money on fuel, and the dining room felt frigid. The few Arabs who still worked in the hotel appeared to be ill at ease.

I introduced the group to Moshe Wolf, the child of my cousin Joel Wolf, who had grown up with me on Wielopole Street in Krakow. At the age of 44

Moshe—a handsome blond, blue-eyed Orthodox Jewish father of four—had just retired from the Israeli army's intelligence division with the rank of colonel. Moshe presented to the group—which had been on the receiving end of anti-Israel propaganda for a long time—the human side of the Israeli army and the role of an Orthodox Jew in the army. The compassionate picture he presented made a strong pro-Israel impression.

Though the volatile political situation dominated the events around which our trip was focused, we also saw other aspects of Israel. For instance, we visited an Israeli agency engaged in the teaching of agriculture to people in African countries, explaining, for example, methods used to produce crops in the desert. The impact of the humanitarian work is great in the starving, underdeveloped countries, yet the fact of Israel's involvement is too often little publicized.

Sometimes in my dreams at night I am back in my grammar school in Krakow, talking to the jolly, rotund and friendly priest who taught religion to my Catholic classmates. Suddenly—as happens in dreams—the priest turns into Sister Rose. And when I wake up, I know I am in the right place.

It took 14 years till they convinced me to take a chairmanship of the Endowment. By then we had educated more than 300 teachers, who had gone on to have an impact on thousands of students.

In 2004 *Sister Rose's Passion* was released: An excellent movie about my friend's work. The film received great accolades, including a nomination for an Academy Award. It is our hope to distribute it to schools to teach tolerance.

Finally, Sister Rose's work is receiving the recognition it deserves. Thanks to the generosity of Leon Cooperman and Eric Ross, an endowed chair dedicated to Sister Rose was established in the Jewish-Christian studies department at Seton Hall University, so that her lifetime work will be a permanent part of the University's curriculum.

Monsignor Robert Sheeran, Luna, Fr.David Bossman and Eli Saks at Yad Vashem Hall of Remembrance, Jerusalem, May 18, 2008

Chapter Thirty-two
Yad Vashem

Jerusalem called to me, and I answered—for Sister Rose's sake.

On Sunday, May 18, 2008, twelve days after the second anniversary of Rose's death, Monsignor Robert Sheeran, president of Seton Hall University, led a delegation to Yad Vashem to honor her memory. Yad Vashem is the nation of Israel's Holocaust memorial in Jerusalem. The occasion served to launch a scholarship in Rose's name, which will permit the Sister Rose Thering Endowment to send one student per year to Yad Vashem, enriching the Jewish–Christian studies program that is offered at Seton Hall. The student's exposure to the museum's resources and teaching will give new depth to our program. A group of Bible students from Summit, New Jersey, organized by Paul Gibbons, was in attendance, as well.

We were also accompanied by a group of students from Seton Hall's College of Education and Human Services. They began a week of study at the Ben Gurion University by attending our event. The group was composed of young men and women from various religions and national origins. I was delighted to see Sister Rose's work bearing fruit.

In his remarks, Monsignor Sheeran reaffirmed Seton Hall's commitment to the continuation of her vision. He offered reminiscences of Rose that illustrated her love for Israel and the Jewish people. He told us of her life devoted to building bridges for people of every religion and her devotion to making a better world.

"Sister Rose's life was a great and remarkable story," he stated. The purpose of this day, he said, was to move the mission of Sister Rose forward into the future. This memorial for Sister Rose at Yad Vashem, he said, was different than the many other honors she had received during her lifetime because it was in the Israel she so loved.

How proud she would be to know that her effort was bearing fruit on the 60th anniversary of Israel's founding! He quoted Sophocles: "You need to wait until the end of a day to see how splendid a day it has been." How appropriately that applies to Sister Rose's splendid life.

Her mission was three-fold: First, to root out anti-Semitism in all its forms wherever it might be found. She found it frequently in Catholic textbooks of the time, and she almost single-handedly eliminated such false teachings. Second, she traveled a road of education. Sister Rose was actually a professor in Seton Hall's College of Education, devoted to educating educators. "She believed the Shoah [Holocaust] needed to be taught by Jews and Catholics- that all people needed to learn from it." And, third, she had a strong dedication to the state of Israel. She took more than 50 trips to this country that she loved.

"One person can make a difference," Monsignor Sheeran emphasized. "That is terribly important." Sister Rose put her unique talents to use in a special calling. "As she moved ahead, she understood that more clearly." He decried the phenomenon of education in hatred and bigotry, rather than education in the truth. He noted that he had attended Israeli President Shimon Peres' Tomorrow Conference of leaders and scholars who discussed the future of Israel, and he thought about how Sister Rose had deeply touched so many lives in Israel as well as around the world.

Monsignor Sheeran concluded: "May we all be worthy of her goodness and her wonderful spirit."

Yitz Greenberg, an Orthodox rabbi and a long-time friend of Sister Rose, rescheduled his planned trip to Israel in order to attend the ceremony. He and his wife, Blu, arrived straight from the airport with her luggage, to make sure they did not miss a moment of the day's activities. Rabbi Greenberg recollected the many weekends Rose spent at his home, celebrating holidays and attending temple services. She had been at his side since the 1960's, launching Holocaust education, protesting the entrapment of Russian Jews, advocating for Israel when it was not yet fashionable. Asked once if she would have helped Jews during the Holocaust, she replied: "I wish I would have had the courage to do it." She was committed to exposing the lack of action by the bystanders, assigning partial blame for the atrocities to their inactivity. Considering her tireless devotion to Jewish causes and to Israel, the Greenbergs applied for a street to be named for her in Jerusalem.

Sister Gemma DelDuca, S.C., of Seton Hill University in Greensburg, Pennsylvania, the founder of Holocaust Education for Christians at Yad Vashem, remembered Sister Rose with great affection. She talked about being introduced to Rose by the Benedictine Father Isaac Jacob, which resulted in a long cooperation between the two scholars. "In the '70's I came to Israel with Sister Rose on two trips." There she visited again with Father Isaac, with Rose's support, and she worked with him over the coming years. She recollected their first conferences in Bet Shemesh, a small village at the time, where the seeds of Holocaust education were planted. Then, in 1987 Seton Hill University began an educational exchange with Yad Vashem.

Sister Gemma read from a note Rose had written to a survivor, "Thank you so much for sharing with us your story. Your life is an inspiration and gives all of us-gives me-courage. I will speak of you to my students and with my mother, whose mother and father came from Germany." Sister Gemma concluded: "For all of us who knew her, she was indeed a great blessing." She also recognized the many Holocaust survivors in the audience

Noami Wish, Ph.D., the director of the Center for Public Service at Seton Hall, spoke of her many years working as a Jew in this Catholic university, of the cooperation she had received from the administration, which she felt had been in great measure inspired by Monsignor John Oesterreicher and Sister Rose Thering. She called Sister Rose an inspiration.

David Bossman, Ph.D., the executive director of the Endowment, echoed the sentiments of other speakers. He spoke of Rose's hard work to bridge the chasm that divided Jews and Christians in history and to make progress on contemporary issues. "Her voice spoke for the millions of Jews silenced in Hitler's death camp," Dr. Bossman said. "Her voice helped move the Church toward issuing the singularly important final document of the Second Vatican Council in 1965, *Nostra Aetate*." This document rejected the notion that the Jews were responsible for the death of Jesus and condemned the persecution of Jews and anti-Semitism. Dr. Bossman urged us all to recommit ourselves to continuing her work.

The representatives of Yad Vashem also recollected Rose with great warmth and appreciation and presented us with a certificate recognizing the establishment of the Sister Rose Thering Scholarship, which will permit us to send a student annually for a teacher-training course at Yad Vashem's International School of Holocaust Studies.

From the ceremony we moved to the Hall of Remembrance where Monsignor Sheeran relit the eternal flame and laid a beautiful wreath with a banner saying, *Am Israel Hai* ("Long live the people of Israel!") a favorite saying of Sister Rose. Father John Morley led the congregation in recitation of the

23rd Psalm, and Paul Gibbons, the current chair of the Sister Rose Thering Endowment, read the poem, "The Shtetl."

The following visit to the Yad Vashem museum illustrated very emphatically the reasons for our commitment. Seeing the atrocities committed against innocent people in Europe made it quite obvious why we need to commit ourselves to eradicating hatred and prejudice. We should be grateful for the people who went to such great pains to document the history of the Nazi atrocities, because in another few years it might otherwise be forgotten or treated as unbelievable. As the time goes by even I, who lived through the horrors, have a hard time reconciling myself to the fact that it really happened. That is why Sister Rose worked so tirelessly educating people and explaining the need to remember.

Have we learned this lesson of vigilance?

Later we dined at the museum, breaking bread with my Israeli friends and family. They were quite amazed to see such devoted Christians working with us. It was equally important for them to meet Christians committed to developing relations with Jews. Luckily most of them speak English, particularly the younger generation, though they live in isolation. Hearing the recollections of Sister Rose's accomplishments created quite an impression.

It was a perfect day. The only thing I personally regret is that I could not attend the Mass at the Mount of Olives celebrated by Monsignor Sheeran. Some last-minute arrangements at Yad Vashem had required my attention.

On Friday evening Monsignor invited us to celebrate the coming of Shabbat at his hotel suite. Overlooking Jerusalem bathed in the golden sun, we understood why Sister Rose loved the city so much. Her favorite song was "Jerusalem of Gold." On this occasion we listened to the reading of an essay by Kerry Close, a granddaughter of one of our Catholic participants. Kerry was the winner of the Luna Kaufman Essay Contest at Brookdale Community College in Lincroft, New Jersey-which had been established unbeknownst to me. This 15-year-old girl wrote the essay from the point of view of a boy returning to his home village after the Holocaust. The sensitivity of the essay drove home the results of the teaching that Sister Rose had advocated. It brought tears to our eyes.

Saturday we visited the magnificent Scrolls of Fire sculpture by Natan Rappoport. The majestic monument stands 20 feet tall in Kisalon, a suburb of Jerusalem. It was originally designed for Riverside Park in New York, but Mayor John V. Lindsay's administration decided that it was too somber for a place where children play. It depicts the history of Jews, culminating in their entrance into Israel.

From Kisalon we went to Abu Gosh, an Arab village were we met a young Muslim girl, a leader in her community in charge of the youth center, who introduced us to their life in Israel, as well as Arab customs.

The more agile members of our trip walked atop the walls surrounding the Old City of Jerusalem. Their experience was rather trying since panhandlers accosted them. But the feisty ladies were not ready to be taken advantage of, and all went well. We then followed the route of the Stations of the Cross. We reunited at the Church of the Holy Sepulcher where Mass was celebrated by Father Morley, with Monsignor Sheeran and Father Bossman as concelebrants. It was interesting that the three Christian denominations who are housed in the same church, each have to observe the demarcation lines while wearing their vestments. Evidently the coexistence of centuries is not always friendly.

Following the official ceremonies, Monsignor Sheeran returned to the States to face his busy schedule. We proceeded in the footsteps of Christ.

Our first step was to visit Bethlehem. The guide brought us across the border, but not being permitted to drive an Israeli bus on Palestinian territory, an Arab guide met us with a bus, which took us into the city. The biggest surprise of my fellow travelers was the friendliness between the two guides. If left alone, I believe the Jews and Palestinians would enjoy a much more friendly relationship than the governments will permit. Here again it was demonstrated, as in Abu Gosh, that they can get along for the benefit of both. The volume of tourists greatly reduced by present discrimination against Christians was striking especially to me, who remembered the crowds from years gone by. In a startling contrast to the developments in greater Israel, Bethlehem was a rather poor city. The bus that took us to the church was also very primitive. But the hospitality was very warm. The narrow passages in the church created a darkly mystical ambience. We lingered there, delaying our return, wanting to absorb the atmosphere of this holy place.

Our next stop was a disappointment for me. It was the visit to the Wailing Wall. I remembered the great open plaza without any buildings, gates or metal detectors, which had created a very spiritual environment; it was now gone. This crowded place did not resemble the holy place where people came to contemplate and pray. I had to reach over women who were crowded by the Wall to insert the traditional little paper wishes of my six- and nine-year-old grandchildren. I looked around, not recognizing the place I had cherished in the past. I recollected the night in 2000, right after the start of the Intifada, when we visited this dark, deserted place with Sister Rose. Now the crowds squeezed into the limited space surrounded by wire fences and the presence of military. While I understand the need for protection, it is difficult to accept the reality of today.

On the way to the Sea of Galilee we stopped at the ancient city of Caesarea. Considering that no heavy mechanical equipment can be used for the archaeological excavations, it was amazing to view the vast extent of the beautiful ruins of this metropolis standing before our eyes. I remember seeing Samson and Delilah, an opera based on the biblical story, staged at this beautiful stone amphitheater. We sat in the outdoor theater with scenery matching the original stones. When Samson destroyed the temple it was impossible to tell which of the fallen stones were the real ones. The acoustics are great for musical performances.

We arrived at the Sea of Galilee. The great blue ripple-free span of water, which mirrors the surrounding mountains, made us aware that 2,000 years ago Christ saw the same image-and this brought us even closer to its history. We pictured the followers of Jesus roaming the shores of this lake. Sailing a boat on the lake and having the group of Christians dance to the tune of Israeli music united us. The place retained its serenity.

The visit to the baptismal site in the Jordan River, where hundreds of people in long white robes, came from all over the world to submerge themselves in the holy water of Jordan, brought us even closer to those long-ago disciples. A Mass celebrated by Father Bossman at the Mount of the Beatitudes where Christ delivered his Sermon on the Mount rounded out our spiritual experience.

What a jolt it was to take a jeep to visit the Golan Heights, an object of contention among Syria, Lebanon and Israel for generations. The barren strip of land is not much larger than many farms in the U.S. It appears to be worthless, yet has created such a great conflict. It brought home to us the reality of today's political situation. So many lives have been lost in this dispute.

On the way to Tel Aviv, we stopped in Nazareth, where I had another disappointment. I remembered my visit in 1951 when it was a small quaint village without vehicular traffic and with primitive housing. Now we confronted a bustling commercial town. We celebrated Mass and Father Bossman's birthday, but it was a far cry from the spirituality of Galilee.

Then we moved to the contemporary world. Our visit to the Hall of Independence introduced us to the proceedings that created the State of Israel. We looked into the Hebrew University department that deals with anti-Semitism where a German student was spending a summer doing research.

The Museum of the Diaspora gave us a picture of the Jewish communities all over the world prior to creation of the State of Israel. It solved many puzzles for me. It was always a question in my mind as to why the Jews remained such a strong, coherent community without a country to call home, while so many cultures disappeared over the ages. An eloquent guide explained the Jewish traditions which contributed to our survival. The need to have ten persons to conduct the prayers made any traveler feel included in the community. So did the invitations for meals-the tradition of hospitality. Keeping kosher also isolated the community, defining it and at the same time uniting it.

The prevention of intermarriage also was a factor in the continuity of Jewish society through all those centuries. Keeping separate and maintaining strong bonds among themselves were the reasons for the survival of Jews until our own day.

To conclude the trip and say good bye to Israel, we were invited by Dafna and Zwi Fuss, my cousins with their three daughters, to their home for a beautiful supper in their garden.

The spirit of friendship blessed the evening, as it had the entire pilgrimage-for me and for my dear Christian companions. Together, we were open to seeing new sights, to learning new ways, to seeking answers to questions of co-existence and reconciliation.

Luna with doll, 2007 (Photo by Jerry Galiano)

Chapter Thirty-three
Final Reflections

I have so many memories of my life's journey – and time ebbs and flows, forward and backward in ways that are mysterious to me. So I share some impressions and reflections from the last decade.

April 30, 1997

I sat at my sewing machine, looking out the window of my 33rd-floor New York City apartment. I could see Central Park and the George Washington Bridge as I sewed a doll for Manya, my cherubic granddaughter, then nine months old, who bears my mother's name.

As I worked on that doll I reflected on the one I had made for the SS guard Anna Lisa 53 years earlier at the Leipzig concentration camp. Little had I known at that time that 1945 would be the year of our liberation. We had been disappointed in that regard so many times that we had almost stopped thinking about being freed.

As I reflected on the different circumstances in which I was making the doll for Manya, the sound of the TV in the background caught my attention. A documentary of the trial in Israel of Adolf Eichmann, the most notorious henchman in Auschwitz, had just begun to air.

What a coincidence! Joy filled my heart. Eichmann had been tried by a sophisticated judicial system. He had been convicted and executed, while I, one of the millions whom he had earmarked for extermination simply because of my religious and racial identity, was sewing a doll for the joy of my life and awaiting another grandchild due in a few months.

The price was very high, but in the end victory was mine.

We survived. Our ranks are thinner, but not weaker. We are like a tree. Sometimes we seem vulnerable, attacked by the elements that have destroyed many of our branches. At other times, though, we are flourishing and gaining a healthy strength. We are a tree of life.

December 20, 2006

Almost 10 years have passed since I put down my pen thinking I had completed my life story. I looked with pride at my children, whose attitude toward their fellow human beings filled me with pride. Their kindness is apparent in their relationships to one another and to the many friends they have. They chose wonderful spouses, who also embrace those values.

When the girls were in their forties, it appeared that my hopes for grandchildren were melting away. But life had delightful surprises in store for me.

First, Bernice and Don had presented me with Manya, who is now a 10-year-old young lady. To give her a sibling we traveled to Siberia and brought back the rambunctious, delightful Elena, who entertains herself with a computer at age four.

Andy, a handsome and kind boy, arrived a year later, and Mark and Katia gave him a little sister, Alexandra, who at two became a pet of the family.

Irene and Daniel blessed us first with Evan, who at age seven is my opera companion, and followed with Dora, the charmer who is now five. Her smile can melt an iceberg.

The time has come for me to smell the roses. I've done my share of work, devoting my time to myriad projects. True, I never had much staying power-that's why I kept moving from project to project. Now I would like to spend more time with my burgeoning family. How rewarding it is to have a family gathering of 14 people! Sixty years ago I could not have dreamed I would be the matriarch of such a brood.

Although my life is filled with the joy arising from the adorable family surrounding me, I do feel that this life would lack an important dimension of meaning if I didn't continue to be involved with the work of Sister Rose Thering.

Rose passed away on May 6, 2006. It was a great loss to all of us, but I committed myself to following in her footsteps, reaching out to people of other religions and hoping to foster ever greater understanding.

November 28, 2006

I celebrated my 80th birthday today. The children arranged a beautiful party for 100 of my best friends, which I decided to make my Bat Mitzvah, a ceremony in which under normal circumstances a 13-year-old girl is called to read from the *Torah* (Jewish scripture) for the first time. It gave me a great opportunity to express my values and hope to motivate my family and friends to follow the golden rule of Sister Rose. As is customary on this occasion I delivered a speech:

It is quite fitting that my Haftarah is dealing with twins. As a mother of twins myself, I am very sensitive to their mutual relationship. It is with great delight that I witness the relationships of all my children and their spouses, which unlike the one of Jacob and Esau are loving and all-inclusive.

How timely is the remark in the commentaries to my Haftarah:

"Have we not all one father? Hath not God created us all? Why do we deal treacherously every man against his brother?"

The time has come for us to act upon those values. We have learned a hard lesson using our differences and bigotry as a model for our behavior. They produced very painful results; so now we have to try to follow the road charted for us by Sister Rose Thering.

The inspiration for this morning's 80th birthday celebration (in the format of a Bat Mitzvah) came from Sister Rose. It was at her memorial service last September that the sisters of the Dominican convent in Racine, Wisconsin, Sister Rose's Motherhouse, presented me with this *tallit* (Jewish prayer shawl), which had been given to Sister Rose by a synagogue and was among the possessions she had left. Cherishing the relations she had established with the Jewish community and devoting her life to fighting anti-Semitism did not make her any less a Christian. That is why I decided to reaffirm my Judaism by having my Bat Mitzvah: to prove that working with the Christian world did not make me any less a Jew. It is my hope to become the Jewish counterpart of Sister Rose, and that all my grandchildren will become a Bar or Bat Mitzvah in this *tallit* and pledge to perpetuate the values fostered by Sister Rose.

Sister Rose devoted her life to building bridges of tolerance in the hope of creating a world that would not thrive on prejudice and bigotry. I think she achieved quite commendable results, but they are only the beginning. There is still a lot of work to be done. Correcting the mistakes committed in the name of centuries of prejudice can't be accomplished in one generation. We must commit ourselves to continuing her work. If each of us will tear down a building block from the wall that divides us, we will create a world where prejudice and bigotry will not rule our actions.

Evening of Roses, Seton Hall University, 2000.
Irene, Evan, Bernice, Manya and Sister Rose

Family Album

Family home, Krakow Wielopole 13

Schneider Family – Grandparents Malka & Jozef, circa 1900

*Hela & Mania
(mother)*

Aunt Regina Kaner,
Budapest, 1939;

Uncle Henryk, Austrian Army,
circa 1916

Salomon, Sala, Henryk, sister and brothers,
a postcard written to mother's aunt Fanny
Silberlust living in New York, 1903

Wir erbitten uns die Ehre Ihrer werthen Gegenwart zur
Vermählungsfeier unferer Kinder

Regina
mit
Max

welche Dienftag den 28 Jänner 1896 um 8 Uhr Abends
in Krakau Methgasse Nr. 7 Hotel Wiedenski stattfinden wird.

Josef Schneider & Frau
Krakau.

Wolf Kanner & Frau
Rzeszów.

Telegramme: **Schneider, Krakau Hotel Wiedeński.**

Wedding invitation, 1896

Grandparents, Pepcia & Noah Fuss, 1937

Oskar, Hela, Julek and Jozek Hilfstein, 1939

Marek Fuss, Krynica, 1938

Luna & Niusia,
Krakow, 1928, 1930 & 1931

Luna, Niusia, Wisia & Edzia Landau, Krakow, circa 1934.
Wisia died of diphteria in Palestine.

Luna and Mala Hoffnung-Sperling, New Jersey, 2008

The memorial card was designed by a Dominican Sister at Racine, Wisconsin, sister Rose's Mother House. She always wore this necklace. Upon her passing away, I wear it now to symbolize the continuity of her mission.

Father (center), visit to Podworska during the war, 1942.

Mother and Luna, Israel, 1950

Below, Tapestry embroidered by mother in 1935 and smuggled from Poland as a bedspread. The leftover yarn was used to embroider blouses for us, such as the ones pictured in the cover photo.

Irene, Alex, Luna, Mark, Bernice, 1976

Unveiling of "LiberationZ" by Natan Rapoport, May 30, 1985

Presidents of Temple Sholom, Plainfield, N.J., 1946-1986.
Back, Martin Kestenbaum, Bill Shuldenfrei, Hy Tobi, Jo Hyman,
Abe Banker, Bill Drier and Mort Rutenberg; Front, Syd Darwin, Art Goldstein,
Harold Schwartz, Morris Vogel, Luna Kaufman, Bill Ginden,
Marty Schwartz and Steve Ritz.

Myself, Elie Wiesel and Sister Rose, April 23, 2005

Day after parents wedding. Krakow, June 16, 1923. Back row, Marek, Lutka, Julek, Salek, Hela, Leon and Henryk; Front row, Mania, Helen, Oskar, Malka and Cyla. Malka and Henry died before WWII. Of the remaining people, only Mania and Oskar survived. The credenza in the background is now in Irene's house in New York.

Luna's 80th birthday party, November 28, 2006. Back, Daniel, Irene Neiden, Don, Benice Gaver, Alex, Mark, Sasha and Katia; Front, Evan & Dora Neiden, Manya & Elena Gaver, Andy Kaufman and Luna

Acknowledgments

Many people were instrumental in completing this work. It took many years to accomplish, and I sincerely thank those whom I remember who were of such great assistance to me.

First of all, my gratitude goes to Monsignor Robert Sheeran, the president of Seton Hall University, who took me under his wing and encouraged me to finish my book.

Now come all the others who worked very hard to keep me in line: It started with Joe Peret, who guided me at the beginning stages. Then followed Ellen Friedland, devoting countless hours. Demise Garrepis also made a contribution toward refining the manuscript. A special gratitude to Dan Creighton for the photography and Irene for creating a beautiful cover. Thanks to Daniel Neiden for going through the book with a fine-toothed comb, finding all my mistakes, and to Mike Meilach for the painstaking job of making sure that all the "i"s were dotted. Many thanks to publisher Rob Huberman for the inspiration of adding a picture album and for his most responsive cooperation and guidance, and to graphic artist Jackie Caplan for the beautiful layout of the book. And finally thank you to Greg Tobin, who lent his professional touch to see it through.

Thanks to all of them, and if I forgot someone, my deepest apologies. This work took twenty years to complete, and I hope it is understandable that I might omit someone.

Luna